The Nature, Tasks and Scope
of the Catechetical Ministry

The Nature, Tasks and Scope
of the Catechetical Ministry:

A Digest of Recent Church Documents

Rev. Berard L. Marthaler, O.F.M. Conv., S.T.D., Ph.D.

With a Foreword by
Most Reverend Donald W. Wuerl, S.T.D.

National Catholic Educational Association

Contents

Foreword xi

Preface xv

Timeline xvii

Abbreviations xix

INTRODUCTION 1

CHAPTER 1—Catechetical Ministry: The Nature, Tasks
and Scope in the Documents of Vatican II 11

CHAPTER 2—First Generation of Post-Conciliar Documents:
Directory and Code 19

General Catechetical Directory 19

Code of Canon Law 33

CHAPTER 3—Post-Conciliar Catechetical Documents in
the United States 41

To Teach as Jesus Did: A Pastoral Message on Catholic Education 41

Basic Teachings for Catholic Religious Education 47

Sharing the Light of Faith—The National Catechetical Directory 49

Guidelines for Doctrinally Sound Catechetical Materials 75

CHAPTER 4—Towards Maturity of Faith 81

A Vision of Youth Ministry 81

The Challenge of Adolescent Catechesis: Maturing in Faith 83

Renewing the Vision: A Framework for Catholic Youth Ministry 85

Adult Catechesis in the Christian Community 86

*Our Hearts Were Burning Within Us: A Pastoral Plan
for Adult Faith Formation in the United States* .89

CHAPTER 5—Liturgy and Catechesis 91
Rite of Christian Initiation of Adults 91
Christian Initiation for Children of Catechetical Age 94
Directory for Masses with Children 95

CHAPTER 6—Synodal Documents: Evangelization and Catechesis . .99
Evangelii nuntiandi 99
Catechesi tradendae 100
Familiaris consortio 102
Reconciliatio et paenitentia 103

CHAPTER 7—Documents for the Millennium 105
Catechism of the Catholic Church 106
Compendium of the Catechism of the Catholic Church 115
Compendium of the Social Doctrine of the Church 116

CHAPTER 8—Evangelizing Catechesis 123
General Directory for Catechesis 123

CHAPTER 9—Catechesis in the American Context 169
National Directory for Catechesis 169

CHAPTER 10—Addressing American Culture 213
United States Catholic Catechism for Adults 213

CHAPTER 11—Ecumenism and Inter-Faith Dialogue 227

Directory for the Application of Principles and Norms on Ecumenism 228

*The Ecumenical Dimension in the Formation of Those Engaged in
Pastoral Work* 231

*Guidelines and Suggestions for Implementing the Conciliar Declaration
"Nostra aetate"* 232

*Notes on the Correct Way to Present the Jews and Judaism in Preaching
and Catechesis* 233

CHAPTER 12—Catechetical Personnel 241

Guide for Catechists 242

National Certification Standards for Lay Ecclesial Ministers 250

CHAPTER 13—Religious Education and Catechesis 257

The Religious Dimension of Education in a Catholic School 257

Appendix 271

About the Author 275

Index 277

Foreword

Catechesis is all about passing on the faith. In the Acts of the Apostles and elsewhere in the New Testament we find inspired examples of the proclamation of the faith. At the beginning of the Patristic era, spanning five centuries, we find the writings of Clement in Rome, Ignatius of Antioch and the "Teaching of the Apostles." Twenty centuries later in an unbroken line of witness to the faith we hear the words of Pope Benedict XVI in his homily at the Mass at Washington Nationals Park, Thursday, April 17, 2008: "In the exercise of my ministry as the Successor of Peter, I have come to America to confirm you, my brothers and sisters, in the faith of the Apostles (cf. Lk. 22:32). I have come to proclaim anew, as Peter proclaimed on the day of Pentecost, that Jesus Christ is Lord and Messiah, risen from the dead, seated in glory at the right hand of the Father, and established as Judge of the living and the dead (cf. Acts 2:1-14 ff.)."

One particularly rich period in the development of catechesis in the Church Universal and especially for the Church in the United States is the nearly four decades culminating in our day but beginning with the preparation in the late 1960s of the *General Catechetical Directory* and its publication on Easter Sunday, 1971.

Father Berard Marthaler, O.F.M. Conv., Professor Emeritus of Religion and Religious Education at The Catholic University of America, begins his highly informative *Digest of Recent Church Documents* on the catechetical ministry with dicastery responsible for the oversight of catechesis and catechetical materials throughout the Church. As Father Marthaler asserts, this was the beginning of a new generation of post-conciliar documents that would give focus, direction and impetus to the catechetical renewal called for by the Second Vatican Council and starting then to take place in parishes, dioceses and episcopal conferences throughout the world. With scholarship and skill, Father Marthaler leads us through the decades of documents that offer magisterial direction to the perennial task of catechizing. In his survey and summary of ecclesiastical documents he concludes with the *United States*

Catholic Catechism for Adults, the work of the United States Conference of Catholic Bishops to provide an inviting and faithful summary of the faith.

Wisely, Father Marthaler, who is himself a master catechist, points out to his readers that "no digest, and even less a summary, is a substitute for an original work…" What he does provide however, is a faithful focus on the main points of the texts in a way that the reader being introduced into this vast body of catechetical guidance has a good idea of what the Church sets forth in each of the documents and a sense of the basic content.

While Father Marthaler issues the disclaimer that "this is not a complete catalogue of the significant documents dealing with Catholic religious education that have appeared since Vatican II," he nonetheless, in my opinion, has chosen the truly important ones that have given direction to catechesis for the Church in the United States.

Throughout the decades, from the *General Catechetical Directory* on through to our own *National Directory for Catechesis* and with the intervening *Catechism of the Catholic Church* and our own *United States Catholic Catechism for Adults*, there is a healthy recognition in these texts of the developments in catechetical method taking into account age-appropriate formation and underscoring the primary role of adult faith formation and at the same time a necessary insistence on the content of the faith—the very substance of the message that introduces us both to the person of Christ and his saving message.

This collection of magisterial documents makes us aware on even preliminary scrutiny that Catholic religious education in whatever form has as its primary task the communication of the person and message of Christ. This takes place through a wide range of efforts, but the goal is always the same. In our Catholic elementary and secondary schools, parish religious education programs, adult faith formation, the Rite of Christian Initiation for Adults, sacramental formation programs, as well as in youth ministry, campus ministry, and even Catholic institutions of higher learning, the threads of the encounter with Christ and his life-giving message must be woven into the fabric of our human experience. A review of the documents in this Digest highlights that what we bring in our catechetical educational effort is our Catholic faith. What we try to communicate is an understanding of the life that only faith can provide.

Looking through the Digest of the various catechetical and educational documents, one is reminded of the words of our Holy Father in his homily in Washington: "In every time and place, the Church is called to grow in unity through constant conversion to Christ, whose saving work is proclaimed by the successors of the Apostles and celebrated in the sacraments. This unity, in turn, gives rise to an unceasing missionary outreach, as the Spirit spurs believers to proclaim 'the great works of God' and to invite all people to enter the communion of those saved by the blood of Christ and granted new life in the Spirit."

To take the time to go through this important work is to travel with the bishops united with Peter on the road that covers well over thirty years of highlighting, encouraging, instructing, teaching and empowering those women and men, priests, deacons, religious and laity who have labored so long and so hard to see that the next generation entrusted to their care hears the Gospel, encounters Christ and comes to experience new life in him.

In holding up this book of catechetical documents, we need as well to hear once again the words of Pope Benedict XVI: "Here I wish to add a special word of gratitude and encouragement to all those who have taken up the challenge of the Second Vatican Council, so often reiterated by Pope John Paul II, and committed their lives to the new evangelization. I thank my brother bishops, priests and deacons, men and women religious, parents, teachers and catechists. The fidelity and courage with which the Church in this country will respond to the challenges raised by an increasingly secular and materialistic culture will depend in large part upon your own fidelity in handing on the treasure of our Catholic faith."

Father Berard Marthaler has done everyone interested in the teaching of the faith a great service in this *Digest of Recent Church Documents*. His decades of scholarship, pastoral ministry and catechetical involvement are evident in this volume which provides us a concise, faithful, clear and digestible summary of a wide range of documents all of which are intended to assist us "in handing on the treasure of our Catholic faith."

Most Reverend Donald W. Wuerl, S.T.D.
Archbishop of Washington

Preface

The genesis for this publication comes from the proliferation of catechetical documents that have emerged since the close of the Second
Vatican Council in 1962. A sure sign of catechetical renewal, these
texts, taken one by one, focus our catechetical attention topically. Collectively,
they articulate clearly what the Church teaches as well as guide and direct catechetical leaders who accept the call to pass on the faith in a post-modern,
technological age. How could one ever hope to read them all? Who possesses
the breadth and depth of knowledge of these documents to highlight key
elements and show their interconnectivity? Those questions prompted the
Department of Religious Education at the National Catholic Educational
Association to invite Rev. Berard L. Marthaler, O.F.M. Conv., S.T.D., Ph.D.,
Professor Emeritus of Religion and Religious Education at The Catholic
University of America, to write a digest of recent Church documents that guide
catechetical ministry. Digested in a single text, these become more accessible
to another generation. Well suited to this task, Father Marthaler has played a
significant role as teacher, author and respected authority in catechesis for over
forty years. He presents the reader with a masterful guide through select
"authoritative" post-Conciliar documents suitable for the novice as well as the
seasoned catechetical leader. Indeed, this Digest is a book whose time has come!

I thank Father Marthaler for accepting the challenge in writing *The
Nature, Tasks and Scope of the Catechetical Ministry: A Digest of Recent Church
Documents*. It reveals the fruit of a lifetime of dedicated service to the Church
as a priest, scholar, teacher and mentor. I am especially grateful to Most
Reverend Donald W. Wuerl, S.T.D., for writing the Foreword to this Digest.
Many others deserve thanks and recognition for having helped to bring the
project to a successful completion: Dan Mulhall for his valuable editorial
assistance; Christina Gergits and Lisa Pannucci for their careful attention to
numerous details during the production process; Cele Edwards for copy editing;
and Deborah Green and Wade Marshall for design and marketing assistance.

In keeping with the Department's tradition of providing publications that serve the field of catechetical ministry and those who labor on behalf of the Gospel, I trust that each reader will find within these pages an occasion of grace to seek the sources "digested" here and go deeper.

Diana Dudoit Raiche
Executive Director
Department of Religious Education

Timeline

1971   *General Catechetical Directory*

1972   *To Teach as Jesus Did: A Pastoral Message on Catholic Education*

1973   *Basic Teachings for Catholic Religious Education*

1973   *Directory for Masses with Children*

1974   *Rite of Christian Initiation of Adults* (Provisional Text)

1974   *Guidelines and Suggestions for Implementing the Conciliar Declaration "Nostra aetate"*

1975   *Evangelii nuntiandi (On Evangelization in the Modern World)*

1976   *A Vision of Youth Ministry*

1979   *Sharing the Light of Faith: National Catechetical Directory for Catholics of the United States*

1979   *Catechesi tradendae (On Catechesis in Our Time)*

1981   *Familiaris consortio (On the Family)*

1982   *Notes on the Correct Way to Present the Jews and Judaism in Preaching and Catechesis*

1983   *Code of Canon Law*

1984   *Reconciliatio et paenitentia (Reconciliation and Penance)*

1986   *The Challenge of Adolescent Catechesis: Maturing in Faith*

1988   *The Religious Dimension of Education in a Catholic School*

1988   *Rite of Christian Initiation of Adults*

1990   *Adult Catechesis in the Christian Community*

1990   *Guidelines for Doctrinally Sound Catechetical Materials*

1992   *Catechism of the Catholic Church*

1993   *Directory for the Application of Principles and Norms on Ecumenism*

1993   *Guide for Catechists*

1994   *Catechism of the Catholic Church* (English Edition)

1997   *General Directory for Catechesis*

1997   *Renewing the Vision: A Framework for Catholic Youth Ministry*

1998   *The Ecumenical Dimension in the Formation of Those Engaged in Pastoral Work*

1999   *Our Hearts Were Burning Within Us: A Pastoral Plan for Adult Faith Formation in the United States*

2000   *Catechism of the Catholic Church* (2nd Edition)

2003   *National Certification Standards for Lay Ecclesial Ministers*

2004   *Compendium of the Social Doctrine of the Church*

2005   *National Directory for Catechesis*

2006   *National Certification Standards for Lay Ecclesial Ministers* (Expanded Edition)

2006   *Compendium of the Catechism of the Catholic Church*

2006   *United States Catholic Catechism for Adults*

Abbreviations

AA	*Apostolicam actuositatem* (*Decree on the Apostolate of the Laity*)
AG	*Ad gentes* (*Decree on the Church's Missionary Activity*)
APNE	*Directory for the Application of Principles and Norms on Ecumenism*
C-CCC	*Compendium of the Catechism of the Catholic Church*
C-SD	*Compendium of the Social Doctrine of the Church*
CCC	*Catechism of the Catholic Church*
CD	*Christus dominus* (*Decree on the Pastoral Office of Bishops in the Church*)
CIC	*Code of Canon Law*
COINCAT	International Council for Catechists
CT	*Catechesi tradendae* (*On Catechesis in Our Time*)
DH	*Dignitatis humanae* (*Declaration on Religious Liberty*)
DMM	Director of Music Ministries
DV	*Dei verbum* (*Dogmatic Constitution on Divine Revelation*)
EDFPW	*The Ecumenical Dimension in the Formation of those Engaged in Pastoral Work*
EN	*Evangelii nuntiandi* (*On Evangelization in the Modern World*)
FC	*Familiaris consortio* (*On the Family*)
GCD	*General Catechetical Directory*
GCM	*Guide for Catechists*
GDC	*General Directory for Catechesis*
GDSCM	*Guidelines for Doctrinally Sound Catechetical Materials*
GE	*Gravissimum educationis* (*Declaration on Christian Education*)
GS	*Gaudium et spes* (*Pastoral Constitution on the Church in the Modern World*)
IM	*Inter mirifica* (*Decree on the Mass Media*)

LG	*Lumen gentium* (*Dogmatic Constitution on the Church*)
MWC	*Directory for Masses with Children*
NA	*Nostra aetate* (*The Relation of the Church to Non-Christian Religions*)
NALM	National Association for Lay Ministry
NCCB	National Conference of Catholic Bishops; now USCCB
NCCL	National Conference for Catechetical Leadership
NCEA	National Catholic Educational Association
NFCYM	National Federation for Catholic Youth Ministry
NDC	*National Directory for Catechesis*
NPCD	National Association of Parish Catechetical Directors
NPM	National Association of Pastoral Musicians
OE	*Orientalium ecclesiarum* (*Decree on the Catholic Eastern Churches*)
OHWB	*Our Hearts Were Burning Within Us: A Pastoral Plan for Adult Faith Formation in the United States*
OT	*Optatam totius* (*Decree on the Training of Priests*)
PA	Lay Ecclesial Pastoral Associate
PC	*Perfectae caritatis* (*Decree on the Adaptation and Renewal of Religious Life*)
PCL	Parish Catechetical Leader
PLC	Parish Life Coordinator
PO	*Presbyterorum ordinis* (*Decree on the Ministry and Life of Priests*)
RP	*Reconciliatio et paenitentia* (*Reconciliation and Penance*)
RCIA	*Rite of Christian Initiation of Adults*
RV	*Renewing the Vision: A Framework for Catholic Youth Ministry*
SC	*Sacrosanctum concilium* (*Constitution on the Sacred Liturgy*)
SLF / NCD	*Sharing the Light of Faith: National Catechetical Directory for Catholics of the United States*
TTJD	*To Teach as Jesus Did: A Pastoral Message on Catholic Education*

UR	*Unitatis redintegratio (Decree on Ecumenism)*
USCC	United States Catholic Conference; now USCCB
USCCA	*United States Catholic Catechism for Adults*
USCCB	United States Conference of Catholic Bishops; formerly USCC/NCCB
YML	Youth Ministry Leader

Introduction

Although the formal sessions of the Second Vatican Council spanned a period of only four years (1962–1965), its impact on Catholic life continues to be felt now, more than a half century since Pope John XXIII convoked it 1959. In no area, save perhaps the liturgy, has the ripple effect of the Council been more evident than in the influence it has had on Catholic religious education. Already in the preparatory stage leading up to the Council numerous proposals were made on how better to communicate the Christian message, and in the years since, the number of documents and directives issued by the Holy See and episcopal conferences dealing with Catholic religious education and catechesis continues to grow. The ranks of individuals who had an interest in reading the post-conciliar publications as they appeared one by one are very thin, and those who are taking their places are overwhelmed by the titles that have accumulated on their bookshelves. Some are of historical interest, some are still normative for religious education and catechesis, but time is limited. How does one get a handle on their contents? This digest is offered as a place to begin.

Disclaimer One

No digest, and even less a summary, is a substitute for an original work, whether it is one of Shakespeare's plays or a Church document. Digests and summaries, focusing as they do on the main points of a text, say little about its background. They may outline the plot, but they gloss over fine points and nuances. Nonetheless, *Reader's Digest* and *Cliffsnotes* stand as evidence that digests and summaries have a function and fill a need.

Disclaimer Two

This in not a complete catalogue of the significant documents dealing with Catholic religious education that have appeared since Vatican II. The thirty publications digested here are "authoritative," that is, they were issued by the Holy See or an agency recognized and approved by the United States

Conference of Catholic Bishops, but they do not include many documents published by Roman dicasteries dealing with specific topics or the catechisms, directories, and pastoral letters published by other Episcopal Conferences and individual bishops.

The authoritative statements regulating the teaching of Christian doctrine promulgated by the Holy See promulgated before Vatican II were few and far between. The most notable was the encyclical letter *Etsi minime* of Pope Benedict XIV in 1742. In the spirit of the Council of Trent, Pope Benedict traced many of the Church's ills to "ignorance of things divine," which in turn he attributed to neglect of catechetical instruction. The main thrust of *Etsi minime* was to remind bishops, in very strong terms, that their first duty, by reason of their Apostolic Office, is to nourish the faith of the people with the rudiments of Christian doctrine and knowledge of the divine precepts. Insofar as he is able, the bishop should be personally involved both in teaching and by overseeing the work of pastors. The laity too have a part to play. Pope Benedict cites the papal brief *Ex debito pastoralis officio* of his predecessor Pius V (1571) who recognized the success of the Confraternity of Christian Doctrine in organizing religious instruction in Rome and elsewhere and recommended that it be established in every parish.

Etsi minime reaffirms two obligations imposed by the Council of Trent on everyone who has the care of souls: namely, on feast days to preach sermons adapted to the listeners, and to teach the basics of the faith to children and all who are ignorant of the Divine Law. Benedict adds, if pastors preach inspirational homilies, exhorting people to virtuous living, they can expect to raise up a people pleasing to God and doers of good things. Preachers should impress on parents the importance of teaching the truths of religion to their children, and if the parents are not up to it, they are to bring their children to Church where they can learn about God's Law. Parish churches should regularly schedule religious instruction at a time convenient to all, and festive celebrations (notably in churches in the care of Religious Orders) should not be an excuse for neglecting the teaching of Christian doctrine.

Knowledge of Christian doctrine, the Divine Law, and the precepts of the Church is a requisite for receiving the sacraments. Without a grasp of the basics, children are not to be admitted to the Eucharist and Confirmation. Confessors are not to give absolution to individuals who do not understand the meaning and obligations of the Sacrament of Penance. Pastors cannot permit couples to marry who are uninformed as to what is necessary for salvation.

In conclusion, Pope Benedict endorsed the catechism of St. Robert Bellarmine for its content and especially as a means to insure uniformity in the teaching of Christian doctrine:

> Following the footsteps of Pope Clement VIII and others among our predecessors, we exhort in the Lord and earnestly recommend that in teaching Christian Doctrine, the booklet written by Cardinal Bellarmine be used. Examined and approved by the proper Congregation of the Holy See deputed for the purpose, the same Pope Clement ordered it to be published. It was his most valid intention that in the future all adhere to one and the same method of teaching and learning Christian doctrine.
>
> There is nothing more desirable nor more opportune than this kind of uniformity to guard against errors that can furtively be introduced when there are many and varied catechisms. If, however, because of the specific needs of a place, some other small work is used, great care must be exercised to see that it not contain nor insinuate anything out of harmony with Catholic truth. Care must also be taken that the dogmas of faith be explained simply and clearly, that any missing elements be added, and anything superfluous be eliminated. (n. 17)

The concern of the post-Tridentine popes to combat error and safeguard truth surfaces again in the encyclical *In Dominico agro* of Pope Clement XIII (1761). Clement attributed many of the errors and confusion to a disregard of the catechism mandated by the Council of Trent. Better known as the *Roman Catechism*, it was to be the norm for pastors and priests in communicating the Church's teaching to the faithful. In the words of *In Dominico agro*:

> ... even though this book, composed with remarkable work and effort, was universally approved and welcomed with the highest praises, at that time, the love of novelty almost wrested it from the priests' hands by inspiring the production of more and more catechisms which could compare in no way with the

Roman Catechism. Thus two evils arose: Agreement on a method of teaching was almost destroyed, and the weak members of the faithful were scandalized at finding that they were no longer united by the same language and topics....

Like Benedict XIV, Clement's remedy was to insist on uniformity in method, content, and language.

The focus of *In Dominico agro* was almost exclusively on the Roman Catechism as the norm and source for catechetical instruction. Other popes in the post-Tridentine years, most notably Pius IX whose pontificate dominated almost a third of the nineteenth century, focused more on the catechesis of children and young people. Early in his pontificate Pope Pius directed that only catechetical books approved by the Holy See be used in the dioceses of Italy (*Nostris et nobiscum,* Dec. 8, 1849). The feasibility of a single catechism for the universal Church dominated the discussions in the early session of the First Vatican Council. The Constitution *De parvo catechismo* made the case for uniformity:

Just as all members of the Church of Christ, spread over the whole world, should be of one heart and soul, so too should they have but one voice and tongue. And since different methods and ways of transmitting to the faithful the essential of faith are known to create no little inconvenience, we shall by our authority and with the approval of this council, see to it that a new catechism is drawn up in Latin, modeled after the Small Catechism of the Ven. Cardinal Bellarmine. Compiled at the command of the Holy See, it is highly recommended to all the local ordinaries. Its use by all will facilitate the disappearance in the future of the confusing variety of other short catechisms.

After protracted debate the constitution was amended and approved, but the Council disbanded before it was officially promulgated and no steps were taken to implement it.

Although bishops in the United States had begun to speak of a common catechism for the faithful as early as the First Provincial Council of Baltimore in 1832, they did not take action until after the First Vatican Council. The

Third Council of Baltimore citing the "great disadvantage that rises from the variety and number of catechisms which are circulated in the provinces," ordered a common catechism to be used through the country. The Council went so far as to recommend that youths "learn the before-mentioned Catechism in the English tongue."

Second only to Pope Pius X's insistence on frequent reception of the Eucharist beginning at an early age was his encyclical letter *Acerbo nimis* in shaping the direction of catechesis in the 20th century. *Acerbo nimis,* published early in his pontificate (1905), echoed the concerns of the Council of Trent and his predecessors about the prevailing ignorance of religion among all classes of people, young and old, cultured and uncultured. He attributed the moral depravity in society at large to the neglect of religious instruction. The first part of the encyclical stressed the importance and obligation of the clergy, especially pastors, to impart Christian doctrine. In the second part, he returns to a point made by both Trent and Pope Benedict XIV, namely, the homily is not to displace the explanation of Christian doctrine to both children and adults. The third part gives practical guidelines as to how catechetical instruction is to be carried out and concludes with a number of regulations:

> We, therefore, Venerable Brethren, desirous of fulfilling this most important obligation of Our Teaching Office, and likewise wishing to introduce uniformity everywhere in so weighty a matter, do by Our Supreme Authority enact the following regulations and strictly command that they be observed and carried out in all dioceses of the world.

> I. On every Sunday and holy day, with no exception, throughout the year, all parish priests and in general all those having the care of souls, shall instruct the boys and girls, for the space of an hour from the text of the Catechism on those things they must believe and do in order to attain salvation.

> II. At certain times throughout the year, they shall prepare boys and girls to receive properly the Sacraments of Penance and Confirmation.

III. With a very special zeal, on every day in Lent and, if necessary, on the days following Easter, they shall instruct with the use of apt illustrations and exhortations the youth of both sexes to receive their first Communion in a holy manner.

IV. In each and every parish the society known as the Confraternity of Christian Doctrine is to be canonically established. Through this Confraternity, the pastors, especially in places where there is a scarcity of priests, will have lay helpers in the teaching of the Catechism.

V. In the larger cities, and especially where universities, colleges and secondary schools are located, let classes in religion be organized to instruct in the truths of faith and in the practice of Christian life the youths who attend the public schools.

VI. Since it is a fact that in these days adults need instruction no less than the young, all pastors and those having the care of souls shall explain the Catechism to the people in a plain and simple style adapted to the intelligence of their hearers. This shall be carried out on all holy days of obligation, at such time as is most convenient for the people, but not during the same hour when the children are instructed, and this instruction must be in addition to the usual homily on the Gospel which is delivered at the parochial Mass on Sundays and holy days. The catechetical instruction shall be based on the Catechism of the Council of Trent; and the matter is to be divided in such a way that in the space of four or five years, treatment will be given to the Apostles' Creed, the Sacraments, the Ten Commandments, the Lord's Prayer and the Precepts of the Church.

Pius X made his strong desire for uniformity known in a number of writings as well. Shortly after *Acerbo nimis* appeared, he addressed a letter titled *Uniformitas* to the Cardinal Vicar of Rome (June 14, 1905) in which he ordered all dioceses in the Roman Province to adopt the catechism used in northern Italy. "We are confident," he wrote, "that other dioceses as well will wish to adopt it in order that we may thus succeed in having one uniform text, at least throughout Italy, as indeed everyone desires." In 1912 when a new, revised edition of the Catechism appeared, Pope Pius pointed out the problems connected with a variety of catechetical texts which, he observed, would be eliminated by the universal adoption of a single and uniform text.

The regulations in *Acerbo nimis* were later incorporated in the Code of Canon Law (an enterprise also initiated by Pius X) almost in their entirety, and were reaffirmed by Pius XI. In the first year of his pontificate Pope Pius XI, by way of the Motu proprio *Orbem catholicum* (June 23, 1923), established within the Sacred Congregation of the Council a catechetical office for the purpose of guiding and promoting the catechetical ministry. It was this new office that, after consultation with bishops throughout the world, in 1935 published *Provido sane consilio*, a comprehensive instruction "On Better Care for Catechetical Teaching."

Provido sane concilio, without rehearsing "more ancient documents," builds on the provisions of Pius X's *Acerbo nimis*, noting that the Code of Canon Law had made them obligatory. It reaffirms the need to impart "the heavenly knowledge necessary for salvation" not only to boys and girls but also to youths and adults. Despite the initial success of *Acerbo nimis*, there remain many obstacles: the indifference and ignorance of parents; mixed marriages; and "a general lack of interest" on the part of the children and youth themselves. To overcome these obstacles, *Provido sane concilio* reaffirms the directives already in Canon Law and enacts new provisions which, "if observed, will give grounds to hope that catechetical instruction will make a greater progress in the future."

In accordance with Canon Law (c. 711:2), the Confraternity of Christian Doctrine, established in every parish, "should embrace all, especially trained teachers, who are engaged in catechetical instruction." Every parish should offer classes in Christian doctrine and children who have not acquired sufficient knowledge of the catechism shall not be admitted to the Sacraments of Penance and Confirmation. The provisions of Canon 1332 should be scrupulously observed, namely, "to explain the catechism on Sundays and holy days to adults," so that over a period of four or five years the material in the *Catechism of the Council of Trent* would be covered. The new provisions instituted by *Provido sane concilio* call on Ordinaries to establish offices to supervise and direct all catechetical education in their dioceses. These diocesan offices shall provide for the training of teachers and the organization of catechetical meetings. In addition, ordinaries are to appoint "competent priest-visitors" to monitor the quality of instruction in diocesan schools. Each parish should make "Catechetical Day" an occasion to preach on the importance of Christian Doctrine and the duty of parents to see that their children are well instructed. In places where the clergy cannot do the work, "the Ordinary should take active steps to supply *capable catechists* of both sexes to help the pastors to impart religious instruction."

The Sacred Congregation concludes *Provido sane concilio* with the command (approved by Pope Pius XI) that all bishops submit an accurate report every five years regarding the catechetical instruction in their dioceses. It appends a questionnaire based on the provision in the *Provido sane concilio* to be used in preparing their reports: twenty questions deal with the catechesis of children; four questions, with the catechesis of adults.

The priority that Popes Pius X and XI gave to the teaching of Christian doctrine tilled the ground and planted the seed for a renewal in catechesis that would flower at the Second Vatican Council. Pope John XXIII anticipated that the Council would bring about "an extensive and deep renewal of catechetical teaching," as in fact it did.

Disclaimer Three

Finally, this digest is not a commentary. Other than brief introductory remarks that provide some background and set the documents in context, the documents are left to speak for themselves. Although no attempt is made to interpret the documents, it soon becomes obvious that they stand in stark contrast, both in number and content, to the earlier documents described in this introduction. The post-Vatican II documents throb with a different spirit and expand the vision of the nature, tasks, and scope of catechesis. Coupled with evangelization, catechesis is seen as central to the Church's missionary mandate to preach the Gospel to all nations. Globalization replaces the Eurocentrism of the Tridentine era. Adaptation to diverse cultural and social milieux overrides the desire for uniformity prevalent in pre-Vatican II documents. The almost exclusive emphasis on imparting Christian doctrine to children shifts to life-long learning and formation so that the mantra in the post-Vatican II documents becomes "catechesis for adults must be considered the chief form of catechesis." Their very number (and still growing) is a measure of the vitality of the catechetical ministry in years since the Second Vatican Council.

1. Catechetical Ministry: The Nature, Tasks and Scope in the Documents of Vatican II

The resurgence of catechesis in the 20th century is without parallel in the history of the Church. Many factors contributed to the new vitality: the hunger of the faithful to know more about their faith; the zeal and vision of catechetical leaders who recognized that more is involved in handing on the faith than rote memorization of traditional formulas; and official directives from popes, Vatican congregations, and bishops stirred by pastoral concerns. None of these factors is independent of the others, nor are they unrelated to cultural and social changes in today's world. The modern catechetical movement was shaped by the interaction of many seemingly unrelated events that brought a new understanding of the nature, tasks, and scope of this ministry of the word.

The renewal of catechesis was already underway when Pope John XXIII convoked the Second Vatican Council, but Vatican II gave the renewal new impetus. The list of Church documents published in the wake of the council records the development and progression of thought regarding the nature and tasks of catechesis. The documents published by the Roman Congregations and episcopal conferences come in many forms and styles: apostolic constitutions and exhortations, *praenotanda* to liturgical documents, pastoral letters, catechetical directories, and guidelines. They touch on every aspect—the who, when, where, how, and means—of catechesis. They address a variety of issues from goals to strategies, methods to media. Some of these issues are perennial, some ephemeral, and some that drive contemporary catechetical efforts. The more recent documents highlight the importance of the *Catechism of the Catholic Church* as the centerpiece and primary reference as to the "what" of catechesis, and provide guidance as to how it can best be used.

The pages that follow are intended as introduction; not so much to the documents themselves, but to the catechetical ministry as it has developed in the post-conciliar Church. They take as their point of departure the constitutions, declarations, and decrees of Vatican II, but the body of the work focuses on the post-conciliar documents: exhortations of Pope Paul VI and Pope John Paul II; publications of the various Roman dicasteries; and statements issued by the American episcopal conference elaborating on principles found in the council documents, updating and adapting them to the concrete circumstances that shape the catechetical ministry.

"The Great Catechism of Modern Times"

In his opening message to the Council, Pope John XXIII said:

> In this assembly, under the guidance of the Holy Spirit, we wish to inquire how we ought to renew ourselves, so that we may be found increasingly faithful to the gospel of Christ. We shall take pains so to present to the men of this age God's truth in its integrity and purity that they may understand it and gladly assent to it. (Abbot)

The Council was less concerned with condemning errors and aberrations than it was with retrieving the richness and beauty of the Christian tradition. In the words of Pope Paul VI, John XXIII's successor, Vatican II sought a "renewal of thought, action, practices, and moral virtue, of joy and hope" that is essential if the Church is to be the light of the world (CCC, FD, n. 2).

Paul VI regarded the Second Vatican Council as "the great catechism of modern times." Certainly it was pastoral in the sense that the Council Fathers sought to address the deepest aspirations of the human heart and to transform society into a kingdom where peace and justice prevail. The Council was catechetical in the sense that it focused on the interior life of the Church, seeking to renew its vitality by reaffirming the importance of living the evangelical message.

Over a period of four years (1962 through 1965) Vatican II produced a body of doctrinal statements and pastoral norms that were later assimilated into the 1983 *Code of Canon Law* and that still continue to inspire the Church. In all, the Council promulgated sixteen documents: four constitutions, nine decrees, and three declarations. The *constitutions* treat matters that pertain to the very essence or "constitution" of the Church and its mission:

1. *Lumen gentium* (LG)—Dogmatic Constitution on the Church
2. *Dei verbum* (DV)—Dogmatic Constitution on Divine Revelation
3. *Sacrosanctum concilium* (SC)—Constitution on the Sacred Liturgy
4. *Gaudium et spes* (GS)—Pastoral Constitution on the Church in the Modern World

The *decrees* amplify norms found in the constitutions and recommend pastoral directives to implement them:

1. *Christus dominus* (CD)—The Pastoral Office of Bishops in the Church
2. *Presbyterorum ordinis* (PO)—The Ministry and Life of Priests
3. *Optatam totius* (OT)—The Training of Priests
4. *Perfectae caritatis* (PC)—The Up-to-Date Renewal of Religious Life
5. *Apostolicam actuositatem* (AA)—The Apostolate of Lay People
6. *Ad gentes* (AG)—The Church's Missionary Activity
7. *Unitatis redintegratio* (UR)—Ecumenism
8. *Orientalium ecclesiarum* (OE)—The Catholic Eastern Churches
9. *Inter mirifica* (IM)—The Mass Media

The *declarations* address specific issues and particular pastoral concerns:

1. *Dignitatis humanae* (DH)—Religious Liberty
2. *Nostra aetate* (NA)—The Relation of the Church to Non-Christian Religions
3. *Gravissimum educationis* (GE)—Christian Education

The Council was an exercise in global evangelization. More than 3,000 church leaders—bishops, theologians, and observers—from all over the world witnessed to the Gospel by drawing on their own experience, keeping one eye fixed on tradition and historical precedent and the other focused on present conditions and needs. They illustrated the dynamics of catechesis by proclaiming the Gospel message anew and expressing it in ways that excited the interest and imagination of a worldwide audience that was watching the proceedings on television and reading about them in the secular as well as the religious press. Not only did the Council publish a decree on the media (*Inter mirifica*), but it illustrated how the media can be used to evangelize and catechize via press releases and news conferences, as well as through formal pronouncements.

Even before the Council convened in 1962, catechetical leaders commonly spoke of "the four signs of catechesis": the Church, the Bible, liturgy, and Christian living. Seen as both source and means of catechesis, the significance of the four signs was enhanced in light of the four constitutions of Vatican II. In presenting "the church, in Christ," as "a sign and instrument" of communion of individuals with God and with each other, *Lumen gentium* establishes the Christian community as the center and context of catechesis. The Constitution *Dei verbum* explains how divine revelation is passed on in the Holy Scriptures and Tradition. The liturgy is not the Church's only activity, but it is the summit and source to which all the activities of the Church are directed and from which all their power flows. Sacramental catechesis encourages the faithful to become informed and actively engaged in celebrating the liturgy so that they can become enriched by it. The *Constitution on the Church in the Modern World* describes in some detail the ideals and experiences that sustain Christians "united in Christ and guided by the Holy Spirit in their pilgrimage towards the Father's kingdom." Because the faithful are bearers of a message of salvation for all the world, "they cherish a feeling of deep solidarity with the human race and its history."

On the basis of the general principles and norms laid out in the constitutions, the decrees and declarations affirmed that catechesis must be biblical (DV, 24), liturgical (SC, 14), rooted in the life of the Church, and guided by the Magisterium (CD, 14). Furthermore, catechesis should utilize the means of social communication (IM, 16) in a manner that responds to the aspirations and problems of people in today's world (GS, 40).

Evangelization

From beginning to end, the *Constitution on the Church* stresses the theme of evangelization, an emphasis that will be reflected in later catechetical documents. The Decree *Ad gentes* bluntly states, "The church on earth is by its very nature missionary" (n. 2). Evangelization "is the responsibility of the whole church" (n. 23), but specific types of ministry "are necessary for the implanting and growth of the Christian community," one of which is catechizing (n. 15). Given the decline in the number of ordained ministers, the role of the catechist takes on increased importance. "Therefore, their training must be in keeping with cultural progress and such that, as true co-workers of the priestly order, they will be able to perform their task as well as possible, a task which involves new and greater burdens." *Ad gentes* goes on to say:

> The number of diocesan and regional schools should be increased where future catechists, while studying Catholic doctrine with special emphasis on the Bible and the liturgy, and also catechetical method and pastoral practice, would at the same time model themselves on the lives of Christian women and men, and tirelessly strive for piety and holiness of life. There should be conventions and courses where at certain times catechists would be brought up to date in those sciences and skills which are useful for their ministry, and where their spiritual life would be nourished and strengthened. In addition, those who give themselves fully to this work should be assured by being paid a just wage, of a decent standard of living and social security. (n. 17)

Vatican II recognized that a great impediment to the Church's missionary efforts is the scandal of a divided church. The *Decree on Ecumenism* took a positive approach in affirming that Catholics "gladly acknowledge and esteem the truly Christian endowments from our common heritage which are to be found among those separated from us" (n. 4). The decree outlined principles and general guidelines that Catholics should observe when joining with other Christians in common efforts to restore unity.

Similarly, the Council also took a positive approach to non-Christian religions. *Nostra aetate*, the Declaration on the Relation of the Church to

Non-Christian Religions, affirms "a high regard for the[ir] manner of life and conduct, the precepts and doctrines." Catholics are encouraged "to enter with prudence and charity into discussion and collaboration with members of other religions" (n. 2). Among the many religions of the world, the declaration cites Hinduism and Islam by name, but it singles out the Jews for special treatment. *Nostra aetate* denounces all forms of anti-semitism, and cautions preachers and catechists against teaching anything about Jews that "is not in accord with the truth of the Gospel message or the spirit of Christ" (n. 4).

The Task of Catechesis

Two documents in particular contain statements that describe the task of catechesis in comprehensive, if general, terms. Although the Decree on Christian Education (*Gravissimum educationis*) is concerned chiefly with schools it affirms the importance of catechesis:

> In the exercise of its functions in education, the church is appreciative of every means that may be of service, but it relies especially on those which are essentially its own. Chief among these is catechetical instruction, which illumines and strengthens the faith, develops a life in harmony with the spirit of Christ, stimulates a conscious and fervent participation in the liturgical mystery and encourages people to take an active part in the apostolate. (GE, 4)

By reason of their role as teachers, parish priests should "by means of catechetical instruction lead all the faithful, according to their capacity, to a full knowledge of the mystery of salvation" (CD, 30). The pastoral formation of priests, therefore, requires training in catechesis and preaching (OT, 19). Pastors should invoke the help of the laity by establishing the Confraternity of Christian Doctrine (CD, 30).

Parents have the primary and principal responsibility for their children's education. It is their duty to create a family atmosphere inspired by love and devotion to God and humanity that promotes an integrated, personal and social education of their children. Above all, it is within the Christian family that children learn to know and worship God and to love their neighbor, and it is also through the family that they are gradually initiated into civil society and the people of God, the Church (GE, 3). The Church supports the family's efforts through schools and catechetical instruction. The Church has a particular responsibility to teach Christian doctrine, in a manner suited to their age and background and adapted to the constraints of time and circumstance, to "the great number" of children who do not attend Catholic schools (GE, 7).

The fundamental principles promulgated by the Decree on Christian Education "should be more fully developed by a special post-conciliar commission and should be adapted to the different local circumstances by episcopal conferences" (Preface). The other document, *Christus Dominus*, addressed specifically to bishops suggests, some ways this should be done. In the exercise of their teaching office, bishops are called to expound the mystery of Christ in its entirety, and stress the value of the human person, justice, and peace (CD, 12). They should make known the Church's solicitude for all peoples, Catholic or not, and especially for the poor and disadvantaged (CD, 13). Preaching and catechetical instruction "always hold pride of place," *Christus Dominus* explains the nature and goals of catechesis as follows:

> Its function is to develop in women and men a living, explicit, and active faith, enlightened by doctrine. It should be very carefully imparted, not only to children and adolescents but also to young people and even to adults. In imparting this instruction, the teachers must observe an order and method suited not only to the matter in hand but also to the character, the ability, the age, and the life style of their audience. This instruction should be based on holy scripture, tradition, liturgy, and on the teaching authority and life of the church. (n. 14)

Then, after a word on the importance of adequate preparation for catechists, the decree adds that bishops "should take steps to reestablish or to improve the adult catechumenate" (CD, 44).

The part of the decree that was to have the most immediate influence on the catechetical ministry was its call for "a directory for the catechetical instruction of the Christian people in which the fundamental principles of this instruction and its organization will be dealt with and the preparation of books relating to it" (CD, 44). How this mandate was carried out is the subject of the next chapter.

2. First Generation of Post-Conciliar Documents: Directory and Code

While the Second Vatican Council presented a fresh look at the Church's mission in the world, it left the specifics and the task of implementing its proposals to various commissions and Roman Congregations under the direction of the pope. These bodies then produced and published new norms governing liturgy, revised sacramental rites, and completed a thorough revision of the *Code of Canon Law*. Following the mandate of the Council, they also published a series of directories, a new genre of canonical document that lays down norms and prescribes policy and practice. The *General Catechetical Directory*, one of the first to appear, describes the nature and purpose of catechesis and provides practical guidelines for those engaged in catechetical ministry. It serves a purpose similar to the *Directory for Ecumenism*, a compendium that applies conciliar decrees and canonical regulations to the work for Church unity without introducing new legislation as such. The *General Catechetical Directory* together with the *Code of Canon Law* (especially Books Three and Four) are foundational documents that gave new impetus to the catechetical ministry and continue to shape it in the years following the Council.

General Catechetical Directory

At the first General Assembly of the Synod of Bishops in 1967 Cardinal Jean Villot asked Episcopal Conferences from around the world to submit "a written memorandum of what it feels the *General Catechetical Directory* (GCD) should include, and especially as it touches upon the matter or content of catechesis." At the time Cardinal Villot was prefect of the Sacred Congregation of the Council (the title was later changed to Congregation for Clergy) that had been assigned the task of producing the GCD mandated by Vatican II (*Christus Dominus*, 44). In May, 1968 an international commission of eight experts including Msgr. Russell Neighbor from the United States and the Reverend Robert Gaudet from Canada proposed an outline of the directory based on the suggestions and recommendations sent in by the Episcopal Conferences. A year later, in April 1969, a draft was forwarded to the Episcopal Conferences for their reactions. The text was revised and edited several times before the final draft was ready for publication. Cardinal John Wright who succeeded Villot as Prefect of the Congregation for Clergy introduced the *General Catechetical Directory* to the public at a news conference on June 17, 1971.

The *General Catechetical Directory* was the first document ever issued by Rome for the universal Church that treated catechesis in a comprehensive and systematic way. As its table of contents shows, the GCD was divided into six parts that described the context and nature, the contents and methods, and the audiences and agents of catechesis:

1. The Reality of the Problem: The World. The Church
2. The Ministry of the Word: Revelation. Pastoral Mission of the Church
3. The Christian Message: Norms or Criteria. Outstanding Elements
4. Elements of Methodology
5. Catechesis According to Age Levels
6. Pastoral Activity in the Ministry of the Word

The GCD also had an Addendum that threatened to overshadow the document itself. It addressed an issue much debated at the time, namely, norms for "The First Reception of the Sacraments of Penance and the Eucharist." It insisted on continuing the "common practice" that introduces children to the sacrament of penance at the time they reach the "age of discretion" (n. 5).

Part One – The Reality of the Problem: The World. The Church

The GCD states, "the essential mission of the Church is to proclaim and promote the faith in contemporary society," and then proceeds to identify features and characteristics of the present age, a time of great socio-cultural change. Faith is no longer mediated—handed on—by a homogeneous culture permeated with Christian principles and values (n. 2). Pluralism is a fact that must be taken into account (n. 3). Science and technology, industrialization and urbanization divert attention from spiritual matters, and the media, with ever widening influence, disseminate faulty opinions and errors about the faith and the Christian way of life, especially among young adults (n. 5).

Factors and change-agents that affect society at large also impact the Church. Although it is no longer a matter of preserving traditional religious customs, popular piety can still serve as a starting point for proclaiming the faith. The challenge is to reevangelize individuals, calling them to a new conversion and educating them to a more mature faith (n. 6). Many baptized persons have become indifferent with regard to practice of religion and, "atheism must be accounted among the most serious problems of this age" (n. 7). Even individuals "who have had an excellent Christian education" find difficulty in expressing the faith:

> They think it is bound up too much with ancient and obsolete formulations and too much tied to Western culture. They are, therefore, seeking a new way of expressing the truths of religion, one which conforms to the present human condition, allows the faith to illumine the realities pressing on men [and women] today, and makes it possible for the Gospel to be brought over to other cultures. (n. 8)

Vatican II "time and again urged renewal of the ministry of the word," but the renewal faces a period of crisis. Some eviscerate the heart of the Gospel message by reducing it to a social manifesto. Others, however, are:

> ...unable to understand the depth of the proposed renewal, as though the issue here were merely one of eliminating ignorance of the doctrine which must be taught... [For them] the remedy would be more frequent catechetical instruction. Once the matter has been considered that way, that remedy is immediately seen to be altogether unequal to the needs. (n. 9)

Part Two – The Ministry of the Word

The two chapters of Part Two outline the premise that is fundamental to the GCD, namely, catechesis as a form of ministry of the word. The first chapter, a quilt of quotes sewn together from *Dei Verbum*, the Constitution on Divine Revelation, centers on five points: divine revelation mediated in words and deeds (n. 10); Jesus Christ embodies the fullness of all revelation (n. 12); ministry of the word gives voice to the living tradition that mediates revelation in today's world (n. 13); ministry of the word is rooted in and nourished by Sacred Scripture (n. 14); humans, moved by grace, respond to revelation in faith (n. 15):

> To put the whole matter in a few words, the minister of the word should be honestly aware of the mission assigned to him. It is to stir up a lively faith which turns the mind to God, impels conformance with his action, leads to a living knowledge of the expressions of tradition, and speaks and manifests the true significance of the world and human existence. (n. 16)

The ministry of the word has many forms, each governed by its own principles, but evangelization, catechesis, liturgical preaching and theology, are closely linked in practice (n. 17) and in fact. In turn, catechetical activity takes on various forms and structures according to circumstances, and all forms of catechesis "must also perform the role of evangelization" (n. 18):

> In regions which have been Christian from of old, catechesis often takes the form of religious instruction given to children and adolescents in schools or outside a school atmosphere. Also found in those regions are various catechetical programs for adults. There are also various catechumenate programs for those who are preparing themselves for the reception of baptism, or for those who have been baptized but lack a proper Christian initiation… (n. 19)

When insisting that catechetical instruction must be "thoroughly renewed," the GCD explains "this renewal has to do with a continuing education in the faith, not only for children but also for adults" (n. 9). The importance it gives to adult catechesis reflects the momentous shift in pastoral ministry initiated by Vatican II. One of the most frequently quoted paragraphs in the Directory states:

> [Shepherds of souls] should also remember that catechesis for
> adults, since it deals with persons who are capable of an adher-
> ence that is fully responsible, must be considered the chief form
> of catechesis. All the other forms, which are indeed always nec-
> essary, are in some way oriented to it. (n. 20)

The text, citing the Decrees on the bishops' office (CD, 14) and the missions
(AG, 14), concludes with the admonition that they should "reestablish or better adapt the instruction of adult catechumens."

At this point the GCD provides another principle (or definition) that
determines the functions proper to catechesis, making clear that more is
involved in catechesis than the instruction of individuals:

> Within the scope of pastoral activity, catechesis is the term to be
> used for that form of ecclesial action which leads both commu-
> nities and individual members of the faithful to maturity of faith.
> (n. 21)

The nine paragraphs that follow (nn. 22-30) explain how catechesis contributes to the attainment of this twofold maturity of faith, singling out for
special mention that catechesis should assist communities in ecumenical efforts
to restore Christian unity (n. 27). Without neglecting the individual believer,
catechesis is concerned with the initiation, education, and formation of the
community as a whole (n. 31). And in turn, to be effective "catechesis demands
the witness of faith, both from the catechists and from the ecclesial community, a witness that is joined to an authentic example of Christian life and to
a readiness for sacrifice" (n. 35).

Part Three – The Christian Message

Although the GCD links it to almost every pastoral activity, catechesis
remains chiefly a form of ministry of the word. Following on, and sometimes
in tandem with, the proclamation of the Christian message, catechesis promotes maturity of faith. Part Three describes the content of that message, the
"faith that we hold"—*the fides quae*— as it is referred to by theologians, but
first it outlines norms and criteria that guide catechesis in "the discovery and
exposition of its content" (n. 36). (These norms and criteria deserve special

attention because they were used as guidelines by the Commission of Cardinals and Bishops that compiled the *Catechism of the Catholic Church*.)

The norms and criteria are found in Chapter One. Catechesis, "as a most excellent opportunity for the prophetic ministry of the Church," has the task of communicating the message of salvation in an intelligible and meaningful way. Consequently, it "must strive to promote a greater accord between the possible formulations of the divine message and the various cultures and diverse languages of peoples" (n. 37). The reference to "the prophetic ministry" seems to have been inspired by the opening verse of the Epistle to the Hebrews that suggests a gradual unfolding of revelation. According to this example of "divine pedagogy," catechesis begins with a rather simple presentation of the Christian message, presenting it gradually in a more detailed and developed manner, until the message is presented in its entirety (n. 38, cf. n. 33). Later, the chapter states, "On all levels catechesis should take account of this hierarchy of the truths of faith" which is interpreted to mean that there are basic truths (e.g. the mystery of creation, redemption and sanctification effected by the Holy Trinity acting in the world) that have a higher priority and illumine other doctrines (n. 43).

The object of catechesis is to present the mystery of salvation as an organic whole. Articles 39-43 show how "the works that God has done, is doing, and will do," relate to one another (n. 39). Catechesis is Christocentric because Christ Jesus, the center of the Gospel message, "is the supreme reason" that God intervenes and manifests himself in the world (n. 40). "The structure of the whole content of catechesis," is theocentric and Trinitarian: because it is through Christ that one is led to the Father in the Spirit (n. 42). Catechesis recalls the supreme event in the history of salvation, the Incarnation, Passion, Death, and Resurrection of Christ, and enables "the faithful to recognize how the saving mystery of Christ works today and through the ages through the Holy Spirit and the ministry of the Church" (n. 44).

Chapter One ends with a word about the sources of catechesis and its methodology. God's word, "written or handed down," celebrated in the liturgy, illumined by saintly witnesses, and "in some way" known from genuine moral values embedded in human society, is the ultimate source of catechesis. It is the task of the catechist to explain how the mystery of Christ, as interpreted and defined by the Church, is the center of each doctrine (n. 45). The paragraph describing "general principles of catechetical methodology," is by way of introduction to Chapter Two. The Directory treats methods in greater detail in Part Four.

As already noted, Chapter One presents norms that catechesis "must observe in the discovery and exposition of its content;" the second chapter of Part Three deals with the content itself. The GCD does not attempt to set forth "each and every one of the Christian truths which constitute the object of faith and catechesis," but limits itself to a broad outline of "The More Outstanding Elements of the Christian Message." Following the criteria laid out in the first chapter, Chapter Two expounds elements that are "organically interrelated, especially those particular features which must be brought out more clearly in a new, adapted catechesis which pursues its goal faithfully." Furthermore, the presentation is not intended to serve as a paradigm for ordering the truths according to an objective hierarchy, a task that is best left to theology (n. 36).

Paragraphs 47-54 spell out in greater detail the Christocentric and Trinitarian focus of creation, redemption, and sanctification. The section returns to a pastoral theme touched on in Part One, namely, catechesis "cannot ignore the fact that not a few men of our era strongly sense a remoteness and even absence of God" (n. 48).

Paragraphs 55-59 explain, however briefly, the notion of sacrament as well as individual sacraments. The Church "is in some way to be considered the primordial sacrament" because, in the words of *Lumen gentium*, she is a kind of "sign and instrument of the intimate union with God, and of the unity of the entire human race" (LG, 1). It is Christ who acts in the sacraments and "the ministers of the Church are his ministers" (n. 55). Catechesis "has the duty" of presenting the Seven Sacraments as efficacious signs of faith and sources of grace "related in some way to the sacramental economy" (n. 56). Sacramental catechesis leads "the faithful through the visible signs to ponder God's invisible mysteries of salvation" (n. 57). The GCD goes into somewhat greater detail regarding the Eucharist and Marriage. Paragraph 58 explains transubstantiation, the relationship of the Eucharistic sacrifice to that of the cross, and how the Eucharistic banquet unites the faithful with God and with each other. Paragraph 59, citing Pope Paul's encyclical *Humanae vitae*, says, "catechesis must make matrimony the foundation of family life, with regard to its values and its divine law of unity and indissolubility . . . [and] its duties of love which by its natural character has been ordered towards the procreation and education of offspring."

Paragraphs 60-64 introduce the classic themes of "Christian anthropology." After a brief explanation of grace and sin, the Directory discusses, at some length, the nature and exercise of human freedom in relationship to the history of salvation, the moral life of Christians, and the virtues, especially charity. In the midst of this discussion, it cautions that catechesis cannot be silent about "the profound reflections found in St. Paul (cf. Rom. 5) concerning the reality of sin and Christ's consequent 'work of justice'," which it numbers "among the principal points of the Christian faith" (n. 62).

Paragraphs 65-67 highlight selected points in Vatican II's *Constitution on the Church*, in particular the image of the Church as the People of God, as *communion*, and as "the universal sacrament of salvation." The GCD also draws on *Lumen gentium* for its presentation of Mary, Mother of God and Model of the Church (n. 68).

Finally, catechesis "can not pass over in silence" the last things—judgment, heaven, hell and purgatory—but they should be taught "under the aspect of consolation, of hope and of salutary fear." The GCD adds, "It is not right to minimize the grave responsibility which every one has regarding his future destiny" (n. 69).

Part Four – Elements of Methodology

Part Four consists of only seven paragraphs (70-76). Its purpose is to acknowledge how the social sciences—"psychological, educational and pedagogical"—have advanced the art of teaching and contributed more effective ways of catechizing. It comments on "certain points" that are much in fashion today, but it leaves specifics to regional directories and other catechetical tools.

Before describing various methods, however, the GCD has a word to say about *catechists*. While acknowledging that their work is of "greater importance than the selection of texts and other tools," it also warns them of their limitations:

[Catechists] are responsible for choosing and creating suitable conditions which are necessary for the Christian message to be sought, accepted, and more profoundly investigated. This is the point to which the action of catechesis extends—and there it stops. For adherence on the part of those to be taught is a fruit of grace and freedom, and does not ultimately depend on the catechist... (n. 71)

Part Four then proceeds to particular methods. It says the inductive method "is in harmony with the economy of revelation" that is mediated through visible signs. It adds that the deductive method is most effective "when the inductive process has already been carried out" (n. 72), and in the next paragraph cautions that the latter "must in no way lead to a forgetting of the need for and the usefulness of formulas." Creeds and traditional prayer forms, "when committed to memory, help toward the firm possession of truth," and make possible, "a uniform way of speaking among the faithful" (n. 73).

Catechesis should be concerned with human experience, both individual and social. Catechesis helps people explore and interpret their experience and "to ascribe a Christian meaning" to it. Furthermore, experience can also make the Christian message more understandable as Christ himself showed by drawing on the experience of ordinary people in his parables (n. 74). Catechesis must stir a faith response, that is, an interior acceptance of the word of God. One means of doing this is by "an active style of instruction" that stimulates learners, especially if they are adults, to be involved in the liturgical life of the Church, the practice of charity, and by encouraging them to express the faith in their own words (n. 75).

And finally the GCD notes the importance of group dynamics in catechizing. In the catechesis of children, group activities nurture their social skills. For adolescents and young adults, the group is a "vital necessity". Study groups for young people and adults explore the relationship of the Christian message to their own experience. The group provides its members "not only an occasion for religious education, but also an excellent experience of ecclesial life" (n. 76).

Part Five – Catechesis According to Age Levels

The GCD recognizes that there are several ways of presenting the Christian message according to the needs of the audience. It names "the method of evangelization" and the initiation of catechumens and neophytes as being especially appropriate to missionary activity. Other forms of catechesis are suited to workers, technicians, etc. because of their socio-economic and cultural backgrounds. It recognizes that different methods and programs are needed to instruct believers in the basics and to nurture in them a deeper and fuller knowledge of the faith, but it leaves to national and regional directories the task of providing specific norms "in accord with concrete local conditions and needs." By way of example to show how this might be done, the GCD outlines "some general principles of a catechesis adapted to various age levels," (n. 77) from infancy to old age.

Paragraphs 78-81 deal with catechesis during infancy and childhood when the influence of the family, especially the parents, is foundational. The GCD outlines the developmental characteristics in each of the stages and suggests catechetical tasks appropriate to each. It acknowledges that a different approach must be taken in places where children do not have opportunity to attend school (n. 80), and the difficult challenge presented by "children living in families who do not practice their religion at all or do so in an entirely inadequate way" (n. 81).

Paragraphs 82-91 focus on ministry to youth which the GCD describes as a "social class" that makes a great impact on adult society and even on the Church, thereby, creating "no small problem." The GCD says the problem is further compounded in catechesis because adults often find it difficult "to acknowledge that adolescents and young adults can contribute anything worthwhile," but the young are "less distrustful" when catechists show understanding and acceptance (n. 82).

The GCD distinguishes between pre-adolescence, adolescence, and early adulthood. With regard to the first, it cautions educators against catechizing pre-adolescents in the same way that they would catechize children on the one hand, and adolescents on the other. With regard to the last—young adulthood—the GCD is more tentative. It says, young adulthood is a period of life that "has not yet been sufficiently studied and investigated, and its special characteristics are not sufficiently known." It concludes:

> The method that seems most desirable is that of treating fundamental problems and problems of most concern to this age with the serious, scholarly apparatus of the theological and human

sciences, using at the same time a suitable group-discussion method. (n. 83)

The GCD has more to say about adolescents. At a time of "profound physical and psychological change," adolescents are looking for their own identity and a place in society, "but this searching often leads to a religious crisis." The principal task of catechesis in this stage of development is "to further a genuinely Christian understanding of life" (n. 84), to help adolescents "discover genuine values" (n. 85) and foster "personal maturity" (n. 86). In order to attain the autonomy they very much desire, adolescents form associations and by means of peer groups protect themselves from adult pressures and values. Although youth groups do not always have positive values, catechesis should work with them as a means of mediating between young people and broader church community (n. 87). However, if catechesis is to awaken "an experience of the life of faith," it must nurture a religious way of thinking built on a solid intellectual foundation (n.88). In dealing with adolescents, catechesis "should encourage personal experience of faith," and gradually make them capable of giving Christian witness before the world (n. 89). The GCD again calls on catechists to be sensitive to the special needs of young people who, for one reason or another, are forced to enter the work force early and "are drawn into an accelerated development of their personality" (n. 90). Similarly, catechesis must take into account the fact that "maladjusted children and adolescents make up no small part of the citizenry," and provide for them "the possibility of living a life of faith" (n. 91).

In paragraphs 92-96 the GCD "earnestly affirms the need of catechesis for adults." Paragraph 92 gives three reasons that are spelled out in more detail in the paragraphs that follow: (a) The responsibilities of family, professional, civic, and political life require Christian formation; (b) Aptitudes, personality traits, and life-experiences that "reach their full development in adult life" must be illumined by the word of God and Christian wisdom (n. 94); and (c) The faith of adults must be "constantly illumined, developed, and fortified" to face the life-crises they face at certain periods in their life. For some, the crisis comes because of loneliness (n. 93), and for others, because of old age. Although not always recognized and appreciated, the aged contribute much to the Christian community by their work and witness. It is the task of catechesis to help them foster "supernatural hope" in the face of death (n. 95).

Paragraph 96 outlines "conditions and circumstances that demand special forms of catechesis." The first, "the catechesis of Christian initiation or the catechumenate for adults," is mentioned without comment, (the GCD was published a year earlier than the promulgation of the RCIA). Then it lists a number of occasions that provide an opportunity for catechesis focused on a special topic or issue: e.g. marriage, the baptism of a child, first communion and confirmation. The GCD also mentions career decisions like entering military life, migrating from one place to another, and even recreation and travel as opportunities for catechetical instruction. In the U.S. these special occasions are commonly called "teachable moments" because they provide ready-made opportunities when individuals are most open to reflect on the meaning of life. In Europe they are spoken of as times of "occasional catechesis" (see GCD, 19). The GCD, however, cautions:

> These special forms of catechesis in no way lessen the need for ... a systematic study of the entire Christian message. This organic and well-organized formation is certainly not to be reduced to a simple series of conferences or sermons. (n. 96)

Finally, the GCD identifies "special functions of catechesis for adults" that it lists under four headings: (a) Catechesis should help adults "evaluate correctly, in the light of faith, the sociological and cultural changes in contemporary society"; (b) Catechesis must address the religious and moral questions raised by today's world; (c) Catechesis should educate Christians to understand how ecclesial action, though it has a transcendent goal, "serves in turn to benefit human society"; and (d) Adults must develop "rational foundations" that move them beyond "fideism". The GCD closes out the norms for adult catechesis, stating:

> Catechesis must show that the Gospel is always contemporary and always relevant. For this reason pastoral action must be promoted in the area of Christian doctrine and Christian culture. (n. 97)

Part Six – Pastoral Activity in the Ministry of the Word

Part Six gives a series of directives and guidelines that episcopal conferences should follow in formulating a "plan of pastoral action." While the GCD acknowledges that the structures and procedures it recommends cannot be implemented in the same way in every country, it says they point to common goals "which are to be accomplished gradually" (n. 98). Each of the eight chapters addresses a different aspect:

A plan of action begins with an analysis of the situation. The GCD describes the purpose, objectives, methods, and expected outcomes of the "Careful study [that] must be made of the way in which the ministry of the word is being practiced and of the results . . .which have been obtained by catechesis or by other ways of presenting the Christian message" (nn. 99-102).

Chapter Two describes the goals (n. 104) and norms (n. 106) that must guide every plan of action, and the means (n. 105) and distribution of responsibilities (n. 107) for implementing it. The norms may vary, but "the norms for preparing the faithful for the sacraments have a special importance" (n. 106).

Chapter Three reaffirms the importance of catechist formation (nn. 108, 115) that must be on-going (n. 110). "Higher institutes" should offer programs for national and diocesan leaders, and dioceses should maintain schools for the training of "full-time catechetical personnel" (n. 109). The GCD says "the summit and center of catechetical formation lies in [acquiring] an aptitude and ability to communicate the Gospel message" (n. 111). Sacred Scripture is "the soul of this entire formation." It should include: (a) "adequate knowledge of Catholic doctrine together with a degree of scientific theology"; (b) enough information about the "human sciences" to communicate well; and (c) pedagogical methods (n. 112). The GCD says "the art of teaching catechesis is acquired from experience, from the guidance of skilled teachers, and from actually performing the function" (n. 113). Catechesis requires that catechists nurture "a fervent sacramental and spiritual life, a practice of prayer, and a deep feeling" for the transformative power of the Christian message (n. 114).

After repeating that catechetical aids are effective only in the hands of properly-formed catechists (n. 108), Chapter Four describes "the chief working tools for catechesis." *Directories* "are concerned with promoting and coordinating catechetical action" (n. 117). *Programs* establish educational goals, methodological criteria, and content to be taught (n. 119). *Catechisms* provide, "under a form that is condensed and practical, the witness of revelation and of Christian tradition as well as the chief principles which ought to be useful for catechetical activity." The GCD, "in view of the great difficulties in putting these works together," suggests some practical procedures, including "limited experiments... before definitive publication" (n. 119). (See, "The Approval of Catechisms and Catechetical Materials," in *Proceedings of the Forty-First Annual Convention. Chicago June 11-14, 1986.* The Catholic Theological Society of America, p. 183.)

Textbooks are valuable in that they present "a fuller exposition of the witnesses of Christian tradition and of principles that foster catechetical activity" (n. 120). *Manuals for catechists* explain the message of salvation, give pedagogical advice, and suggest methods. They should be accompanied by companion works for the use of parents when it is a question of catechizing children (n. 121). *Audiovisual aids* enrich catechetical instruction by cultivating "the powers of the senses and the imagination" (n. 122). (The GCD links "programmed instruction," very popular at the time, to the use of audiovisuals.) *Mass media* present both an opportunity and challenge. The modern means of social communications offer the possibility of advancing the cause of religion in the public forum. On the other hand, catechesis also has the task of educating the faithful to "discern the nature and value of things presented through the mass media" (n. 123).

Chapter Five promotes the need for diocesan, regional, and national structures (nn. 125-128). Among other purposes these structures can be expected:

> ... to cooperate with other apostolic undertakings and works (for example, with the liturgical commission, with associations for the lay apostolate, with the ecumenical commission, and so on), because all these activities of the Church have a part even though in different ways, in the ministry of the word. (n. 125)

The same theme is struck in Chapter Six which emphasizes the coordination of pastoral catechetics with all pastoral work, including social action. Chapter Six makes explicit mention of the adult catechumenate because it engages the entire Christian community and brings together a number of pastoral activities (n. 130).

Chapter Seven consists of one paragraph outlining the importance of "scientific study" and suggesting broad areas for research (n. 131).

"International Cooperation and Relations with the Apostolic See," is the heading of the eighth and last chapter. The GCD singles out work among immigrants and tourists as areas that call for international cooperation in various forms of ministry of the word. The Roman Pontiff exercises "his universal office of teaching and of ruling" for the welfare and spiritual development of the People of God "together with the bishops of the entire Church" (n. 133). The pope generally acts through agencies of the Roman Curia. The Congregation for the Clergy has responsibility for coordinating and moderating pastoral activities that have to do with ministry of the word. Among its other duties it reviews and approves catechetical directories, catechisms, and programs for preaching the word of God produced by Conferences of Bishops (n. 134).

Code of Canon Law

At the same time in 1959 that Pope John XXIII announced plans for a Second Vatican Council he called for a revision of the *Code of Canon Law*. After the Council the first Synod of Bishops set down guidelines for updating the Code and bringing it more in line with the spirit and needs of the time. Finally, in 1983, Pope John Paul II promulgated a new Code radically different in spirit and organization (if not in content) from the 1917 Code that had been the norm until then. One difference is the prominence that the new Code gives to the teaching office of the Church. Book Three reflects the primacy that Vatican II gave to the ministry of the word, and it draws heavily on three post-conciliar documents imbued with the same spirit, namely, the *General Catecheical Directory*, the apostolic exhortations *Evangelii nuntiandi* and *Catechesi tradendae* of Popes Paul VI and John Paul II respectively.

The ministry of the word is the thread that runs through all the canons of the third book. By way of introduction, canons 756-759 make it clear that proclaiming the Gospel is a common task of all Christians according to one's office and status in the Church. The two canons that best capture the spirit and summarize the contents of Book Three are canons 760 and 761. Canon 760 stipulates that the ministry of the word "must be based upon sacred scripture, tradition, liturgy, the magisterium, and the life of the Church," and it must "set forth the mystery of Christ completely and faithfully." Canon 761 describes means to be used to proclaim Christian doctrine: First there is preaching and catechetical instruction which the canon says "always hold the principal place." The canon also speaks of "the presentation of doctrine in schools, academies, conferences, and meetings of every type and its diffusion through public declarations in the press or in other instruments of social communication by legitimate authority on the occasion of certain events."

The eighty-six canons in Book Three fall under five headings or as the Code refers to them "titles". The first, "The Ministry of the Divine Word," deals with preaching (cc. 762-772) and "catechetical instruction," (cc. 773-780). The second, "The Missionary Action of the Church," (cc. 781-792) makes the point that evangelization is a responsibility of all the people of God. The third "Catholic Education," (cc. 793-821) deals with the administration and personnel in schools, universities, and institutions of higher learning. Title Four "Instruments of Social Communication and Books in Particular" (cc. 822-832) includes a section on catechisms and textbooks. The last and shortest, "The Profession of Faith" (c. 833) lists persons who are obliged to make such a formal profession. (See, James A. Corriden, "The Teaching Ministry of the Church—A Commentary," in *The Living Light 20:2* (January 1984): 119-145. See, John P. Beal, James A. Coriden, Thomas J. Green, eds., *New Commentary on the Code of Canon Law*. New York, NY;Mahwah, NJ, 2000; pp. 911-993.)

A number of canons that fall under the heading of preaching are related to the work of catechists. "The proclamation of the gospel of God to all" is among the principal duties of those charged with preaching (c. 762), and this includes preaching by lay persons "if necessity requires it in certain circumstances or it seems advantageous in particular cases" (c. 766). The Code instructs preachers "to propose first of all to the Christian faithful those things one must believe and do for the glory of God and the salvation of humanity," as well as Church teaching "concerning the dignity and freedom of the human person, the unity and stability of the family and its duties, the obligations which people have from being joined together in society, and the ordering of temporal affairs according to the plan established by God" (c. 768). They are to set forth Christian doctrine "in a way accommodated to the condition of the listeners and in a manner adapted to the needs of the times" (c. 769). Pastors of souls are to make special provision that the word of God is proclaimed to the faithful who for one reason or another are deprived of pastoral care, and they are to see to it that the Gospel message reaches non-believers (c. 771).

After setting down norms for preaching, Book Three turns to the Church's catechetical task. Canon 773 paraphrases *Christus Dominus* in speaking of the "grave duty" of pastors "to take care of the catechesis of the Christian people so that the living faith of the faithful becomes manifest and active through doctrinal instruction," to which the Code adds, "and the experience of Christian life." The canons that follow spell out what was already implied in canons 756-759, namely, "solicitude for catechesis belongs to all members of the Church," parents above all (c. 774).

Canon 775 describes the responsibilities of diocesan bishops and episcopal conferences. It lists three ways the bishop can fulfill his obligation: (1) by issuing norms or regulations that guide the catechetical ministry; (2) by making available suitable catechetical tools and resources, even if it means publishing a catechism "if it seems opportune"; and (3) fostering and coordinating catechetical endeavors within the diocese. The canon recognizes the authority of episcopal conferences to compile catechisms for use in their territory, but they need the approval of the Holy See. The conference of bishops also has the prerogative of establishing a catechetical office to assist individual dioceses.

One of the most important tasks of the pastoral office is to foster the catechetical formation of adults, youth, and children (see cc. 528, 761, 773). Canon 776 specifies that this is to be done by enlisting the help of clerics attached to the parish, of members of institutes of consecrated and apostolic life, and of laity. The pastor is also obliged "to promote and foster the function of parents" in family catechesis described in c. 774.

Canon 777 singles out five particular duties for which the pastor has a special responsibility, namely:

1. That suitable catechesis is imparted for the celebration of the sacraments;

2. That through catechetical instruction imparted for an appropriate period of time children are prepared properly for the first reception of penance and the Most Holy Eucharist and for the sacrament of confirmation;

3. That having received first communion, these children are enriched more fully and deeply through catechetical formation;

4. That catechetical instruction is given also to those who are physically or mentally impeded, insofar as their condition permits;

5. That the faith of youth and adults is strengthened, enlightened, and developed through various means and endeavors.

This canon recognizes the close interrelation between the teaching and sanctifying offices in the Church, especially in regard to sacramental catechesis. Also noteworthy is the mention of catechesis adapted to the needs of the physically and mentally impaired.

Canon 778 calls on superiors of religious congregations and apostolic life to see to it that catechetical instruction is provided in churches, schools, and ministries under their care. The focus here seems administrative and supervisory in institutions rather than on the endeavors of individual members.

Canon 779 echoes c. 761. It encourages the use of every available manner and means, teaching aid and medium. For these means to serve catechesis effectively they must be adapted to the character, capabilities, age, and life-conditions of the faithful.

Canon 780, the final canon in the section on catechetical instruction, focuses on the formation of catechists. It puts the obligation on local ordinaries to take care that they:

> ... are duly prepared to fulfill their function properly, namely, that continuing formation is made available to them, that they understand the doctrine of the Church appropriately, and that they learn in theory and in practice the methods proper to the teaching disciplines.

The Missionary Action of the Church

The second major part of Book Three sets down norms to guide the Church's missionary activity. Canon 781 establishes the premise of the entire section when it states, "the whole Church is by its nature missionary and the work of evangelization must be held as a fundamental duty of the people of God." Consequently all the Christian faithful have a part to play in the Church's missionary outreach. Canon 785 describes in some detail the role of catechists in missionary countries:

> ... catechists are lay members of the Christian faithful, duly instructed and outstanding in Christian life, who devote themselves to setting forth the teaching of the Gospel and to organizing liturgies and works of charity under the direction of a missionary.

The canon stipulates that catechists should receive special training "in schools designated for this purpose or, where such schools are lacking, under the direction of missionaries." (Vatican II's *Decree on the Church's Missionary Activity*, the principal source of this canon, recommends that a canonical mission be conferred on properly trained catechists in a public ceremony so as to enhance the importance of their work and give it official standing. AG, 17). (Note: A "canonical mission" (*missio canonica*) grants authorization to exercise ministry of the word in the name of the Church. It applies to preaching, teaching, and catechetical instruction (See, S.A. Euart in Beal, Coriden, Green, p. 967).)

It is clear from canon 787 that the missionaries themselves are responsible for catechetical instruction in that they are "to take care that they teach the truths of faith to those whom they consider prepared to receive the gospel message so that they can be admitted to receive baptism when they freely request it." Canon 788 describes how the catechumenate "through instruction and the first experience of Christian life" initiates individuals "into the mystery of salvation" and introduces them "into the life of the faith, the liturgy, the charity of the people of God, and the apostolate." Catechetical instruction of the neophytes continues after baptism. They are to be brought "to understand the gospel truth more deeply and to fulfill the duties assumed through baptism; they are to be imbued with a sincere love for Christ and his Church" (c. 789).

Catholic Education

The longest part of Book Three begins by laying down some general principles describing the duty and rights of parents and the Church with regard to education (cc. 793-794). Canon 795, based on the first paragraph of Vatican II's *Declaration on Christian Education*, states that "true education" should be holistic (in that it addresses the formation of the whole person as well as the common good of society), developmental (in that it nurtures the physical, moral, and intellectual growth of young people in a harmonious way), personal (in that it fosters a sense of responsibility and the right use of freedom), and social (in that it forms the faithful to participate actively in social life). Book Three focuses on institutions—schools, universities and institutions of higher education, and ecclesiastical faculties—and uses the terms religious education, religious instruction, and religious formation rather than catechesis. Canon 804 prescribes that religious instruction "imparted in any schools whatsoever or are provided through the various instruments of social communication are subject to the authority of the Church." The canon continues:

> The local ordinary is to be concerned that those who are desig-
> nated teachers of religious instruction in schools, even in non-
> Catholic ones, are outstanding in correct doctrine, the witness of
> a Christian life, and teaching skill.

From this it follows that "the local ordinary has the right to appoint or approve teachers of religion and even to remove them . . . if a reason of religion or morals requires it" (c. 805). He also has "the right to watch over and visit the Catholic schools in his territory, even those which members of religious institutes have founded or direct" (c. 806).

Textbooks and Catechisms

The fourth section of Book Three, "Instruments of Social Communi-cation and Books in Particular" (cc. 822-832), encourages the use of all forms of print and electronic media in evangelization and teaching. It recognizes, however, that along with its great potential for good, the media can also have a negative impact:

In order to preserve the integrity of the truths of faith and morals, the pastors of the Church have the duty and right to be watchful so that no harm is done to the faith or morals of the Christian faithful through writings or the use of instruments of social communication. (c. 823)

In addition to general norms governing the print media—including Bibles, liturgical books, and prayer books—the Code requires that catechisms and textbooks have an *imprimatur.* Canon 827 states:

1. To be published, catechisms and other writings pertaining to catechetical instruction or their translations require the approval of the local ordinary...

2. Books which regard questions pertaining to sacred scripture, theology, canon law, ecclesiastical history, and religious or moral disciplines cannot be used as texts on which instruction is based in elementary, middle, or higher schools unless they have been published with the approval of competent ecclesiastical authority or have been approved by it subsequently.

It further "recommends that books dealing with the matters mentioned in #2, although not used as texts in instruction, as well as writings which especially concern religion or good morals are [to be] submitted to the judgment of the local ordinary" (c. 827, #3).

The Church's Sanctifying Mission

Book Four of the Code, "The Sanctifying Function of the Church" (cc. 834-1253), is divided into three parts—the sacraments, divine worship, and sacred times and places. The Church's sanctifying mission is fulfilled chiefly in the sacred liturgy (c. 834), but the Church carries out this mission in other ways by prayers and works of penance and charity (c. 839). Each member of the community has a role to play in this mission and everyone has special responsibility for the fruitful celebration of the sacraments:

Pastors of souls and other members of the Christian faithful, according to their respective ecclesiastical function, have the duty to take care that those who seek the sacraments are prepared to receive them by proper evangelization and catechetical instruction... (c. 843, #2).

The introductory canons (cc. 834-838) echo the language of Vatican II's *Constitution on the Sacred Liturgy*. Canon 836 in speaking of the ministry of the word links Book Four to Book Three. It first explains that faith is necessary for the exercise of the common priesthood of the Christian faithful and then enjoins the ordained to support the faith of the community especially through the ministry of the word. A theme running through the canons expounding the Church's sanctifying mission is "liturgical actions are not private actions but celebrations of the Church itself." They touch individual members in different ways "according to the diversity of orders, functions, and actual participation" (c. 837). Parents, for example, "share in a particular way in this function by leading a conjugal life in a Christian spirit and by seeing to the Christian education of their children" (c. 835, #4).

It is clear from the Code that the community takes an active part in the Church's sanctifying mission. The community is expected not only to promote the work of evangelization and catechesis but it plays a part in preparation for individual sacraments (c. 843, #2).

3. Post-Conciliar Catechetical Documents in the United States

The same decree that mandated a general directory to set down universal norms for catechesis ordered that specialized directories be developed to provide guidelines for nations, regions, and particular groups. In 1979 the National Conference of Catholic Bishops (NCCB) published a directory for the United States with the title *Sharing the Light of Faith* (SLF). In that it was published by the NCCB and approved by the appropriate Roman Congregations, SLF had the authority of the magisterium behind it; in that it was the product of protracted and broad consultation with every segment of the U.S. Church, it was truly a collegial document. Conceived in the euphoria characteristic of the post-Vatican II years, *Sharing the Light of Faith* adapted the guidelines of the *General Catechetical Directory* (GCD) to the American scene and incorporated several documents that had been previously published by the U.S. hierarchy.

Before outlining the contents of SLF, it is well to say a word about two of the documents that were assimilated into this national catechetical directory. *To Teach as Jesus Did: A Pastoral Message on Catholic Education* and *Basic Teachings of Catholic Religious Education* (January, 1973) were published within a few months of each other, shortly after the GCD appeared. These two documents focused on themes that were—and continue to be—principal concerns of the American hierarchy: Catholic education in general and orthodoxy. The bishops' continuing concern that catechesis present authentic Church teaching prompted them, a decade after SLF appeared, to publish *Guidelines for Doctrinally Sound Catechetical Materials*.

To Teach as Jesus Did: A Pastoral Message on Catholic Education

Despite the euphoria of Vatican II, by the mid 1960s many Catholics had grown pessimistic about the future of Catholic education in the United States. The American hierarchy found it necessary to reassure everyone of their commitment to Catholic schools. In November 1967, the National Conference of Catholic Bishops went on record saying that "Catholic elementary and secondary schools are an indispensable component of the Church's total commitment to education in the United States." At the same time the bishops promised "at a later date" to issue a more comprehensive statement on Catholic education that would apply the norms of Vatican II's *Declaration on Christian Education* to conditions in the U.S.

This promised document had a long period of gestation caused in part because the newly established United States Catholic Conference (USCC) reorganizing the previously autonomous offices of the old National Catholic Welfare Conference into the newly constituted Department of Education and by the insistence of the Reverend Raymond Lucker, the director of this new department, on a broad consultation with educational leaders and people working in the field.(1) After several drafts and hundreds of amendments, the bishops approved the text of *To Teach as Jesus Did: A Pastoral Message on Catholic Education* (TTJD) at their fall meeting in 1972.

Although TTJD acknowledged the important roles of the family and pastoral programs in the Church's educational ministry, it is chiefly concerned with "those agencies and instruments" that are commonly recognized as having "educational" objectives. The document does "not discount the educational/formational roles" of the media and liturgy (described as "one of the most powerful and appropriate educative instruments at the disposal of the Church"), but its main focus is on schools, youth programs, and adult religious education (n. 3). *To Teach as Jesus Did* recognized the "rapid institutional changes" being felt at every level of church life, and invited all who are engaged in the Church's educational ministry—priests, religious, laity—to cooperate in planning and promoting measures that would assure the future of Catholic education at all levels.

In the original printing *To Teach as Jesus Did* ran forty-two pages. It had 155 numbered paragraphs subdivided into a preface and five chapters to which were added study questions and a comprehensive index:

1. To Teach as Jesus Did: Message, Community, Service
2. A World in Transition: Faith and Technology

3. Giving Form to the Vision:

    a. The Educational Ministry to Adults

    b. The Educational Ministry to Youth

4. Planning the Educational Mission: An Invitation to Cooperation

5. A Ministry of Hope

The Preface explains that although expansive, TTJD is not intended to be all-encompassing, nor is it intended as the final word on the Church's educational mission. The main point of the document was to reaffirm the Church's commitment to the educational ministry in general and to Catholic schools in particular, and to articulate ways its mission should be implemented (nn. 3-4).

Chapter One – To Teach as Jesus Did: Message, Community, Service

The organizing principle (later assimilated into *Sharing the Light of Faith*) outlined in Chapter One inspires the entire document:

> The educational mission of the Church is an integrated ministry embracing three interlocking dimensions: the message revealed by God (*didache*) which the Church proclaims; fellowship in the life of the Holy Spirit (*koinonia*); service to the Christian community and the entire human community (*diakonia*). While these three essential elements can be separated for the sake of analysis, they are joined in the one educational ministry. Each educational program or institution under Church sponsorship is obliged to contribute in its own way to the realization of the threefold purpose within the total educational ministry.... (n. 14)

The three tasks are interlocking and mutually dependent. One cannot be fully accomplished apart from the others:

> All three aspects of the educational mission are present, for example, in a well organized, comprehensive parish program of education where the teaching of authentic doctrine supports and is supported by the building of the community, and teaching and fellowship in turn support and are supported by Christian

service through sharing spiritual and temporal goods with those in need. In such a parish Catholic education's lessons are learned in classroom and pew; yet not only there, but also in the experience of living in a Christian community of faith actively engaged in service of God, Church and neighbor. (n. 32)

Chapter Two – A World in Transition: Faith and Technology

"A World in Transition: Faith and Technology," (nn. 33-41) describes the "distressing paradox" of the "knowledge explosion" made possible by computers and advances in technology. Sophisticated means of communication via satellite, television, and the telephone make information of all kinds accessible to the most remote corners of the earth and foster unity among peoples, but at the same time these same means "destroy ancient patterns of life and uproot peoples from their traditions and history." Technology enhances the quality of life while at the same time "makes possible violence and destruction on a scale hitherto undreamed of." In the face societal turbulence, personal uncertainty, and skepticism towards institutions including the Church, Catholic education needs to pursue a policy of "balanced discernment in place of simplistic solutions." Nonetheless, in acknowledging the inevitability of change, TTJD welcomes "the opportunity of proclaiming the Gospel of Christ in our times" (n. 41).

Chapter Three – Giving Form to the Vision

"Giving Form to the Vision," is the heart of the document. It focuses on concrete forms and structures of the Church's educational ministry and suggests ways that each can foster knowledge of doctrine, build community, and encourage a commitment to service as they apply to adults and to youth.

Adults. The influence of the *General Catechetical Directory* is evident throughout TTJD, no place more than in the importance it accords adult education. *To Teach as Jesus Did* states, "the continuing education of adults is situated not at the periphery of the Church's educational mission but at its center" (n. 43). It paraphrases the GCD saying, "religious education for adults is the culmination of the entire catechetical effort" adding, catechesis "for children and young people should find completion in a catechetical program for adults" (n. 47). Paragraph 48 (also see nn. 60-61) outlines a program that follows the guidelines of the GCD (n. 97) cited above.

Under the heading of adult education, TTJD treats a wide range of topics. It stresses the need for marriage preparation and the importance of education for family life (nn. 49-51). Paragraphs 52-59 address parents as educators, acknowledging that changes have disturbed many "in part at least because the training their children now receive seems to bear little resemblance to their own" (n. 53). "The Catholic community," it continues, "today faces the challenge of combining these complementary values—orthodoxy and relevance—in viable programs.... The steps to achieving this cannot be spelled out in the abstract but must instead be worked out in dialogue and cooperation on the parish, diocesan and national levels" (n. 54). The neglect of parental involvement "can only contribute to further misunderstanding and polarization in catechetics, the same is equally true of the sensitive subject of education in human sexuality" (n. 56). While acknowledging the rights of parents and the importance of moral and spiritual values, TTJD condemns "indiscriminate opposition to all forms of classroom education in sexuality," and insists on "the child's need and right to adequate knowledge and guidance" on the topic (nn. 57-58).

Also under the heading of adult education TTJD has a lengthy excursus on higher education that in itself reflects the changed social status of Catholics in the U.S. It calls for support of higher education in general and for Catholic universities and colleges in particular, and speaks of the contribution they make to society and the Church. It states the importance of pastoral ministry for the entire academic community at Catholic institutions and state schools, at four-year residential campuses and two-year "commuter colleges". It singles out the department of theology as being "an integral part of the Catholic university" (n. 78), and explains the many functions it has in the world of academia and the intellectual life (nn. 79-81).

Youth. In speaking of the educational ministry to youth (nn. 82-136) *To Teach as Jesus Did* describes the ideal program as one that includes "the widest opportunities for students to receive systematic catechesis, experience daily living in a faith community, and develop commitment and skill in serving others" (n. 83). "Merely 'teaching about' religion is not enough" (n. 87).

Although the document recognizes "inherent limitations" in part-time programs offered for young people who do not attend Catholic schools, including parental indifference and scheduling problems, it acknowledges that they have "considerable strengths that should be built upon" (n. 88). The fact that they depend largely on volunteers, for example, contributes to the building of a Christian community, provides creative planners to develop innovative approaches, and expands opportunities for Christian leadership and service.

To Teach as Jesus Did was originally conceived at a time when many within and without the Church wondered whether Catholic schools had a future. There was no doubt in the mind of the bishops about the importance of schools in the Church's educational mission:

> Of the educational programs available to the Catholic community, Catholic schools afford the fullest and best opportunity to realize the threefold purpose of Christian education among children and young people. (n. 101; see also n. 118)

TTJD quotes the declaration of Vatican II on Christian education emphasizing that the Catholic school "strives to relate all human culture eventually to the news of salvation" (GE, 8) so that instruction in religious truth and values is not simply one more subject alongside the others but the unifying principle of the program (n. 103). This integration of religion and life in both the curriculum and in the private and professional lives of the teachers (n. 104), is the distinguishing feature of the Catholic school (n. 105). Everyone engaged in the educational ministry are called on to "contribute to making Catholic schools true communities of faith in which the formational efforts of Catholic families are complemented, reinforced and extended" (n. 107). TTJD attributes the crisis in Catholic schools mainly to financial problems that could be solved were a way found to transcend the court decisions that have erected "the impenetrable barrier" that precludes government funding. It outlined an agenda that calls for action to guarantee the continuance of Catholic schools, to establish collaborative programs with public schools, to assure quality education for the poor and disadvantaged of the nation, and to continue the "search for new forms of schooling" (nn. 119-126).

Youths have special needs. Some young people feel alienated from society in general, some disenchanted with organized religion, but even the ones who are positive about society and Church have a spiritual hunger and feel a need for guidance and support. TTJD identifies "three distinct tasks for the ministry to youth":

> … to enable young people to take part in the Church's mission to the world… to give a specific dimension—education in service—to religious education; and to interpret young people, their problems and their concerns to the Christian and general communities. (n. 131)

The efforts of youth ministers "complement the formal religious education carried on in Catholic schools and out-of-school programs" (n. 133). Those working with youth should recognize the value of "peer group ministry" that involves the young people ministering to one another and should welcome young people as co-workers.

Chapter Four – Planning the Educational Mission: An Invitation to Cooperation

Chapter Four (nn. 137-143) stresses the need for planning based on clearly defined goals and the involvement of "the entire Catholic community" (n. 139). It must identify needs, establish priorities, and plan strategies to recruit lay teachers and administrators as the number of religious women and men who traditionally staffed the schools diminishes.

Chapter Five – A Ministry of Hope

For all the problems facing Catholic education at the time, *To Teach as Jesus Did* is upbeat. The final chapter concludes the document saying, "The Christian community has every reason to hope…"

Basic Teachings for Catholic Religious Education

Another document published by the U.S. hierarchy and later assimilated into the *National Catechetical Directory* was an outline of basic doctrines that the bishops expected in religious education programs. At their November 1970 meeting the bishops approved a resolution introduced by John Cardinal Krol of Philadelphia calling for a positive statement of irreducible doctrinal principles to serve as a guide to publishers and religious educators. Published in January

1973, *Basic Teachings for Catholic Religious Education* was intended to provide a syllabus for religious education programs and textbooks (2). In the words of the Introduction:

> No list of documents can bring about real religious education, but certain basic teachings are necessary for doctrinal substance and stability....

> This text makes clear what must be stressed in the religious formation of Catholics of all ages... in every type of religious education: in the home, in Catholic schools, in programs of the Confraternity of Christian Doctrine, in courses of adult education in religion.

Work on *Basic Teachings* was well underway when the *General Catechetical Directory* was published in June 1971. The episcopal oversight committee chaired by Archbishop John Whealon of Hartford decided to pattern their document on the section in the GCD titled "The More Outstanding Elements of the Christian Message" (Part Three, Ch. Two). The twenty-five headings in *Basic Teachings* correspond to the topics treated in the *General Directory* and the text itself is at times little more than an a paraphrase or an elaboration of the GCD. The most notable elaboration is an excursus titled "Specifics in the Teaching of Morality" (n. 19). The Introduction makes it clear, that *Basic Teachings* should be read in the light of the *General Directory.*

For all their similarity, the two documents do differ in places with regard to emphasis and content. The most obvious difference is in the title. The GCD uses the terms *catechesis* and *catechetical* throughout and describes it as a form of ministry of the word. *Basic Teachings* adopts the American term *religious education*, and while it acknowledges the formational aspect of religious education, it emphasizes instruction and the teaching of doctrine.

A second difference reflects pastoral concerns of the Church in the U.S. By way of preface to the list of doctrines that forms the body of the text, the *Basic Teachings* singles out three themes that "carry through all religious education," namely, prayer, participation in the liturgy, and Bible study. The GCD presumes that prayer, liturgical participation, and Bible study are fundamental to catechesis, but *Basic Teachings* highlights them in a way that the GCD does not.

The third noteworthy difference is in the two Appendices at the end of *Basic Teachings*. The first lists the Ten Commandments and the Beatitudes stating that they are of "special importance in teaching the specifics of morality." Appendix B lists *seven* "Precepts of the Church." The six precepts named in the nineteenth century Baltimore Catechism are updated, given a more pastoral turn and added to. The seventh precept, for which there is no precedent in the old catechism, directs Catholic Christians "to join in the missionary spirit and apostolate of the Church." Both appendices are later incorporated as appendices to the National Catechetical Directory, *Sharing the Light of Faith* (3).

Sharing the Light of Faith

Even before *To Teach as Jesus Did* and *Basic Teachings for Catholic Religious Education* appeared in print, the U.S. bishops had shifted their attention to the production of a national catechetical directory as called for by the GCD. At their annual meeting in November 1971, they established an *ad hoc* committee chaired by the Most Reverend Joseph McKinney, auxiliary bishop in Grand Rapids, Michigan, to propose a plan and procedures for creating a national directory. The committee outlined three "guiding principles" that were to govern its composition:

1. That the broad directives of the *General Catechetical Directory* be adapted to the needs and conditions of the United States.

2. Taking into consideration established principles of Sacred Scriptures, the human sciences, contemporary theology and the teachings of Vatican II, the national directory should give priority to pastoral concerns. It should give prominence to liturgy.

3. The national directory should be the fruit of the widest consultations feasible, so that the process by which it is developed has an educational value, and at the same time creates an environment that will assure broad acceptance of the finished product. (n. 4)

The bishops voted to implement the proposals of the *ad hoc* committee at their spring meeting in April 1972, but it was 1977 before the consultation process had run its course. After discussing the text in plenary session (November, 1977), the National Conference of Catholic Bishops submitted it to the Congregation for the Clergy (October, 1978) for review and final approval. The Directory itself makes reference to the lengthy consultation process (n. 4), and describes the sources (n. 5), the audience for whom it is intended (n. 6), and the document's authority (n. 7). With regard to the last, it states:

> Not all parts of this document are of equal importance. The teaching of the Church in regard to revelation and the Christian message is to be held by all; the norms of criteria identified in article 47 pertaining to all catechesis must be observed. The other portions of the NCD are also important, but the treatment of such matters as stages of human development, methodology, catechetical roles and training, organization and structures, resources, etc., is subject to change in light of new knowledge or different circumstances.

Sharing the Light of Faith: National Catechetical Directory for Catholics of the United States (SLF or NCD) assimilates the main principles of the GCD, and applies them to the U.S. scene, adding chapters on liturgical catechesis and catechesis for social ministry. The original edition, copyrighted 1979, ran to 182 pages (with index) and was illustrated with photographs. In all, SLF has 266 numbered articles distributed in a Preface and through eleven chapters of varying length. It also reproduces the two appendices from *Basic Teachings* omitting, however, the list of the Beatitudes in Appendix A. Two of the many features of the National Directory that make it user-friendly are the comprehensive index of topics and the short introductory paragraph at the beginning of each chapter. The introductory paragraph is as much a summary as an explanation of the chapter's relevance to the overall catechetical ministry:

Preface

1. Some Cultural and Religious Characteristics Affecting Catechesis in the United States

2. The Catechetical Ministry of the Church

3. Revelation, Faith and Catechesis
4. The Church and Catechesis
5. Principal Elements of the Christian Message for Catechesis
6. Catechesis for a Worshiping Community
7. Catechesis for Social Ministry
8. Catechesis toward Maturity of Faith
9. Catechetical Personnel
10. Organization for Catechesis
11. Catechetical Resources

Preface

By way of introduction, the Preface explains the connection of SLF to the GCD and gives a brief overview of developments that had shaped contemporary catechetical efforts up to that time. In the first part, the Preface makes the point that the National Directory represents a collaborative effort of the Eastern and Western Catholic Churches. It describes briefly the consultation process that fed into the National Directory, the sources, and Directory's intended audience. The NCD "is an official statement of the National Conference of Catholic Bishops," but "not all parts... are of equal importance." Nor did the bishops present the SLF as the last word: "Because the methods and cultural context of catechesis are very likely to change and new Church documents on the subject will be published, this document will be reviewed periodically for updating and improvement" (n. 7).

Among the "hopeful signs" in contemporary catechesis, SLF singles out lay involvement, the emphasis on adult catechesis, and the use of electronic media in communicating the message. The Preface also cites "contemporary problems," some arising from "errors of judgment, misplaced emphasis, and ill-timed innovations," some arising from changing social conditions:

> Recent difficulties and disagreements revolve largely around the orthodoxy and adequacy of doctrinal content in contemporary catechetical methodology.... No small part of the difficulty arises from the fact that today most children are catechized in a way which bears little resemblance to the ways in which their parents received religious instruction. (n. 10)

Chapter One – Some Cultural and Religious Characteristics Affecting Catechesis in the United States

Taking its cue from Part One of the GCD, Part One of SLF describes major social and cultural conditions that shape catechesis in the U.S. under four headings: (1) racial, ethnical, cultural and religious diversity; (2) the opportunities and the dangers presented by advances in science and technology including communications media and nuclear armaments; (3) a brief profile of U.S. Catholics with reference to their devotional life, attitudes towards the Church and church teachings; and (4) the importance of the home and changing family structures. Part One concludes, "The picture presented here and elsewhere in this NCD is a sober one" (n. 29) that needs to be taken into account in doing catechesis in the United States.

Chapter Two – The Catechetical Ministry of the Church

Many who participated in the consultation complained that the first draft of the National Directory lacked a theoretical framework. It made no attempt to explain the nature and aims of catechesis or how catechesis relates to other forms of ministry of the word. It was to answer this criticism that the present Chapter Two was inserted. Following the lead of the GCD it describes catechesis as a form of ministry of the word whose task is to foster maturity of faith (a topic taken up again in Chapter Eight).

At the time that work on the NCD began the controversy over nomenclature had not yet run its course. There were those who preferred the Anglo-American term "religious education" (e.g. the *Basic Teachings* document) to "catechesis" and its cognates. The NCD, following the GCD, uses the latter term throughout. It states, "Catechesis is an esteemed term in Christian tradition," saying its purpose is, in the words of Vatican II, to make a person's "faith become living, conscious, and active, through the light of instruction" (n. 32), and explaining further, "Catechesis is a lifelong process for the individual and a constant and concerted pastoral activity of the Christian community."

The chapter has four subheadings:

A. Catechesis – A Form of Ministry of the Word

B. Forms of Catechesis

C. Source and Signs of Catechesis

D. Catechetical Criteria

The first two sections rehearse the general norms found in the GCD (Part Two, Chapter Two). They explain the relationship of catechesis vis-a-vis other forms of ministry of the word, "pre-evangelization" (much discussed at the time), evangelization, liturgy (not simply liturgical preaching), and theology. A final article in Section A, "Catechesis in Morality" (n. 38), could just as well have been put under the second heading which mentions the diversity and variety of catechetical activities singling out adult catechesis for special emphasis (n. 40).

Taking its inspiration from the *General Catechetical Directory*, the NCD moves well beyond the slogan of "creed, code, and cult" that once was used to describe the source and content of catechesis. Sections C and D expand on the norms in Part Three, Chapter One of the GCD.

Section C explains that the source and content of catechesis are one, namely:

> God's word, fully revealed in Jesus Christ and at work in the lives of people exercising their faith under the guidance of the magisterium, which alone teaches authentically. God's word deposited in scripture and tradition is manifested and celebrated in many ways: in liturgy and "in the life of the Church, especially in the just and the saints"; moreover, "in some way it is known too from those genuine moral values which, by divine providence, are found in human society." Indeed, potentially at least, every instance of God's presence in the world is a source of catechesis. (n. 41)

Sharing the Light of Faith reflects an important development in contemporary catechesis. Before Vatican II the catechetical movement had begun to include the Bible as a principal source of catechesis and to speak of the "four signs of catechesis," namely, Bible, doctrine, moral teaching, and liturgy. The reason they are called signs is, as the NCD explains:

The various manifestations of the source of catechesis are called signs because they point to a deeper reality: God's self-communication in the world. (n. 42)

The insights of Vatican II further expand the understanding of the manner and means of God's self-communication to include God's self-manifestation in creation (see n. 49) and "signs of the times." Thus the NCD, adopting language that had come into use in Europe, speaks of *biblical signs* (especially creation and covenant); *liturgical signs* (sacramental celebration and liturgical year); *ecclesial signs* (doctrinal and witness of Christian living); and *natural signs.* "Catechesis seeks to teach the faithful to test and interpret all things, including natural signs," in light of the Gospel (n. 46).

Section D summarizes the main points of articles 37-46 including the caution:

While it is neither possible nor desirable to establish a rigid order to dictate a uniform method for the exposition of content, certain norms or criteria guide all sound catechesis. These are developed further throughout this NCD. (n. 47; see GCD, 46)

Chapter Three – Revelation, Faith and Catechesis

Chapter Three of SLF corresponds to Part Two, Chapter One of the GCD that, in turn, relied heavily on the *Constitution on Divine Revelation* of Vatican II. Revelation is God's self-communication; faith is the grace-inspired human response. Although "revelation" can be understood in both "a general and strict sense," *Sharing the Light of Faith* insists on using it in the strict sense:

The word "revelation" is used in this document to refer to that divine public revelation which closed at the end of the Apostolic Age. The terms "manifestation" and "communication" are used for the other modes by which God continues to make Himself known and share Himself with human beings through His presence in the Church and the world. (n. 50)

In setting down guidelines for "A Catechetical Approach to Revelation and Faith," Chapter Three expands on the explanation of biblical, liturgical, ecclesial, and natural sources described in the previous chapter. Catechists are instructed to "use examples from daily life, the arts, and sciences to draw out the meaning of God's revelation and show its revelation for contemporary life." Other guidelines direct catechists to:

A. Note the historical character of revelation and faith,

B. Understand the development of doctrine,

C. Situate catechesis within the community of believers,

D. Pray for discernment of the Spirit,

E. Emphasize God's living presence, and

F. Give guidance on private revelation. (n. 60)

Chapter Four – The Church and Catechesis

The National Directory is based on the premise that catechesis is a ministry carried on by the Church and is integral to the Church's own mission. Chapter Four outlines "catechetical principles and guidance concerning the Catholic Church's mission and concerning its relationship to other Christian churches and communities, the Jewish people, other major religions, and those who profess no religion" (n. 62).

In addition to the catechetical guidance found in the articles explaining the Church's mission, Chapter Four lists a number of practical directives. Article 74 focuses on points that should be emphasized in expounding ecclesiology. Article 75 outlines principles of ecumenism and Article 76 gives general norms for dialogue with other Christian churches: "Catechetical textbooks should conform to the guidelines found here and in the *Directory for Ecumenism* according to the age and readiness of learners" (n. 76).

The NCD calls for sensitivity regarding relationships with the Jewish people, and recommends that Catholics and Jews "cooperate in scholarship, particularly in reference to sacred scripture, and in social action programs" (n. 77). The Directory names "certain beliefs" that Catholics and Moslems have in common, and states that Catholics have an obligation to collaborate "in promoting spiritual and moral values in society." It also urges that Catholics gain "familiarity with the history of Islam, especially the centuries old quarrels and hostilities between Christians and Moslems" (n. 78).

Similarly, catechists should manifest a positive and respectful attitude toward other non-Christian religions and search for common bonds with such religions as Hinduism and Buddhism (n. 79). "Catholics must strive to understand those who profess no faith and to collaborate with all persons of good will in promoting human values common to all." In addition, *Sharing the Light of Faith* cautions against "religious indifference," that is, "the idea that it makes no difference whether one believes in Christ or not as long as one follows one's conscience and is sincere" (n. 80).

Article 73 deserves special mention. The Preface to SLF explains that the National Directory, though "written largely from the perspective of the Western Church," makes a special effort to inform and interest Catholics of the Church's "rich diversity" and the traditions of the Eastern Churches (n. 3). Article 73 is one of the places that the NCD explains the diversity and gives some of the background for the different rites and traditions. Later in the chapter, it singles out the "unique contribution" that members of the Eastern churches in communion with Rome make "to the ecumenical movement by remaining faithful to their Eastern heritage" (n. 76).

Chapter Five – Principal Elements of the Christian Message for Catechesis

The introduction to Chapter Five describes its purpose and outlines its contents:

> Having spoken of the Church, we now consider the more outstanding elements of the message of salvation, which Christ commissioned the Catholic Church to proclaim and teach to all nations and peoples. (n. 82)

An important footnote confirms that the chapter is based on *Basic Teachings for Catholic Religious Education*, which in turn "was largely inspired by the *General Catechetical Directory*, articles 47-69," (n. 5) but the text is not a verbatim transcript of the earlier documents. Its description of the "principal elements of the Christian message" departs from the earlier documents in minor ways:

A. Mystery of the One God

B. Creation

C. Jesus Christ

D. The Holy Spirit

E. The Church

F. The Sacraments

G. The Life of Grace

H. The Moral Life

I. Mary and the Saints

J. Death, Judgment, Eternity

The first three headings, A, B, and C, summarize revealed doctrine about the mystery of God, creation, and Jesus Christ. Part D describes the role of the Holy Spirit in the Church and the life of the Christian. In describing the nature and mission of the Church, Part E introduces several articles dealing with hierarchical structures that were not in the text of *Basic Teachings*. Where the *Basic Teachings* document treated the sacraments at some length, Part F of *Sharing the Light of Faith* presents only a brief statement, remanding a fuller, updated treatment to Chapter Six, "Catechesis for a Worshiping Community." Parts G and H depart substantially from both the GCD and *Basic Teachings*. They incorporate material from two documents that were published after *Basic Teachings* appeared: *To Live in Christ Jesus,* a pastoral letter on the life of grace and the Church's moral teaching issued by the bishops of the United States in 1976; and the *Declaration on Certain Questions Concerning Sexual Ethics* issued by the Congregation for the Doctrine of the Faith in 1975. SLF gives specific guidance as to what should be taught regarding morality under the headings of duties: (a) towards God; (b) toward other people; and (c) towards oneself (n. 105). Parts I and J outline Church doctrine regarding Mary (6) and the saints, and the "last things," death, judgment, eternity,

Among the specific items that should have a place in catechesis in Christian living, SLF includes the Precepts of the Church. The *National Catechetical Directory,* following *Basic Teachings*, lists seven precepts that add references to the Catholic's responsibilities regarding the Sacrament of Confirmation and the Church's missionary apostolate (see Appendix B, p. 162).

Without compromising the intent and purpose of the *Basic Teachings* document, *Sharing the Light of Faith* presents the "principal elements of the

Christian message," with greater sensitivity to catechesis and pastoral concerns. A conscious effort was made to avoid giving the impression that "content" can be neatly separated from "method". By repeating material found in other sections (n. 82) and cross-referencing other parts of the directory, the NCD subtly confirmed that content and method, message and medium, substance and structure are inseparably entwined.

Chapter Six – Catechesis for a Worshiping Community

From the very outset *Sharing the Light of Faith* makes a concerted effort to highlight the close relationship between catechesis and liturgy. The ad hoc committee that devised the plan for developing a national directory of the United States had urged that the document "give prominence to the liturgy."

The main sources for Chapter Six were Vatican II's *Constitution on the Sacred Liturgy* and the various decrees and instructions dealing with sacramental practice that were issued after the Council (n. 7). Every sacramental rite was reviewed and, when needed, revised in the light of principles and norms set down by the Council. The *praenotanda* ("prefatory notes") that introduce each of the revised rites proved especially helpful in compiling the NCD because they explain the rites and sketch the main principles that should guide catechetical instruction. Many of the guidelines regarding sacramental catechesis are prescriptive and are to be interpreted according to the norms of liturgical law:

- A. Liturgy and Catechesis
- B. Sacraments/Mysteries
  - i. Sacraments – Mysteries of Initiation
  - ii. Sacraments – Mysteries of Reconciliation and Healing
  - iii. Sacraments – Mysteries of Commitment
  - iv. The Eucharistic Liturgy for Groups with Special Needs
- C. Prayer
- D. Sacred Art and Sacramentals

In drafting Chapter Six, the directory committee faced three challenges: (1) the need to emphasize the mutual dependence of liturgy and catechesis and at the same time safeguard the integrity of both; (2) the challenge of bringing adult Catholics to a new understanding of the liturgy and to teach a language and terms that were unfamiliar to most; and (3) to account for the different ecclesial traditions of the Eastern and Western Churches in an informed and sensitive manner.

Sharing the Light of Faith addresses the first in Part A. The NCD had already identified a twofold relationship of liturgy and catechesis in Chapter Two (n. 36); here in Chapter Six it describes how catechesis helps prepare the faithful to participate in the liturgy and then reflect on the community's experience of worship:

> Both [liturgy and catechesis] are rooted in the Church's faith, and both strengthen faith and summon Christians to conversion, although they do so in different ways. In the liturgy the Church is at prayer, offering adoration, praise, and thanksgiving to God, and seeking and celebrating reconciliation: here one finds both an expression faith and means for deepening it. As for catechesis, it prepares people for full and active participation in liturgy (by helping them understand its nature, rituals, and symbols) and at the same time flows from liturgy, inasmuch as, reflecting upon the community's experiences of worship, it seeks to relate them to daily life and to growth in faith. (n. 113)

The second challenge was more difficult because the novel language and terms imported from the Constitution on the Liturgy and other documents of Vatican II carried a new (or more accurately, retrieved an old) understanding of liturgy and sacraments. The language resurrected from the rites of the early Church would have been more readily understood by Christians of the fourth and fifth centuries than by modern Catholics nurtured on the catechisms of the past two or three hundred years. Gone was the language of the Baltimore Catechism that spoke of "sacraments of the living" and "sacraments of dead". Instead, *Sharing the Light of Faith* speaks of Sacraments of Initiation, Sacraments of Reconciliation and Healing, and Sacraments of Commitment. It makes no mention of "extreme unction," but gives catechetical guidelines for the "anointing of the sick," noting that the revised rite also treats ministry to the dying (n. 127).

The manner of addressing the third challenge is evident even in the chapter's subtitles which use sacrament and mystery as synonyms. Part B explains that spirit of the liturgical tradition in the Churches of the East is captured in the Greek word *mysterion* ("mystery"). It emphasizes the reality, hidden in the rites, that centers on the working of the Holy Trinity in the world and the Church (n. 114). Although the Latin word *sacramentum* translates *mysterion*, the two terms have a slightly different nuance. Sacramental theology in the Western Church centers more on the coming of the Spirit and the salvific work of Christ in the life of the Church and its members. (Of course, a sound Christology does not exist apart from the Holy Trinity, and vise versa.) *Sharing the Light of Faith* gives further explanation of differences between the Eastern and Western traditions in connection with the sacraments of initiation (see, nn. 119, 122). Further, the Eastern Churches attach great importance to the epiklesis in the sacramental rites—the invocation of the Holy Spirit—a practice that has also come into common use in the West with the reform of the Eucharistic liturgy (n. 114).

In Part B, the heart of Chapter Six, *Sharing the Light of Faith* presents a significant advance from the General Catechetical Directory. SLF incorporated the *praenotanda* and directives of the new *Rite of Christian Initiation of Adults* (RCIA) that was published after the GCD. The influence of the RCIA is evident in three themes that run throughout the chapter and, to some extent, throughout the entire National Directory: (1) "Full initiation into the Church occurs by stages." (2) Catechesis of both adults and children should emphasize "the intimate relationship of the sacraments of Baptism, Confirmation, and the Eucharist." (3) Catechesis involves "many members of the parish community who support and pray with the catechized, besides instructing them so that they may grow in understanding the Christian message" (n. 115).

The attention it gives to two pastoral issues reflects the times in which SLF was created: (1) the appropriate age for the sacrament of Confirmation and (2) the catechesis of children in preparation for First Penance. The NCD, content to legitimize present practice, did not resolve the first:

> The revised rite of Confirmation says episcopal conferences may designate the appropriate age for Confirmation. Practice in this matter now varies so much among the dioceses of the United States, that it is impossible to prescribe a single catechesis for this sacrament. (n. 119)

The issue of catechesis for First Penance reflected a controversy that had erupted in the early 1960s when several dioceses in the U.S. and Europe (specifically, Holland) allowed small children to receive First Eucharist before they learned to go to Confession. The arguments for and against the practice seem in most cases to have been born of pastoral experience; whatever their merits, the *General Catechetical Directory* exacerbated the controversy by including an Addendum that took up the question, "The Reception of the Sacraments of Penance and the Eucharist." *Sharing the Light of Faith*, aware that children who were initiated according to the adapted rite for children in *Rite of Christian Initiation of Adults* could not make a sacramental confession before receiving the Eucharist, made a distinction between *catechesis* for the sacrament and *reception* of the sacrament:

> Catechesis for the Sacrament of Reconciliation is to precede First Communion and must be kept distinct by a clear and unhurried separation.... The Sacrament of Reconciliation normally should be celebrated prior to the reception of First Communion. (n. 126)

Part B outlines the principle points to be covered in a catechesis for each of the sacraments, including special guidelines for First Communion (n. 122). In addition, it provides norms for the celebration of "the Eucharistic liturgy for groups with special needs." The Directory mentions young people, cultural, racial, and ethnic groups, and handicapped persons; it draws on the *Directory for Masses with Children*, in identifying factors that must be taken into consideration in ministering to them. The NCD notes, "Catechists are frequently asked to assist such groups in preparing for their Masses. In doing so, they should take into consideration the nature of the liturgical celebration" (n. 134).

SLF describes various forms and emphasizes the importance of both community and private prayer in Part C. It presents a long list of devotional practices and describes the feasts and seasons that make up the liturgical year. In addition to providing catechetical guidelines for prayer (n. 145), the NCD makes explicit reference to *The Commentary on the Revised Liturgical Year* and *The General Norms for the Liturgical Year and Calendar*, saying they "provide an ample model for catechesis" (n. 144; see endnotes 33, 34, and 45, p. 167).

SLF includes mention of devotional practices in the Eastern Church in parts C and D. In discussing the use that catechesis can make of literature, dance, drama, music, and other art forms, Part D singles out the way that icons in the Eastern tradition seek "to express in painting what is divinely mysterious in reality" (n. 146).

Chapter Seven – Catechesis for Social Ministry

Chapter Seven builds on Vatican II's dogmatic and pastoral constitutions on the Church (*Lumen gentium* and *Gaudium et spes*) and the statement of the Second Assembly of the Synod of Bishops, *Justice in the World* (n. 160). The chapter directs individuals involved in catechesis for social ministry to "keep abreast of the pronouncements of the Holy See, the United States bishops, and other sources in the Church" (n. 166). Divided into three parts, the chapter explains the foundations of Catholic social teaching; briefly sketches its development, and offers guidance as how to address contemporary social issues.

In explaining the foundations of Catholic social teaching Part A begins by describing the "urgent, recurring summons to practice justice and mercy" in the Old Testament (n. 152), and in the teaching and example of Jesus in the New Testament (nn. 153-154). It then goes on to explain that "the fundamental concept in Catholic social teaching is the dignity of the human person" and that "human beings are social by nature" (nn. 156, 158). Although Christ did not give the Church a "distinct mission in the political, economic, or social order," its religious mission is "a source of insights and spiritual motivation which can serve to structure and consolidate the human community according to divine law." Part A ends noting, "action on behalf of justice is a significant criterion of the Church's fidelity to its missions," and that the Church must submit "its own policies, programs, and manner of life to continuing review" (n. 160).

Catechesis should indicate how the Church's involvement in social ministry evolved over the centuries (n. 161). Part B, in a few deft strokes, traces the development of Catholic social teaching from its early days to the papal encyclicals of the nineteenth and twentieth centuries. It cites the wide variety of topics that the Church has addressed, from education to international justice and peace, from women's role in society and the alienation of youth to "the political vocation" of Christians (nn. 162-164).

Before honing in on contemporary problems, Part C stresses the importance of having a clear understanding of three concepts: "social justice, the social consequences of sin, and the relationship of justice and charity." The first, "social justice focuses not only on personal relationships but on institutions, structures, and systems of social organizations." Social justice "helps us evaluate our responsibility for the kind of society we are willing to support and share in." In explaining the social consequences of sin, SLF affirms that the choice of sin is "expressed through personal choices and actions," as well as unjust systems and structures. It cites "institutionalized racial or ethnic segregation" as an example of "social sin," and puts the responsibility on "all who participate in the society in question." In the Christian concept of social responsibility, justice and charity are complementary. "Justice reaches its fulfillment in charity" (n. 165).

"In order to suggest the scope and content of catechesis for social justice" *Sharing the Light of Faith* "mentions a variety of issues currently of particular concern to the United States." It lists them under three general headings: respect for human life, national problems, and international issues. It cautions that, in actuality, social issues are often complex and "catechists should avoid treating in isolation social problems which are in fact related" (n. 166), for example, "respect for life should also underlie one's assessment of issues pertaining to warfare and defense policy, as well as the question of capital punishment" (n. 167). Among the more pressing social problems in the United States are racism and other forms of discrimination as well as "encroachments on basic rights by the federal and state governments and courts." Many on the long list of issues have been addressed in pastoral letters by the U.S. bishops and, "in a more global manner, by papal statements that deserve close study" (n. 168). In addition, Popes Pius XII, John XXIII, and Paul VI (and later, John Paul II) addressed international issues: peace, human rights, world hunger, and a variety of other social problems (n. 169).

Catechesis "should include efforts to motivate" people to act on behalf of justice, mercy, and peace. Chapter Seven concludes with a long series of principles, values, and concerns—fifteen in all—that summarize its main thrust (n. 170): "Catechesis for justice, mercy, and peace is a continuing process which concerns every person and every age" (n. 170, #11). Principles of social justice should be given priority in adult catechesis (n. 170, #13), and catechists are enjoined:

… to point out the harm which can be done to children's values, attitudes, and behavior by toys and games which make war and its weapons seem glamorous. They should call attention to the damage which excessive exposure to violence and immorality in the mass media, especially television, can do to children and adults. (n. 170, #15)

Chapter Eight – Catechesis Toward Maturity in Faith

Chapter Eight, by far the longest in the national directory, focuses on the recipients of catechesis. It has four principal parts with a number of subdivisions. Part A considers the relationship between the life of faith and human development. Part B, the centerpiece of the chapter, describes various characteristics of life stages from infancy to old age, and shows they are factors in one's moral and sexual development. Part C explains the need to adapt catechesis to the cultural background and special needs of certain individuals. Part D describes "some significant factors affecting catechesis in the United States."

Revelation, grace, and theological aspects of the life of faith are dealt with in Chapter Three. Chapter Eight reaffirms the use of biological, social, and psychological sciences in pastoral care, and then quotes the GCD (n. 131) saying, "the catechetical movement will in no way be able to advance without scientific study." After directing manuals for catechesis to "take into account psychological and pedagogical insights, as well as suggestions about methods," SLF adds, "the behavioral sciences cause neither faith nor growth in faith; but for that matter, neither does the catechist." While these sciences "make a significant contribution to catechesis, catechists should not be uncritical in their approach to them" (n. 175).

Quoting the GCD n. 72, SLF endorses a balanced use of the inductive and deductive methods: "Although certain norms or criteria apply to all catechesis, they do not determine a fixed methodology, nor even an order for presenting truths of faith." The experiential approach, described as a form of inductive learning, "is not easy," but it does encourage people "to reflect on their significant experiences and respond to God's presence there." Catechists, moreover, should use both cognitive (intellectual) and affective (emotional) techniques in their effort "to reach the whole person" (n. 176).

Following on the guidelines for inductive and deductive methods the same article adds a word on memorization:

> While catechesis cannot be limited to the repetition of formulas … memorization has nevertheless had a special place in the handing-on of faith throughout the ages and should have such a place today, especially in catechetical programs for the young.

Among items to be committed to memory are common prayers (Sign of the Cross, Our Father, et. al.); factual information contributing to an appreciation of the major themes in the history of salvation, the major personalities of the Old and New Testaments and key biblical texts; factual information regarding the Church year, important practices in the devotional life (e.g. list of sacraments, mysteries of the Rosary, etc.); and formulas dealing with Christian moral life including "the commandments, beatitudes, the gifts of the Holy Spirit, the theological and moral virtues, the precepts of the Church, and the examination of conscience."

Part B corresponds to Part Five, "Catechesis According to Age Levels" in the *General Catechetical Directory*, but it goes into greater detail. After describing developmental characteristics and appropriate emphases in catechesis during infancy and early childhood (birth to age 5), in pre-adolescence and puberty (ages 10-13), and adolescence ("no specific age bracket"), SLF lists thirteen guidelines that "offer supplementary assistance to catechists" (n. 181). The supplementary guidelines emphasize that "children and young people have a dignity of their own" and that "they are important not only for what they will do in the future, but for what they are here and now" (n. 2).

The NCD identifies several stages in its reflection on catechesis for adults. After identifying developmental tasks characteristic of early and middle adulthood (nn. 182-184), it then provides some general guidelines (n. 185). They highlight "those universally relevant elements which are basic to the formation of an intelligent and active Catholic Christian" and the particular responsibilities of adults in the Christian community. The guidelines present a list of principles ("adults play a central role in their own education") and methods commonly used in adult catechesis (reading, workshops, etc.). This section ends with the statement, "all catechetical programs, including those for adults, should be evaluated periodically." Where the GCD speaks of "old age" (n. 93), the U.S. directory provides recommendations for catechesis in "later adulthood," including reflection on the meaning of Christian death (nn. 186-187). (Without mentioning Elizabeth Kubler-Ross by name, it cites the stages she identified in coming to terms with impending death: "denial, anger, bargaining with God, depression, and finally acceptance.") This section of Part B concludes by emphasizing once again the importance of adult catechesis (n. 188), and suggesting ways to motivate people to become involved. "The best inducement to participate is an excellent program" (n. 189).

Part B has two other sections that have no parallel in the *General Catechetical Directory*. The first deals with conscience formation. *Sharing the Light of Faith*, as already noted, has a lengthy discussion on conscience in Chapter Five (nn. 101-105). The consideration in Chapter Eight is on *formation* of conscience. Emphasizing that "an individual's conscience should develop as he or she matures," it comments that knowledge of the stages of growth identified by psychology and the process by which moral judgments are made "can be helpful when interpreted in a Christian context" (n. 190). The second deals with sexuality and catechesis (n. 191). It begins quoting Vatican II's *Decree on Christian Education,* "as they [children and young people] advance in years, they should be given positive and prudent sexual education" (GE, 1). *Sharing the Light of Faith* then continues:

> Education in sexuality includes all dimensions of the topic: moral, spiritual, psychological, emotional, and physical. Its goal is training in chastity in accord with the teaching of Christ and the Church... Sexuality is an important element of the human personality, an integral part of one's overall consciousness. It is both a central aspect of one's self understanding (i.e. male or female) and a crucial factor in one's relationships with others.

SLF's guidance on the subject situates it in Christian context. It insists that "the primacy of the parental right in education obviously extends to children's formation in relation to sexuality," but parents "should not let their feelings express themselves in indiscriminate opposition to all classroom instruction in sexuality."

Sharing the Light of Faith provided norms and principles to guide the celebration of the Eucharistic liturgy with children, youth, and groups with special needs in Chapter Six (nn. 134-139). Under the heading "The Church in Dialogue," Chapter Four outlined catechetical guidelines with regard to the Church's relationship to other religious traditions (nn. 75-79). In Part C Chapter Eight provides guidelines for the adaptation of catechesis to cultural, racial, and ethnic groups, "persons with handicapping conditions," and other persons with special needs (nn. 192 -196).

Within the fundamental unity of faith, catechesis takes into account the social, educational, and economic circumstances of people being cate-chized. "The preparation of catechists is of greatest importance." They must use the language of the particular group, "not just its vocabulary, but its thought patterns, cultural idioms, customs, and symbols." Adaptation involves more than translations and picture changes; it generally necessitates the devel-opment of new materials (n. 194).

"The goal [of catechesis] is to present Christ's love and teaching to each handicapped person in as full and rich a manner as he or she can assimilate" (n. 195). The diocese and parishes should collaborate in planning special programs, preparing appropriate resources, and providing special training for catechists, especially with regard to the blind, the deaf, and the mentally challenged. Even "the possibility of ecumenically sponsored and conducted programs should be investigated" (n. 195).

Catechesis for people with special needs is part of the Church's total pastoral ministry. SLF recognizes that "the list of groups with special needs is almost endless:" the aged, the illiterate and educationally deprived, young sin-gles, unmarried people with children, young married couples, couples in mixed marriages, middle-aged singles, the divorced, the widowed, the imprisoned, persons with a homosexual orientation, etc. To which it adds "people in the caring professions—such as doctors, nurses, and social workers—who have their own special requirements along with many opportunities for witness and for catechizing..." (n. 196).

The final section, Part D of Chapter Eight "Some Significant Factors Affecting Catechesis in the United States," refers back to Chapter One and specifically to articles 24-28 that present a "profile" of Catholics in the United States. The factors are many and varied: adults spend less time parenting, youths create their own subculture (n. 197). Despite the fact that youth culture changes rapidly, SLF describes "some current traits with their significance for catechesis":

> In general, young people mirror the values and standards of society. Their problems tend to be essentially symptoms of malaise in the larger community; they are more the victims than the source of religious and social ills. Most are conscientious persons growing toward maturity, really concerned about their mistakes and interested in their fellow human beings. Such qualities offer a starting point for effective catechesis.

The remainder of article 200 offers detailed observations and recommendations regarding the catechesis of youth.

Article 201 focuses on the characteristics of young adults, and offers suggestions regarding the catechesis of college students and non-college students alike. Article 202 returns to "later adulthood," describing special needs of the elderly and the importance of developing catechetical programs to address them.

Chapter Nine – Catechetical Personnel

Although all members of the community of believers share in the catechetical ministry by witnessing to the faith, some—parents, teachers, principals in Catholic schools, coordinators or directors of religious education, deacons, priests, and bishops—are called to exercise more specific roles. *Sharing the Light of Faith* uses the term catechist "in a broad sense to designate anyone who participates formally or informally in catechetical ministry" (n. 204). Part A of Chapter Nine describes the "the ideal qualities of catechists" and Part B describes their various roles and the preparation required for them.

The description of the qualities of catechists is "meant to be a challenge as well as a guide" (n. 205). "A clear understanding of the teaching of Christ and His Church" in not enough; a catechist "must also receive and respond to a ministerial call from the local church." (n. 213, #8 speaks of "some form of commissioning ceremony".) The person called must manifest "an aptitude and ability to communicate the Gospel message," that presumes he or she is a person of prayer and deeply committed to Christ (n. 207).

SLF puts a great deal of emphasis on commitment to the Church and community building. In exercising the ministry of the word the catechist represents the Church (n. 208). The National Directory borrows a phrase from *To Teach as Jesus Did* (n. 23) to describe the catechist as one who has "learned the meaning of community by experiencing it." The catechist must have the patience and skills—including conflict resolution—to foster community. The catechist needs to experience and witness to the unity of the community "through frequent participation in the celebration of the Eucharist with other catechists and with those being catechized." The catechist collaborates with other leaders in "making the parish a focal point of community in the Church" (n. 209). He or she is a servant of the community in educating the members and supporting them in social action and missionary activity (n. 210).

The ultimate success of the catechetical ministry depends on the action of the Holy Spirit. Nonetheless catechists should "seek to acquire the knowledge, skills, and abilities needed to communicate the Gospel message effectively":

> They must have a solid grasp of Catholic doctrine and worship; familiarity with scripture; communication skills; the ability to use various methodologies; understanding of how people grow and mature and of how persons of different ages and circumstances learn. (n. 211)

The Directory moves from this general description of knowledge, skills, and abilities to the specific responsibilities of the faithful in various roles beginning with parents and works its way up to bishops. SLF repeats the statement of the *Decree on Christian Education,* "parents are the first and foremost catechists of their children" (GE, 3), and reminds the church community—diocese and parish—that it has an obligation to help them in various ways (n. 212). Similarly, programs should be designed to help parish catechists, "many of whom are volunteers," acquire the particular knowledge and skills they need. Their training should direct them to participate in liturgical experiences, classes, retreats, service programs, study clubs, and other teaching/learning activities that SLF spells out in some detail (n. 213).

Part B recognizes that "an increasing number of men and women have assumed positions as parish or inter-parish directors and coordinators of religious education." The exact title and specific functions vary from place to place depending on size of staff, scope of program, and other factors, but in general the work requires appropriate background in religious studies, educational theory, administrative ability, and practical experience with children and adults. Pastors or parish boards "must formulate clear and specific agreements with them concerning their duties in line with diocesan policies," as well as "the spiritual, psychological, and financial support to be provided by the parish" (n. 214).

One of the few articles in SLF (see, nn. 232-233) that deals explicitly with Catholic schools states that although the role of the principal varies according to circumstances, "certain functions relating to catechesis are basic":

> Recognizing that all faculty members share in catechetical ministry, principals recruit teachers with appropriate qualifications in view of the Catholic school's apostolic goals and character. They provide opportunities for ongoing catechesis for faculty members by which they can deepen their faith and grow in the ability to integrate in their teaching the fourfold fundamental dimensions of Catholic education: message, community, worship, and service. In collaboration with the faculty, principals see to it that the curriculum reflects these dimensions.

Among other responsibilities the principal collaborates with parish and diocesan personnel "in planning and implementing programs for a total, integrated approach to catechesis" (n. 215).

Because of the varied roles of permanent deacons as ministers of the word, their preparation should include catechetical formation. Similarly, candidates for the transitional deaconate and priesthood "should have supervised catechetical experiences in parishes, hospitals, or other institutional settings" (n. 216). The pastor has the primary responsibility for catechesis in the parish but priests in general "exercise a uniquely important role and have a special responsibility for the success of the catechetical ministry." Preaching and the priest's liturgical-sacramental ministry are central factors in the catechesis of the Christian community (n. 217).

Not only does the bishop, "the chief catechist in the diocese," devote himself personally to the ministry of the word but he has the responsibility for seeing that sound catechesis is provided for all the faithful in his care. In seeing to it that "all involved in this ministry receive continuing catechetical formation," he chooses qualified personnel to assist him in the work. *Sharing the Light of Faith* presents a lengthy checklist of tasks carried out by the diocesan staff. Diocesan personnel should have experience and good training for the catechetical ministry, and it "is highly desirable" they join together frequently in the celebration of the Eucharist. "In this way they foster communication among themselves, grow in their ability to proclaim the message in truth, intensify their prayer life, and make their work truly a service of the Lord" (n. 218).

Chapter Ten – Organization for Catechesis

Before going on to explain the need for organizational structures Chapter Ten states, "One can hardly emphasize too strongly the catechetical importance of the witness to faith given by individuals" (n. 220). In laying down general organizational principles, moreover, it "does not propose structures without reference to the people involved" (n. 221). Part A proposes other general guidelines with regards to planning ("an essential part of any serious organizational effort"); evaluation "made in light of established goals and objectives," and research to ascertain needs and to develop models for local use (nn. 222-223).

The other parts, B through F, discuss parish, diocesan, regional and national, structures, higher education, and structures in other settings. Several of the topics are discussed elsewhere in SLF, notably in Chapter Eight, but here they are examined from the point of view of organization.

Part B insists every parish needs "a coherent, well-integrated catechetical plan," and programs that are adequately "financed, staffed, and evaluated in light of the goal of meeting the needs of everyone in the parish" (n. 224): adults (n. 225); families (n. 226); young adults, youth, and children of all ages (nn. 227-230); as well as persons with special needs (n. 231). Although schools "necessarily" have their own independent identity, "a parochial school is also a community within the wider community, contributing to the parish upon which it depends and integrated into its life." Teachers as catechists are expected "to meet the standards" and "possess qualities" described in Chapter Nine (n. 232; see, nn. 205-211 above). Schools serving "disadvantaged children in poverty areas of large cities" provide "a complete education which includes catechesis and guidance" (n. 233).

It is important that parish planners be aware of courses and programs in public schools "which in one way or another bear upon religion and values," and they should see to it that parish catechetical programs be prepared to address the questions and issues they raise. "When young people or their parents object to a program on religious or moral grounds, the public schools should exempt such pupils from participation without embarrassing them" (n. 234). SLF discusses the pros and cons of "released time," and suggests, "parishes, individually or collectively," explore "viable alternatives" (n. 236).

"Representatives of national parishes and of cultural and ethnic groups should be the prime movers in planning and organizing catechetical programs for themselves." They should also seek ways for sharing their traditions and values with neighboring parishes and the Church at large (n. 236). Parishes on large military bases and posts must address special needs of personnel and their families, but they require the services of professional catechists and coordinators, the means to procure catechetical materials, ways to develop parental and lay leadership for their programs. Military parishes offer good opportunities for ecumenical efforts (n. 237).

Sharing the Light of Faith (1978) was published before the revised *Code of Canon Law* (1983). Thus it is the spirit rather the details of the diocesan organization described in Part C that apply. Most dioceses have some structure that corresponds to the "catechetical office" called for in the *General Catechetical Directory* (n. 131), but the name of the office and the ordering of catechetical activities differs from place to place. "Whatever its structure," SLF says, "the Diocesan Catechetical Office should have sufficient professional personnel to serve as resources... in relation to all aspect of catechesis," and it should collaborate on regular basis "with other diocesan offices which have a catechetical dimension: i.e., offices for continuing education of the clergy, liturgy, ecumenism, communications, social justice, etc." (n. 238). Similarly, regional and provincial cooperation and the sharing of programs and personnel is desirable (n. 239). SLF, following the GCD (n. 128), enjoins that the conference of bishops "should have a permanent structure to promote catechesis at the national level (n. 240). The United States Conference of Catholic Bishops has such an office but its title, procedures, and some of its responsibilities described in article 240 have changed in the years since SLF was published (8).

Under the heading "Higher Education," Part E considers seminaries, colleges and universities, and campus ministry. "Seminaries serve the local Church by making their faculties and facilities available as far as possible to the diocese and community-at-large," and in turn the diocesan office should collaborate in preparing seminarians for the catechetical ministry. (n. 241). Catholic colleges and universities are encouraged to offer undergraduate and graduate degree programs in catechetics and theology for individuals who wish to work full time in the catechetical ministry and for those who may assume other leadership roles in the Church. "The cooperation of Catholic colleges with diocesan catechetical offices, neighboring parishes, and other institutions … is highly desirable" (n. 242).

SLF enjoins campus ministry to provide a variety of pastoral services to the entire campus community: students, administrators, faculty, and staff in confronting "a range of concerns which reflect in microcosm the catechetical concerns of the entire Church." It is important, especially on the nonsectarian, non-Catholic campus for campus ministry to emphasize "worship, community, and tradition through the development of a community of faith." It should be of service to the entire community by promoting responsible governance and showing concern as to how the institution's policies, programs, and research impact on "human development". "Campus ministry should be carried on in cooperation with local parish communities" (n. 243).

Part F, the final section of Chapter Ten, is a catch-all that describes aspects of the catechetical ministry appropriate for a variety of settings: nursing homes, child-care centers, facilities and schools for the handicapped (n. 244), hospitals, prisons, and chaplaincies in police and fire departments (n. 246). The emphasis in this section is on training centers that prepare individuals, clerical and lay, professional and nonprofessional catechists, for ministry in these institutions.

Chapter Eleven – Catechetical Resources

SLF makes the point in several places that the character of the catechist is more important that methods and structures (e.g., n. 206), but it also recognizes the principle "good tools in the hands of skilled catechists can do much to foster growth in faith" (n. 249). Chapter Eleven considers the tools in common use at the time the Directory was written: "human and organizational resources, the communications media, textbooks, and audiovisual materials."

Although advances in electronic technology have radically transformed the means of social communications in recent years, the general observations outlined by *Sharing the Light of Faith* in Part A are still valid. Many of the associations, agencies, offices, institutes, etc. it lists have changed their names or have gone out of existence (see, n. 257), but there are other information services and libraries that provide resources and services helpful in catechesis (n. 250). From its earliest years the Church used various art forms—stained glass, mosaics, painting, sculpture—to communicate Christ's message, "just as television, films, photography, film-strips, and tapes do so today" (n. 251). Although contemporary media "present serious challenges and problems," they have the potential for uniting people, facilitating the exchange of ideas, promoting justice and peace, and spreading the Gospel message. "Not all catechists can or need be media specialists, but all should have some understanding of media for their work" (n. 252). In Part D, the Directory instructs catechists "to learn how to take the media into account as a crucial part of the cultural background and experience of those being catechized… and how to help their students understand and evaluate media in the light of religious values" (n. 261).

Part B encourages catechists "either to acquire specialized media training or collaborate with others experienced in broadcast production" (n. 253). Radio and television can "be the most effective means of communicating with people in isolated and rural areas, as well as with… the aged and shut-ins" (n. 255). In order to hold the broadcast media accountable (n. 254) and to avail themselves of free air time and public service they provide (nn. 256–257), "Church-related communicators" should keep informed of "significant changes in technology, organizational structure, and policy now occurring or anticipated in the broadcasting industry" (n. 258).

Despite the emergence of electronic communications, the print media has not lost its importance. Part C includes Catholic newspapers and parish bulletins on its list of "useful catechetical tools." Catechetical leaders and Catholic publishers should dialogue on ways to "exchange ideas and information about catechetical needs and about the effective use of the Catholic press for catechetical purposes" (n. 259). Although it is "unrealistic" to expect the secular press to be "a vehicle for direct catechesis," it can be of service in reporting information of interest to catechists. Diocesan communications offices, even catechists themselves, ought to supply the secular press with news releases and "to be prepared to respond to press inquiries" (n. 260).

The final section, Part E, directs that "written materials and material in other media" be considered in planning curricula, and adds, "the classroom learning situation itself is only one element in total catechesis" (n. 263). In addition to presenting "the authentic and complete message of His Church," textbooks must employ graphics "in the best tradition of Christian art, chosen with sensitivity to the age, psychological development, intellectual capacity, and background of learners" (n. 264). Later it expands on this point:

> Today most people, especially the young, are accustomed and
> even expect to experience much of their learning through sophis-
> ticated media presentations. The Church needs to make creative
> use of these tools in communicating with them. (n. 265)

Textbooks series should include teachers' manuals ("essential compo-nents") and notes for parents, and the Bible should be used along with text-books in catechizing older children, youth, and adults (n. 264). "All catechetical textbooks and other materials are to be prepared according to the criteria and guidelines in this NCD" (n. 266).

Almost as an afterthought, SLF inserts a word about correspondence courses that "are of particular importance in the catechesis of families and individuals in isolated areas,... those who wish to study the faith privately, and any others who find it difficult to participate in organized catechetical programs." Correspondence courses can also be helpful for training teachers and for assisting parents in the catechesis of their children (n. 265).

Guidelines for Doctrinally Sound Catechetical Materials

By 1988 a new generation of bishops had replaced those who had attended Vatican II and created *Basic Teachings* or *Sharing the Light of Faith*. Furthermore, these new bishops had come to realize that while the National Conference of Bishops publishes documents and issues pastoral directives for the country as a whole, individual bishops do not have jurisdiction over publishers outside their dioceses. "And for their part, publishers," were said to "have on occasion asked for national norms and standard criteria that can help them in presenting the Church's doctrine on faith and morals." Consequently, one of the objectives adopted by the USCC/NCCB for the years 1988-1990 was:

> ... to support the catechetical ministry of the Church in the United States by developing policy guidelines for the creation of doctrinally sound textbooks and by providing for their implementation.

At their November meeting in 1990 the bishops approved the short document *Guidelines for Doctrinally Sound Catechetical Materials*, (GDSCM). These guidelines were created by a task force of catechetical leaders "generally representative of the geographic, cultural, and social profile of the Church in the United States" under the chairmanship of Bishop John Leibrecht of Springfield-Cape Girardeau.

The Introduction to GDSCM says the guidelines are based on the Church's major catechetical documents and the teachings of Vatican II. It quotes the GCD describing catechesis as a pastoral ministry "which leads both communities and individual members of the faithful to maturity of faith" (n. 21). It cites SLF regarding the variety of catechetical resources and their usefulness "as effective instruments for teaching." It accepts catechesis as a form of ministry of the word and reviews the fourfold dimension of catechesis— proclaiming the message; building community; leading people to worship and prayer; and motivating them to Christian living and service. The Introduction then outlines the "Principles and Criteria of Doctrinally Sound Catechetical Materials" on which the guidelines are based. The specific criteria are based on two principles: (1) that the presentation of the Christian message be both *authentic* and *complete*: that is, it must be in harmony with the doctrine and traditions of the Catholic Church; and it must be presented in its entirety and in a balanced way; and (2) the recognition that the message of faith is *incarnate* and *dynamic*; that is, "God's creative power is mediated in the concrete experience of life, in personal development, in human relationships, in culture, in social life, in science and technology, and in 'signs of the times'" (pp. 3-8).

The guidelines are not intended to supplant—"and in fact should be studied in conjunction with"—*Basic Teachings*, Chapter Five of SLF, "and any exposition of doctrine found in a future *Catechism for the Universal Church*."

(Such a catechism had been proposed by the Extraordinary Synod of Bishops in 1985.) But the guidelines differ from the earlier documents in two ways: (1) they make reference to Church documents that were published after the earlier texts appeared; and (2) "they single out certain doctrines that seem to need particular emphasis in the life and culture of the United States at this time" (p. 11).

The document presents two sets of guidelines corresponding to the above principles. The first outlines core teachings and the second, "Guidelines for Presenting Sound Doctrine" is a restatement of instructions in earlier documents. The first set lists sixty-eight specific items under the headings: General Doctrinal Content; Father, Son, and Holy Spirit; Church; Mary and the Saints; Liturgy and Sacraments; Life of Grace and Moral Issues; Death, Judgment, and Eternity. Each section begins, "Doctrinally sound catechetical materials..." and is followed by directives that use such action verbs as help, present, describes, explains, maintains, emphasizes, nourishes, etc. Most doctrinal directives reference the GCD and/or the NCD. Some cite constitutions and decrees of Vatican II and others, more recent papal documents or episcopal instructions such as the Apostolic Exhortations *Catechesi tradendae* and *Christifideles laici*, and *Economic Justice for All: Pastoral Letter on Catholic Social Teaching and the U.S. Economy*. The most obvious example of a point that seemed "to need particular emphasis... at this time," reads:

> Doctrinally sound catechetical materials...
>
> [17] maintain the traditional language, grounded in the Scriptures, that speaks of the Holy Trinity as Father, Son, and Spirit, and apply, where appropriate, the principles of inclusive language approved by the NCCB (see, *Criteria for the Evaluation of Inclusive Language Translations of Scriptural Text Proposed for Liturgical Use*.)

The second set of guidelines, based on pastoral principles and pastoral concerns, also draws heavily on *Sharing the Light of Faith*. "They are reminders that catechetical materials must take into account the community for whom they are intended, the conditions in which they live, and the ways in which they learn." The guidelines acknowledge that "no single text or program can address the many cultures and several groups that make up society in the

United States, but all catechetical materials must take this diversity into account." The first set of guidelines emphasizes that catechesis must present the Church's teaching "correctly and in its entirety." The second set recognizes for catechesis to be effective "it is equally important" to present Church doctrine in ways that are attractive, appealing, and understandable by the individuals and communities to whom it is directed.

Notes

1.   William E. McManus, "To Teach as Jesus Did: A Chronicle," *The Living Light* 10:2 (Summer 1973), 278-283; Berard L. Marthaler, "A Pastoral on Catholic Education: The Process and the Product," *The Living Light* 28:2 (Winter 1992), 101-113.

2.   See, Chas. C. McDonald, "The Background and Development of 'The Basic Teachings' Document," *The Living Light* 10:2 (Summer 1973), 264-277.

3.   Edw. G. Pfnausch, "Precepts of the Church in the *Catechism of the Catholic Church*," *The Living Light* 33:2 (Winter 1996), 32-37.

4.   For more detailed information on the consultation process, the membership of the various committees that worked on the national directory, and the final approval of the document by the NCCB and Rome, see *Sharing the Light of Faith: An Official Commentary*, (Washington, DC: United States Catholic Conference, 1981).

5.   Note 1 (p. 165) cites specific points where SLF modifies the text of the earlier documents.

6.   Endnote 48 (p. 166) cites the bishops' pastoral letter, *Behold Your Mother, Woman of Faith*, published in 1973, which, it says, "can be very helpful in catechizing on this subject." It also refers to the 1974 Apostolic Exhortation of Pope Paul VI, *Devotion to the Blessed Virgin Mary (Marialis cultus)*.

7.   The Vatican agency governing sacramental practical has gone through a metamorphosis in the years since the Council. At the time of the Council it was known as the Sacred Congregation of Rites. After 1967 it was called the Congregation for Divine Worship until 1988 when another reorganization

during the pontificate of Pope John Paul II renamed it the Congregation for Divine Worship and Discipline of the Sacraments.

8.   The organizational structures of the Catholic Church in the United States have undergone several mutations so that the description of the various offices and departments in *Sharing the Life of Faith* are outdated. Even the name of the episcopal conference has changed. In 2001 the National Conference of Catholic Bishops (NCCB) and the United States Catholic Conference (NCCB) morphed into the United States Conference of Catholic Bishops (USCCB). For an up-to-date description of the USCCB, its departments and offices, see *The Official Catholic Directory* for the current year.

4. Towards Maturity of Faith

The 1971 *General Catechetical Directory* (GCD) put new emphasis on maturity of faith. In stating that "catechesis for adults, since it deals with persons who are capable of an adherence that is fully responsible, must be considered the chief form of catechesis" (n. 20), the GCD focused on the goal, and set new criteria for, catechesis. It added, however, that other forms are "always necessary" and "in some way oriented" to adult catechesis. The GCD outlined considerations that should be taken into account in "catechesis according to age levels" (nn. 77–97). At the time it was published the GCD was praised for explicitly acknowledging in Part Five that the age level of learners should be given due consideration. *Sharing the Light of Faith: The National Catechetical Directory for Catholics of the United States*, (SLF or NCD, 1979) further elaborated on how human development—age, family, social and economic conditions—impact on a person's ability to respond to God's revelation in Chapter Eight "Catechesis toward Maturity in Faith."

These two directories inspired a number of other documents that describe in greater detail the needs and recommends approaches that are appropriate to particular age groups. Among the most important of these are: *A Vision of Youth Ministry* (1976); *The Challenge of Adolescent Catechesis: Maturing in Faith* (1986); *Renewing the Vision: A Framework for Catholic Youth Ministry* (1997); *Adult Catechesis in the Christian Community: Some Principles and Guidelines* (1990); *Our Hearts Were Burning Within Us: A Pastoral Plan for Adult Faith Formation in the United States* (1999).

A Vision of Youth Ministry

The document that did most to shape youth ministry in the post-Vatican II years was *A Vision of Youth Ministry* (1976) published by the Department of Education of the U. S. Catholic Conference (USCC). In 1975 the USCC's Advisory Board for Youth Activities commissioned an in-depth study of "the developing field" of youth ministry. *A Vision of Youth Ministry*, published the following year, describes youth ministry as "the response of the

Christian community to the needs of young people, and the sharing of the unique gifts of youth with the larger community" (p. 5). A basic principle underlying the document (and the documents it influenced) is "any description of youth ministry must grow out of and be confirmed by the lived experience of the persons who exercise this ministry on a daily basis" (p. 1). *Vision* "offers a focus for the work of youth ministry," and outlines its major components as seen by hundreds of individuals involved in this ministry on a daily basis.

A Vision of Youth Ministry has three parts. The first presents an overview of "the mission and ministry of the Church," that it says, is guided by Word, Community, and Service. The second, the real meat of the document, offers "a vision of youth ministry," under five headings:

A. **Dimensions**. The driving principle that runs throughout is "youth ministry is TO, WITH, BY and FOR youth."

B. **Goals**. Youth ministry is "a multidimensional reality" united in the twofold goal of fostering "the total personal and spiritual growth of each young person," and drawing young people into the life, mission, and work of the faith community."

C. **Principles**. Youth ministry recognizes: 1. During the teenage years the "physical, psychological and social growth is more concentrated than at any comparable time span in life." 2. Concern for the total person entails sensitivity for the concrete living situations of individuals—social, cultural, developmental, and spiritual. 3. The utmost importance of enabling relationships that allow "a mutual opening to change and willingness to grow." 4. Youth ministry is most effectively carried out in communal settings—family, parish, and school. 5-6. When individuals recognize their personal worth and gifts they awaken their potential to minister to others, an essential dimension of youth ministry.

D. **Context**. Peer pressure, a powerful force for conformity, exercises both a positive—constructive—and negative—destructive—influence in the lives of adolescents. It often creates conflict situations and alienates young people from family and Church. The faith community in general and youth ministry in particular must help them resolve these differences and display "a prophetic witness" against the false values of the general culture.

E. **Components**. The document singles out seven aspects of the
Church's mission that youth ministers identify as especially
important in their work: Word, Worship, Creating Community, Guidance and Healing, Justice and Service, Enable-
ment, and Advocacy. Running through them all is an
emphasis on peer ministry, the need of youth to experience
the Christian message and the reality of the Christian community in their daily lives.

The third part of *A Vision of Youth Ministry* incorporates several
observations made by representatives at the 1975 convention of national
Catholic youth organizations. There was a consensus among them that the
Church "is neglecting its responsibilities to youth and young adults," and if
ministry to youth is to be taken seriously, dioceses and parishes need to train
adults and budget a significant portion of their funds to planning and supporting it. They caution against fragmentation and competition and call for collaboration of all involved in this "multi-faceted" ministry. The document
concludes, "the vision has been presented. There are many possibilities. It
remains to be made a living reality."

The strength and weakness of *A Vision of Youth Ministry* was that it is
based on "the lived experience of the persons who exercise this ministry on a
daily basis" (Preface). It presented a comprehensive overview of the situation
as it appeared to them at the time. It was weak in not acknowledging and
drawing lessons from successful efforts—many dating from before Vatican II—
like the CYO, YCW, and CSMC. It was a timely and needed reminder that youth
ministry is an integral part of the Church's life, ministry, and mission.

The Challenge of Adolescent Catechesis: Maturing in Faith

In 1986 the National Federation for Catholic Youth Ministry
(NFCYM), Inc., in collaboration with the National Conference of Diocesan
Directors of Religious Education (NCDD), and the youth desk of the
Department of Religious Education at the USCC, developed a document
"addressed to leaders in ministry with youth and in catechetical ministry in
parishes, Catholic schools, and diocesan offices." Published in English and

Spanish the paper, including an Introduction and Conclusion, consists of six parts.

The Introduction acknowledged the contribution of *A Vision of Youth Ministry* and at the same time asserted that "adolescent catechesis is clearly in a state of transition." Furthermore, a "dramatic increase" of people working in youth ministry "has resulted in confusion and tension regarding responsibilities for adolescent catechesis at every level of the Church—schools, parishes, and diocesan offices" (n. 3). This document represents an effort "to speak in a fresh way to the gifts and needs of young people" (n. 4). It builds and expands on themes found in *A Vision of Youth Ministry*. It shows the influence of Pope John Paul II's Apostolic Exhortation *Catechesi tradendae* (CT), notably in the emphasis it puts on catechesis and its link to evangelization which, it says, "is the energizing core of all ministries" (CT, 20).

Despite the fact that the document acknowledges that "catechesis is a broad reality" with many facets, it focuses chiefly on "that aspect of catechesis that is systematic and intentional and that can be planned" (n. 9). The document uses italics to emphasize that "*the primary aim of adolescent catechesis is to sponsor youth toward maturity in Catholic Christian faith as a living reality*" (n. 21). It singles out six "key faith themes"—Jesus Christ, Scripture, Church, Prayer, Interpretation, and Critical Reflection—that provide "a systematic, orderly, and focused presentation of the Catholic Christian tradition" (n. 25). Recognizing that the maturation process differs according to age levels, the document presents a framework outlining these faith themes according to the learning needs of younger (11/12–14/15 years) and older adolescents (14/15–18/19 years). *The Challenge of Adolescent Catechesis* asserts that the principles it proposes apply to catechesis for Confirmation at whatever age it is administered because "catechesis is lifelong and the Christian community needs to provide learning opportunities for continuing growth in faith" (n. 43).

Insisting throughout that adolescent catechesis is a well-integrated and collaborative venture of the entire Christian community, in Part Five the paper sketches the responsibilities of a "variety of leaders with specialized roles" that extend from catechists and school teachers, to youth ministers, to priests, diocesan personnel, and bishops themselves. It outlines the training and competencies they must cultivate for adolescent catechesis to be effective.

Renewing the Vision:
A Framework for Catholic Youth Ministry

In 1996 the Department of Education of the U.S. Catholic Conference commemorated the twentieth anniversary of the foundational document *A Vision of Youth Ministry* with the publication of *Renewing the Vision: A Framework for Catholic Youth Ministry*. It credited the 1976 document with initiating "a transformation in the Church's thinking and practice" (p. 3), and added it "was the catalyst for a dramatic increase in new and innovative pastoral practice with adolescents" (p. 4). *Renewing the Vision*, however, identifies "three new challenges" confronting the Church's ministry with adolescents. The first, the consequences of social and economic changes, includes the media as it affects family life and values. The second, explained at greater length in Part Three of the document, refers to new research into the factors that make for healthy adolescent development. The third is rooted in the Church's more expanded and holistic understanding of ministry, including youth ministry. It lists a number of publications that provide insights and strategies: *The Challenge of Adolescent Catechesis: Maturing in Faith* (NFCYM, 1986), *The Challenge of Catholic Youth Evangelization: Called to Be Witnesses and Storytellers* (NFCYM, 1993), *A Family Perspective in Church and Society* (USCC, 1988), *Putting Children and Families First* (USCC, 1991), *Follow the Way of Love* (USCC, 1994), *Communities of Salt and Light* (USCC, 1993), and *A Message to Youth: Pathway to Hope* (USCC, 1995).

The "Goals for Ministry with Adolescents" outlined in Part Two of *Renewing the Vision*, basically the same as in the earlier document, puts greater emphasis on catechesis as "an essential component of youth ministry" (p. 10). Part Two has a number of eloquent quotes from Pope John Paul II, notably statements he made in connection with World Youth Days, that stress the need to assist young people in seeing how their activities advance the Church's mission in the world.

The longest section and the heart of *Renewing the Vision* is Part Three. Again it takes as its starting point the vision of youth ministry first set out in the 1976 document, and like the earlier document, is content to present a broad framework rather than recommend a single model or endorse a specific program. "Ministry with adolescents," it insists, "creates flexible and adaptable program structures that address the changing needs and life situations of today's young people and their families within a particular community" (p. 24). *Renewing the Vision* sees the need for "an integrated approach to achieving the three goals described in Part Two" (p. 20). It expands on the "eight fundamental ways to minister effectively with adolescents"—advocacy, catechesis, community life, evangelization, justice and service, leadership development, pastoral care, prayer and worship—and adds a ninth, namely, "vocational discernment."

The publication of the *Catechism of the Catholic Church* (1992) and the revised edition of the *General Directory for Catechesis* (1997) account for the new emphasis that *Renewing the Vision* gives to the ministry of catechesis. (Although the GDC, following Pope John Paul II's Apostolic Exhortation *Catechesi tradendae*, emphasizes the link between evangelization and catechesis, *Renewing the Vision* treats them separately.) *Renewing the Vision* outlines "several distinct features that give direction to catechetical programming" for Catholic youth, and it is in this context that the document (following the *Challenge* document) introduces the distinction between "the faith development of young and older adolescents." It goes to some length in outlining "faith themes" for the two groups based on the "four pillars"—creed, sacraments, commandments, prayer—in the *Catechism of the of the Catholic Church* (pp. 29-34).

Adult Catechesis in the Christian Community

The International Council for Catechists (COINCAT), meeting in Rome in 1988, took as its theme "Catechesis of Adults in the Christian Community." The results of the discussions, summarized and edited by Caesare Bissoli, S.D.B., Secretary General of COINCAT, were published in 1990 with the title *Adult Catechesis in the Christian Community: Some Principles and Guidelines*. The subtitle makes it clear that COINCAT did not intend the document to be an exhaustive treatise or to present a paradigm for adult catechesis. Since the Council is an international group and the document intentionally incorporates the contributions of all its members, the principles and guidelines are general and sometimes repetitious. The document is filled with valuable insights and recommendations but its main contribution is summarized in the statement, "by reasons of its special position and the contribution it makes to the growth of the whole community's faith journey, the catechesis of adults must be regarded as a preferential option" (n. 29). COINCAT sought to correct the "grave imbalance" that "devoted considerable attention to children" while neglecting the catechesis of young people and adults (n. 21).

The document is divided into three sections. The first begins by drawing attention "to the *difficulties and sufferings* which weigh heavily on so many adults, including Christians." It singles out the lack of opportunity available to adults for "self-development (humanization); lack of respect for the basic right to freedom... as well as the right to follow one's own conscience... and the obstacles to carrying out one's responsibilities to society and the family." It is necessary to investigate the causes of these complex and multiple evils and to recognize "the various conditions and challenges in the ecclesial communities" that influence the proclamation of the Gospel to adults (nn. 13, 14). The members of COINCAT recognized the need for new approaches in adult catechesis, among them a great need for "a more adequate language of faith, which will be comprehensible to adults at all levels from those who are illiterate ... to those who are highly educated," and "more accessible places where unchurched adults will feel welcomed" (n. 17, a, b).

The second section gives the rationale for adult catechesis, sets down basic criteria, and outlines some "points of reference". According to the COINCAT document there are several, complementary motives for adult catechesis, but the fundamental rationale is based on "the right and obligation of all Christians," independent of any role or service they are called to fulfill, to be catechized. The specific rationale for *adult* catechesis is bound up with their responsibilities in public life, including the family and workplace, and in the Christian community where they are called on to contribute to the pastoral care of the members, to share their wisdom, and to promote the missionary vocation of the Church. The document repeats the refrain, "it is not only legitimate, but necessary, to acknowledge that a fully Christian community can exist only when a systematic catechesis of all its members takes place and when an effective and well-developed catechesis of adults is regarded as the *central* task in the catechetical enterprise" (n. 25).

Adult catechesis does not ignore two operative principles common in all forms of catechesis. First, it must be "integrated with liturgical formation and formation in Christian service," and second, it must be coordinated with the catechesis of other age groups (n. 29). In addition, adult catechesis is characterized by certain basic criteria: it treats adults as *adults*, that is, it is always attentive to and respectful of their problems and experiences. Another criterion, based on the Apostolic Exhortations *Evangelii nuntiandi* and *Christifidelis laici*, is that adult catechesis recognizes and appreciates the "secular character which is proper and peculiar to the laity." And "one of the most valid criteria," often overlooked, is "the *involvement of the community.*" This last is of particular importance because "adults do not grow in faith primarily by learning concepts, but by sharing the life of the Christian community" (n. 28).

The "points of reference" that conclude this second section of the COINCAT document refer to the difficult task of defining adulthood "in an univocal way" because of the variety of ethnic, cultural, and religious factors that play a significant role. Consequently "it is not at all easy, from a practical viewpoint, to provide a precise and uniform definition of the *catechesis of adults*" (n. 31). Citing other church documents COINCAT reaffirms, however, that catechesis is "one moment in the total process of evangelization," different from "formal religious education" and "informal occasions" that arise in the faith life of adults (n. 32).

The third section of the COINCAT document, "Guidelines for Practical Implementation," repeats, underscores, and expands on principles found in the first two sections. It emphasizes the need for the Church "to build *adult Christian communities*" (n. 35) whose members are characterized by "an obedient listening to the Word of God, communion with the Faith community, and the service of charity and witness in the world" (n. 38). The third section again emphasizes the importance of taking the widely diverse experiences of adults into consideration, that is, "by accepting adults where they are," their economic, social and cultural status (n. 56). The *dialogical approach* is of "fundamental importance" because it affords adults the opportunity to "make known their needs" and encourages them to become "subjects or agents in their own catechesis and in that of others" (n. 57). COINCAT applauds "the emergence of *lay catechists of adults*" (n. 75) with "solid theological, anthropological and cultural preparation" (n. 78). On the one hand they must foster personal strong relationships and ties to the local church while on the other hand remain conscious of "the secular character" of their identity and mission (n. 79). Finally, the document returns to a point that it made at the beginning: While the bishop has primary responsibility for all catechesis, "the *whole*

Christian community should be involved in it, all the more so because adults determine the quality of Church life and guarantee its smooth operation" (n. 24).

Our Hearts Were Burning Within Us

In 1999 the National Conference of Catholic Bishops/United States Catholic Conference (NCCB/USCC) at the urging of the USCC's Committee on Education and the National Advisory Committee on Adult Religious Education, authorized the publication of *Our Hearts Were Burning Within Us: A Pastoral Plan for Adult Faith Formation in the United States*. It builds on and makes frequent reference to the COINCAT document, and like *Adult Catechesis in the Christian Community* recognized "that placing ongoing adult faith formation at the forefront of our catechetical planning and activity will mean a real change in emphasis and priorities" (p. 4). The NCCB/USCC, however, attempted what COINCAT, given its international and diverse constituency, could not do, namely, sketch out a concrete plan to be implemented in the parishes of the country.

Our Hearts Were Burning has four parts: Part One describes concrete challenges and opportunities that shape adult faith formation; Part Two describes "qualities of mature adult faith and discipleship" (pp. 15-20); Part Three sets goals, outlines guiding principles, identifies content areas and recommends approaches to "sound and diversified faith formation" (p. 6); Part Four focuses on the parish ("The parish is the curriculum."), and on "parish culture" and leadership as well as diocesan support (pp. 41-43).

Although Parts Three and Four draw heavily from the COINCAT document and the *General Directory for Catechesis*, they move beyond the previous documents. These sections reaffirm the major goals, the core content, and general principles of adult faith formation before moving on to specific recommendations and concrete approaches. Regardless of the approach chosen, however, the general principle is constant: "adult faith formation should always actively challenge participants to get involved with their own faith journey— passive listening is never enough; the goal is always conversion" (p. 26).

Since no single approach can encompass "the broad scope of content" and "the diverse range of adult interests and responsibilities" a variety of "systematic and occasional, individual and community, organized and spontaneous" learning activities are necessary (p. 34). *Our Hearts Were Burning* groups under five headings a variety of activities that can in some way be used in any Catholic community: liturgy, family/home, small and large groups, and individual activities. The activities range from the Sunday homily to reading the parish bulletin and diocesan newspaper, "family-to-family ministry," small faith communities, lectures and social events, as well as private prayer and personal reflection. Since the parish is the locus where Christian community is formed and most Catholics experience Church, it is of pivotal importance to the pastoral plan outlined in *Our Hearts Were Burning*. It goes so far as to say, "while the parish may *have* an adult faith formation program, it is no less true that the parish *is* an adult faith formation program" (p. 41). The quality of the liturgies, the priorities in the parish budget, the commitment to social justice, and the quality of its catechetical programs—in short the "total fabric of parish life" contributes to adult faith formation. The document encourages pastoral leaders to examine certain procedures and lists a number of pointed questions that they should ask in assessing the success of their programs (pp. 41-42).

5. Liturgy and Catechesis

The Second Vatican Council called for "a general restoration" of the sacred liturgy that would help make both the texts and rites more expressive of the holy things they signify (LG, 21). *Sacrosanctum concilium*, the Constitution on the Liturgy, set down general norms for the restoration. The Instruction on the Proper Implementation of the Liturgy (*Inter oecumenici*), on the implementation of the Council's directives, stated further that its aim was "to foster the formation of the faithful and that pastoral activity of which the liturgy is the summit and source" (n. 5). A translation of the rites and texts prepared by the International Commission on English in the Liturgy gives the rubrics and texts of the new rites for Christian Initiation, Penance, Holy Communion and Worship of the Eucharist outside of Mass, the blessing of Oils and Consecration of Chrism, Marriage, Anointing and Pastoral Care of the Sick, Funerals, the Institution of Readers and Acolytes and Admission to Candidacy for Ordination as Deacons and Priests. (New York: Pueblo Publishing Co., 1976) An introduction to each of the rites outlining the principles that guided the changes together with an explanation of the rites themselves provide a basis for a catechesis to enable the faithful to participate in the celebrations "fully, actively, and as a community" (LG, 21).

The Rite of Christian Initiation of Adults

First on the list are the restored rites of Christian Initiation and foremost of these is the *Rite of Christian Initiation of Adults* (RCIA). Just as post-conciliar documents describe catechesis for adults as "the chief form of catechesis," so these same documents hold up the RCIA with the restored catechumenate as the paradigm for all catechesis. The *General Catechetical Directory* (1971) explains why:

> The catechumenate for adults, which at one and the same time includes catechesis, liturgical participation, and community living, is an excellent example of an institute that springs from the cooperation of diverse pastoral functions. Its purpose is to direct

the spiritual journey of persons who are preparing themselves for the reception of baptism, and to give direction to their habits of thought and changes in moral living. It is a preparatory school in Christian living, an introduction to the religious, liturgical, charitable, and apostolic life of the People of God (c.f. AG, 13-14; SC, 65; CD, 14). Not only the priests and catechists, but the entire Christian community, through sponsors who act in its name, is engaged in this work. (GCD, 130)

Guidelines for the reestablishment and adaptation of the baptismal catechumenate, inspired by the practice of the early Church, were published almost simultaneously with the GCD in 1972. Two innovations are immediately noticeable in the *Rite of Christian Initiation of Adults*: (1) Initiation takes place step by step. It is, as recommended by the *Constitution on the Liturgy*, a period of instruction "sanctified by sacred rites to be celebrated at successive intervals of time" (SC, 64). And (2) it bundles Baptism, Confirmation, and Eucharist together as the "Sacraments of Christian Initiation" stating, they "combine to bring the faithful to the full stature of Christ and to enable them to carry out the mission of the entire people of God in the Church and in the world" (n. 2).

The *Rite of Christian Initiation of Adults* is the model for all sacramental catechesis for, as the GCD quoted above states, it combines instruction based on the Scriptures, liturgical participation, prayer, and bonding with the ecclesial community. According to "the principles and guidelines" laid down by the COINCAT document previously quoted, "every form of catechesis should be inspired by the catechumenal model," and "should be encouraged everywhere" (n. 66). The American bishops make the same point in *Our Hearts Were Burning Within Us* (p. 26). The reasons for this emphasis are found in the *praenotanda* to the RCIA and the individual rites that make it up. The *praenotanda* explain the nature and goal of all catechesis, the principal means by which it is achieved, and its ecclesial character:

1. Catechesis is concerned chiefly with the shaping of a Christian outlook, Christian values, and Christian behavior.

2. It has as its twofold goal, the individual's conversion—a change of lifestyle—and an interactive bonding of the catechumen with the Christian community, the Church.

3. The principal means is a grounding in "the basic fundamentals of the spiritual life and Christian teaching" gained through meditation on the Scriptures during the early stages of the catechumenate and through the liturgical rites in final stages. The principal agents are the pastoral ministers—sponsors, catechists, deacons and priests—acting in the name of the Church because in final analysis it is the local community that forms the outlook, values, and behavior of its members.

This last point is central to all catechesis. Christian initiation is the "concern and business of all the baptized." The community must, therefore, "help the candidates and catechumens throughout their whole period of initiation" in formal and informal ways. Members of the community are urged to invite the catechumens to their homes, to engage them in private conversation, and to include them in community gatherings. The faithful should take an active part, (n. 41) and at times "the whole community should be assembled for some of the celebrations" of the catechumenal rites (n. 105).

The 1997 *General Directory for Catechesis*, following Canon Law (cc. 204-206), notes "a fundamental difference" between catechumens and others, already baptized, who are in need of catechesis. Nonetheless it emphasizes that the baptismal catechumenate is the model of all catechizing activity when it states:

> Post-baptismal catechesis, without slavishly imitating the structure of the baptismal catechumenate, and recognizing in those to be catechized the reality of their Baptism, does well, however, to draw inspiration from 'this preparatory school for Christian life', and to allow itself to be enriched by those principal elements which characterize the catechumenate. (n. 90)

Vatican II decreed that not only the solemn rite but also the simple rite of adult Baptism, sometimes called for by "extraordinary circumstances," be revised in light of the restored catechumenate. The General Instruction to the

RCIA directs further that the catechetical formation of adults who were baptized as infants but who were neither confirmed nor received the Eucharist "should correspond to the one suggested for catechumens" (n. 297). Although they are already members of the Church by reason of Baptism, they should advance through the same stages as the catechumens, including the period of post-baptismal catechesis, on their way to full integration into the Christian community.

The Christian Initiation for Children of Catechetical Age

Vatican II also called for a revision of the rite of Baptism for children in order that, among other reasons, it be better adapted to the actual condition of children and more clearly express the role and responsibilities of parents and godparents. The Roman Ritual describes "children or infants," as "those who have not yet reached the age of discernment and therefore cannot have or profess personal faith" (n. 1). The Introduction (*praenotanda*) to the revised rite explains the importance of baptism of infants and small children (nn. 2-3), the community's role and ministry, especially that of the parents (nn. 4-7), the appropriate time and place (nn. 8-14) as well as a description of the baptismal rite itself.

The baptism of older children "who have reached the age of reason and are able to be taught" is described in Chapter Five of the 1974 edition of the *Rite of Christian Initiation of Adults*. This chapter entitled the "Rite of Initiation for Children of Catechetical Age" is intended for children "who have been brought by their parents" or "who have come of their own accord with parental permission." They are judged suitable candidates for Christian initiation "if they have developed and nourished their faith and are trying to develop their consciences" (n. 306).

The first version of the adaptation for children, Chapter Five of the 1974 RCIA edition, follows the general outline of the process for adults in the RCIA as does a second version, which appears in the 1988 ritual text with new numbering in Part Two, Rites for Particular Circumstances, Chapter One, "Christian Initiation of Children Who Have Reached Catechetical Age." The initiation of these children should proceed in stages "enriched by liturgical rites," and they should be grouped as in the adult catechumenate with others in a similar situation or with children of their own age who are preparing for Confirmation and Eucharist. The English translations of the instructions and prayers should be adapted to the children's understanding (n. 312, 1974 ed.), and ministers using this rite "may freely and wisely use the options" in the General Introduction (nn. 34-35, 31, 1988 ed. and 67, 1974 ed.). Parents, sponsors, family, classmates, and "a suitable number of faithful," are to take an active part in the liturgical celebrations, but the General Instruction states that it is best, when dealing with children of this age, "not to have the whole parish community present; it is enough to have it represented" (n. 311, 1974 ed. and n. 257, 1988 ed.):

1. The first stage in the RCIA adapted for children, the rite of becoming catechumens, "should take place in the church or in a suitable place so that according to their age and understanding the children's experience of a warm reception will be increased." (n. 315, 1974 ed.)

2. The second stage focuses on penitential rites "which are among the main stages of the catechumenate for children" (n. 330, 1974 ed.). Their purpose is similar to that of the scrutinies which may be adapted for use with the children. A principal part of the penitential rites is preparation for and the reception of the sacrament of penance.

3. The third stage, the celebration of the sacraments of initiation, should be celebrated at the Easter Vigil or at a Sunday Mass. The neophytes share in the eucharist ("First Communion") and are confirmed by the bishop or the presbyter who baptizes. (n. 344, 1974 ed.)

Directory for Masses with Children

"The Church must show special concern for baptized children who have yet to be fully initiated through the sacrament of confirmation and Eucharist as well as for children who have only recently been admitted to holy communion." Thus begins the *Directory for Masses with Children* (MWC, 1973). The scope of the document is more encompassing than the title indicates. Almost every paragraph in the introductory chapter presents important insights regarding the role of ritual in the life of the family and local church.

Although "liturgical, and especially eucharistic celebrations," are said to have "of their very nature" an educative value, MWC recognizes that the words and symbols of the Mass are often beyond the understanding of children (nn. 2, 12). The first chapter lays down basic principles, the second deals briefly with "adult Masses in which children also participate," and the third deals with Masses celebrated primarily for children. Compiled in response to "repeated requests from all over the Catholic world," it is the work of men and women from many countries who specialize in the catechesis of children (n. 4).

The basic principles and the pastoral norms discussed in the introductory chapter seem to apply broadly to catechesis for all children who have not yet reached "pre-adolescence". MWC itself suggests that the general principles can be adapted to the needs of physically or mentally handicapped children (n. 6). One basic principle in the first chapter states "liturgical and eucharistic formation must not be divorced from the child's general education as a human being and a Christian" (n. 8). In addition to "having some idea of God and the supernatural," children should, in proportion to their years, have some experience of "human values" involved in Eucharistic celebration. Citing the *General Catechetical Directory* it singles out:

> ... acting together as a community, exchanging greeting, the capacity to listen, to forgive and to ask for forgiveness, the expression of gratitude, the experience of symbolic actions, conviviality, and festive celebration. (n. 9; see GCD, 25)

It is important for the Christian community, "the best school of Christian and liturgical education," (n. 11), to encourage and support parents and other educators in their efforts to bring children into active participation in Eucharistic celebrations (n. 10). Care must be taken, however, that their efforts not be "excessively didactic in character" (n. 13).

The principles outlined in Chapter One are basic to the detailed description of "children's Masses in which only a few adults participate" in Chapter Three. Although the guiding principle is that the children's liturgy "have the same thrust" as that described in the General Instruction of the Roman Missal, MWC acknowledges "for pastoral reasons one cannot always insist on absolute identity" and adaptations must often be made (n. 20). It says, for example, "there is no reason why one of the adults should not preach a homily to the children after the Gospel, especially if the priest has difficulty in adapting himself to the mentality of the children" (n. 24). Music and singing, especially the acclamations, are encouraged, and MWC even envisions the use of "recorded music" in accordance "with the rules laid down by episcopal conferences" (n. 32). Chapter Three discusses the more general adaptations at some length (nn. 38-54).

6. Synodal Documents: Evangelization and Catechesis

Made newly aware of their collegial responsibility for the Church's mission, the bishops at the Second Vatican Council urged the formation of a Synod—a standing body that advises the pope on matters of importance to the whole Church. Periodically, the Synod polls the worldwide episcopate regarding issues that need attention. On the basis of the feedback received, the Synod convokes a General Assembly made up of representatives from the national episcopal conferences and members of the Roman curia to address the issue and propose action items. Catechesis is a recurrent theme in the discussions of the General Assemblies. Pope Paul VI began the practice of writing Apostolic Exhortations based on the discussions and recommendations of the General Assemblies.

At the first General Assembly in 1967, Cardinal Villot, Prefect of the Sacred Congregation for the Clergy asked for input from the episcopal conferences around the world regarding the *General Catechetical Directory* that had been mandated by Vatican II (see, *Christus Dominus*, 44). "Evangelization in the Modern World" was the theme of the third General Assembly in 1974. Many of the bishops at the synod took the position that evangelization and catechesis are two forms of ministry of the word that feed off one another. The *General Catechetical Directory* published two years earlier had recognized evangelization and catechesis as two closely linked forms of ministry of the word, adding that it is important to keep them distinct because each is governed by it's own laws (GCD, 17).

Evangelii nuntiandi

For Pope Paul VI, however, the distinction seemed less important than did the close relationship between evangelization and catechesis. In the Apostolic Exhortation *Evangelii nuntiandi*, issued following the 1974 Assembly, Paul VI explicitly stated that catechetical instruction is a means of evangelization. Paragraph 44 describes the goals, content, and agents of catechesis. For catechesis to be effective it must "be given to form patterns of Christian living," and not simply remain "notional". *Evangelii nuntiandi* once again reiterated that "present conditions" make catechetical instruction for young people and adults "under the form of the catechumenate" ever more urgent (n. 44). It is the task of evangelization with the solid support of catechesis "to educate people… to live the Sacraments… and not to receive them passively" (n. 47). It must "nourish and make more mature the faith of believers… especially through a catechesis full of Gospel vitality and in a language suited to people and circumstances" (n. 54).

Catechesi tradendae

In light of the bishops' concern for catechesis as the "pedagogy of evangelization" the bishops returned to the topic in the Fifth General Assembly of the Synod in 1977. The *instrumentum laboris*—the "working paper" for the Synod—announced the topic as "Catechesis in Our Time, With Special Reference to the Catechesis of Children and Young People." However, many bishops immediately widened the perspective to included adults and, in the end, everyone who needs to be catechized (See, Moreira Neves in *Going Teach*, p. 78-79). The Church's evangelizing mission guided the 1977 Synod in exploring the nature, goals, and outreach of catechesis as an ecclesial activity basic to proclaiming the Gospel in today's world.

As this Fifth General Assembly was drawing to a close, the bishops addressed a "Message to the People of God." It was an effort to share their deliberations and concerns and to encourage the entire Christian community to enter into the discussion. The Message had three parts: (1) It described the challenges and complexity of doing catechesis in the world of today, especially among young people. (2) It emphasized that the mystery of Christ is the center of catechesis under the threefold heading (borrowed from *Evangelii nuntiandi*) of word, memory, and witness. (3) It stressed the point that catechesis is the task of everyone in the Church. The bishops also prepared a list of thirty-four *propositions* highlighting the main concerns that emerged in the synodal discussions. They asked that Pope Paul VI take them as the basis of an apostolic exhortation along the lines of *Evangelii nuntiandi*. In addition, the bishops appended a list of thirty-eight particular topics that had not found a place in the *propositions* but which they felt deserved further development and comment in the apostolic exhortation (ibid. p. 84).

Catechesi tradendae makes frequent references to the 1977 Synod: It begins by noting the fact that the Synod "stressed the Christocentricty of all authentic catechesis" (CT, 5). The apostolic exhortation following the preparatory work and the discussions throughout the course of the Synod examines the specific character of catechesis in relation to the Church's pastoral and missionary activity as a whole (CT, 18). *Catechesi tradendae* reminds readers that many synod fathers insisted "the Church's social teaching should in appropriate forms, find a place in the general catechetical education of the faithful" (CT, 29). The exhortation cites the synod in a number of other places as well: CT 21, 35, 43, 51, 55, 61, and 63.

Because his two predecessors died before they were able to complete the apostolic exhortation, it fell to Pope John Paul II to put the finishing touches on *Catechesi tradendae*. Pope John Paul explained, "In essence, the exhortation takes up again the reflections that were prepared by Pope Paul VI, making abundant use of the documents left by the synod. Pope John Paul I... had taken them in hand and was preparing to publish them when he was suddenly called to God." In the end, however, the apostolic exhortation gives evidence of John Paul II's personal touch. While still Archbishop of Krakow, Cardinal Wojtyla had taken an active part in the Synod's proceedings, first in the preparatory stages as a member of the Council of the General Secretariat of the Synod that recommended the theme and later as chairman of the Council when the *instrumentum laboris* was drawn up. During the General Assembly he took an active part in the discussions making several interventions from the floor and as a participant in one of the Italian groups that also included Cardinal Luciani of Venice, the future Pope John Paul I. *Catechesi tradendae* incorporates parts of Cardinal Wojtyla's interventions almost verbatim (see, CT, 14, 19, 39, 67).

Although there is some repetition, the apostolic exhortation's nine chapters follow each other in a clear and orderly fashion:

Chapter 1 emphasizes the Christocentricity of catechesis;

Chapter 2 reviews insights that can be gleaned from a history of catechesis in the Church;

Chapter 3 examines specifics of catechesis in connection with other components of evangelization;

Chapter 4 dwells on the content of catechesis;

Chapter 5 identifies the recipients of catechesis (everyone needs to be catechized);

Chapter 6 outlines ways and means, including catechisms, of developing effective catechesis;

Chapter 7 comments on catechetical methods;

Chapter 8 acknowledges difficulties and obstacles that demand creative use of pedagogical resources and adaptation of language; and

Chapter 9 calls on all members of the People of God to recognize their responsibility in the work of catechesis.

A broad outline like the above cannot summarize the many and varied aspects of catechesis touched on in *Catechesi tradendae*. Each chapter offers direction and pastoral insight into a number of topics, for example, Chapter Nine notes that the parish is the privileged place of catechesis (CT, 67) and states in another place, family catechesis "precedes, accompanies, and enriches all other forms of catechesis" (CT, 68).

Familiaris consortio

The Church's "profound interest" in the family was highlighted by the 1980 Synod that emphasized the right and duty of the parents to educate their children in the faith received. In the introduction to the apostolic exhortation *Familiaris consortio* (FC), Pope John Paul II wrote that it "was a natural continuation of the two preceding Synods: the Christian family, in fact, is the first community called to announce the Gospel to the human person during growth and to bring him or her, through a progressive education and catechesis, to full human and Christian maturity" (FC, 2).

"The parents' ministry of evangelization and catechesis," he wrote, "ought to play a part in their children's lives also during adolescence and youth, when the children, as often happens, challenge or even reject the Christian faith received in earlier years" (FC, 53).

To foster the health of family life, the Church is called on to "promote better and more intensive programs of marriage preparation" grounded in a "solid spiritual and catechetical formation" that begins in childhood. *Familiaris consortio* says catechesis for "young people and others preparing for Christian marriage is absolutely necessary," and recommends structuring programs "in such a way that those preparing for marriage will not only receive an intellectual training but will also feel a desire to enter actively into the ecclesial community" (FC, 66).

Reconciliatio et paenitentia

The theme of the Synod's Sixth General Assembly in 1983 was "Reconciliation and Penance in the Mission of the Church." At the end, the participants forwarded to Pope John Paul II a set of *propositions* born of their discussions. He incorporated these propositions in large part in his Apostolic Exhortation *Reconciliatio et paenitentia* (RP).

As the title suggests the pope closely linked the fourfold need for reconciliation (to God, within self, to each other and to the environment) to the Sacrament of Penance. There was a time, he notes, when the faithful seemed to see sin everywhere, but now, many seem not to recognize it anywhere. He attributes the faithful's confused state to "differences of opinions and teachings in theology, preaching, *catechesis* [emphasis added] and spiritual direction on serious and delicate questions of Christian morals" (RP, 18).

Reconciliatio et paenitentia puts a great deal of emphasis on catechesis as "the first means to be used" in helping people to form a right conscience. It describes in great detail the proper approach and the content of catechesis for a complete catechesis regarding reconciliation and penance. Biblical examples and church teaching, including its social teachings, will yield "a theological catechesis, which in its synthesis will also integrate the elements of psychology, sociology, and the other human science which can serve to clarify situations, describe problem accurately and persuade listeners or readers to make concrete resolutions" (RP, 26). *Reconciliatio et paenitentia* not only provides guidelines for catechesis but is itself a good catechetical resource.

Pope John Paul also issued apostolic exhortations after the General Assemblies of the Synod in 1987 (*Christifideles laici*), 1990 (*Pastores do vobis*), 1994 (*Vita consecrata*), and 2002 (*Pastores gregis*). All of these exhortations coupled catechesis with evangelization and emphasized that everyone in the Church, according to his or her state of life—bishops, parents, priests and religious—are called to be catechists.

7. Documents for the Millennium

Pope John Paul II convoked an extraordinary assembly of the Synod of Bishops in 1985 to commemorate the 20th anniversary of the closing of the Second Vatican Council. Its purpose was, he wrote, "to celebrate the graces and spiritual fruits of Vatican II, to study it's teaching in greater depth in order that all the Christian faithful might better adhere to it and to promote knowledge and application of it." In order to achieve this threefold purpose Boston's Bernard Cardinal Law proposed a "Conciliar Catechism," a catechism for the universal Church: "In a shrinking world—a global village—national catechisms will not fill the current need for clear articulation of the Church's faith." Cardinal Law's proposal found its way into the final report of the Extraordinary Synod, and Pope John Paul acted on it.

Pope John Paul's Apostolic Constitution *Fidei depositum* serves as a preface to the *Catechism of the Catholic Church*. It briefly explains the development of the *Catechism* from when it was first proposed by the Extraordinary Synod of Bishops in 1985 to its publication in 1992, and describes the arrangement of the materials. In explaining the "Doctrinal Value of the Text," the pope wrote that the *Catechism*:

> ... is a statement of the Church's faith and of catholic doctrine, attested to or illumined by Sacred Scripture, the Apostolic Tradition, and the Church's Magisterium. I declare it to be a sure norm for teaching the faith and thus a valid and legitimate instrument for ecclesial communion. (n. 3)

The *Catechism* is to be seen as "a sure and authentic reference text for teaching catholic doctrine and particularly for preparing local catechisms" and a means that the faithful can use to deepen "their knowledge of the unfathomable riches of salvation." It is an instrument to support ecumenical efforts "by showing carefully the content and wondrous harmony of the catholic faith."

The *Catechism* is a weighty volume of more than 700 pages. Recognizing its merits as a reference text and also its size, the participants at the International

Catechetical Congress held in Rome in 2002 voiced a need for something more concise to use locally. Pope John Paul II assigned the task of developing this work to a Special Commission of Cardinals chaired by Joseph Cardinal Ratzinger, "assisted by various experts." By the time the work was published in June, 2005 Cardinal Ratzinger had become Pope Benedict XVI. Early in his pontificate (2005) Pope Benedict introduced this *Compendium* that he described as "a faithful and sure synthesis of the *Catechism of the Catholic Church.*"

The *Compendium of the Social Doctrine of the Church* "offers a complete overview of the fundamental framework of the doctrinal corpus of Catholic social teaching" (n. 9). Compiled by the Pontifical Council for Justice and Peace in consultation with other dicasteries of the Roman Curia, episcopal conferences, individual bishops, and experts in the field, it draws on papal statements of all kinds beginning with Pope Leo XII's *Rerum novarum* through the encyclicals of Pope John Paul II. It makes frequent reference to documents of Vatican II and the *Catechism of the Catholic Church.* It is intended as "an instrument for the moral and pastoral discernment of the complex events that mark our time; as a guide to inspire, at the individual and collective levels, attitudes and choices that will permit all people to look to the future with greater trust and hope..."

This chapter will examine briefly these three documents, the *Catechism of the Catholic Church* (CCC), the *Compendium of the Catechism of the Catholic Church*, (C-CCC) and *Compendium of the Social Doctrine of the Church* (C-SD). An outline will be provided for the *Catechism* and the social doctrine compendium. Because the *Compendium of the Catechism of the Catholic Church* presents "in concise form all the essential and fundamental elements of the Church's faith," a digest of its contents would be redundant. However, comments concerning the C-CCC will be made later in this chapter.

Catechism of the Catholic Church

The following outline presents a general overview of the CCC, highlighting where applicable the guidelines it offers for teaching the doctrine.

The *Catechism* begins with a short Prologue that situates the catechetical ministry in the context of the Church's pastoral mission (nn. 4-10). It quotes *Catechesi tradendae* (CT, 8) in stating:

Catechesis is an *education in the faith* of children, young people, and adults which includes especially the teaching of Christian doctrine imparted, generally speaking, in an organic and systematic way, with a view to initiating the hearers into the fullness of Christian life. (n. 8)

Again quoting CT, the Prologue affirms "catechesis is intimately bound up with the whole of the Church's life." Both her numerical increase and inner growth "depend essentially on catechesis" (n. 7; CT, 13).

The Prologue describes the CCC's intended readership "primarily" as bishops. And through them, "it is addressed to redactors of catechisms, to priests, and to catechists. It will also be useful reading for all other Christian faithful" (n. 12). The Prologue gives some practical directions for using the *Catechism*.

Like other church documents, the paragraphs in the CCC—2865 in all—are numbered. The italicized numbers in the margins refer to other paragraphs that deal with the same theme, and at the end of the volume there is an analytical index (n. 18). The *Catechism* uses different size fonts to set off certain passages. Some paragraphs are set in small print to indicate "observations of an historical or apologetic nature, or supplementary doctrinal explanations," as are a number of quotations from patristic and liturgical sources (nn. 20-21). Each thematic unit concludes with a series of summary statements under the heading "In Brief" that lend themselves to memorization (n. 22). The manner of doctrinal presentation and choice of catechetical methods ("indispensable adaptations" required "by differences of culture, age, spiritual maturity, and social and ecclesial condition") are "the responsibility of particular catechisms and, even more, of those who instruct the faithful" (n. 24).

The Prologue ends by quoting the *Preface to the Catechism* of the Council of Trent that in part states, "The whole concern of doctrine and its teaching must be directed to the love that never ends" (n. 25).

The *Catechism* builds on the traditional "four pillars" of catechesis: the Creed, Sacraments, Commandments, and the Lord's Prayer. Part One treats the faith professed; Part Two, faith celebrated; Part Three, faith lived; and Part Four, faith prayed. Each of the four parts is subdivided into sections, chapters, and articles of unequal length that are outlined in the detailed Table of Contents.

Part One – The Profession of Faith

Part One begins with a discussion on faith considering: (1) the insatiable desire of the human heart for God; (2) Revelation by which God reaches out to humans; and finally (3) the response of faith. The first chapter describes ways of coming to know God (nn. 31-38) and the limits of language in speaking about God (nn. 39-43). "Since our knowledge of God is limited, our language about him is equally so" (n. 40).

The Profession of the Christian Faith. Early on, the Church gathered "the essential elements of its faith into organic and articulated summaries, intended especially for candidates for Baptism." These are commonly known as "creeds," from the Latin *credo*, "I believe". The Creeds ("symbols of faith") became "a sign of recognition and communion between believers" (nos. 186-188). Although Christians had other formulas, "two occupy a special place in the Church's life:" The *Apostles' Creed*, based on the ancient baptismal symbol of the Church of Rome, "is rightly considered to be a faithful summary of the apostles' faith." The *Niceno-Constantinopolitan Creed*, dates to the first two ecumenical councils, Nicea (325) and Constantinople (381). Generally known simply as the *Nicene Creed*, it "remains common to all the great Churches of both East and West to this day" (nn. 192-195).

These traditional professions of faith consist of three segments that together affirm the Church's belief in the work of the triune God. Consequently, the first Part of the *Catechism of the Catholic Church* like the *Catechism of the Council of Trent* before it has three parts:

The first part speaks of the first divine Person and wonderful work of creation; the next speaks of the second divine Person and the mystery of his redemption of men; the final part speaks of the third Person, the origin and source of our sanctification. (n. 190)

The mystery of the Most Holy Trinity is the central mystery of Christian faith and life. It is the mystery of God in himself. It is therefore the source of all the other mysteries of faith.... It is the most fundamental and essential teaching in the "hierarchy of the truths of faith." The whole history of salvation is identical with the history of the way and the means by which the one true God, Father, Son, and Holy Spirit, reveals himself to men "and reconciles and unites with himself those who turn away from sin." (n. 234)

The *Catechism of the Catholic Church*, "in accordance with an ancient tradition," identifies twelve articles in the Apostles' Creed, "thus symbolizing the fullness of apostolic faith by the number of the apostles" (n. 191). Although the CCC follows the Apostles' Creed in this regard, its presentation of the faith is "completed by constant reference to the Nicene Creed which is often more explicit and more detailed" (n. 196).

I believe in God the Father. "This first affirmation of the Apostles' Creed is also the most fundamental. The whole Creed speaks of God, and when it also speaks of man and of the world it does so in relation to God. The other articles of the Creed all depend on the first…" (n. 199).

Creator of heaven and earth. The *Catechism* explains that "catechesis on creation is of major importance" because:

It concerns the very foundations of human and Christian life: for it makes explicit the response of the Christian faith to the basic question that men of all times have asked themselves: "Where do we come from?" "Where are we going?".... The two questions, the first about the origin and the second about the end, are inseparable. They are decisive for the meaning and orientation of our life and actions. (n. 282)

Among the many Scriptural texts that speak about creation, "the first three chapters of Genesis occupy a unique place":

Read in the light of Christ, within the unity of Sacred Scripture and in the living Tradition of the Church, these texts remain the principal source for catechesis on the mysteries of the 'beginning': creation, fall, and promise of salvation. (n. 289)

I believe in Jesus Christ. The transmission of the Christian faith and the very heart of catechesis consists primarily in proclaiming Christ and his work. To emphasize this point the *Catechism* cites a passage from *Catechesi tradendae*:

To catechize is "to reveal in the Person of Christ the whole of God's eternal design reaching fulfillment in that Person. It is to seek to understand the meaning of Christ's actions and words and the signs worked by him." Catechesis aims at putting "people... in communion... with Jesus Christ: only he can lead us to the love of the Father in the Spirit and make us share in the life of the Holy Trinity." (CCC, 426; CT, 6)

Although the Creed speaks only about the Incarnation and the Paschal mystery, catechesis presents the richness of the mysteries of Christ's entire life. Everything in Jesus' life—his deeds, miracles, and words—"appeared as 'sacrament,' that is, the sign and instrument, of his divinity and the salvation he brings" (nn. 512-515).

I believe in the Holy Spirit. Everything in the second part of the Creed is to be read in light of the fact that "Christ's whole work is a joint mission of the Son and Holy Spirit" (n. 727). The article on the Church "depends entirely on the articles concerning Christ Jesus," and on the article about the Holy Spirit that immediately precedes it. When we say "I/we believe in the one, holy, catholic, and apostolic Church," we are not professing faith "in" the Church, in the same sense that we profess faith "in" God. We must not confuse God with his works (nn. 748-750).

The laity [also] share "in the priestly, prophetic, and kingly office of Christ." They participate in Christ's priestly office by prayers and personal sacrifices, family and married life, apostolic undertakings, etc. They fulfill their prophetic mission by evangelization "in the ordinary circumstances of the world." With proper training they "may collaborate in catechetical formation, in teaching the sacred sciences, and in use of the communications media." They participate in Christ's kingly office when called to "cooperate" in the exercise of the power of governance "in accord with the norm of law" at particular councils, diocesans synods, pastoral councils, finance committees, and ecclesiastical tribunals (nn. 897-913).

Part Two – The Celebration of the Christian Mystery

The Catechism incorporates the statement of the Second Vatican Council that declared, "it is through the liturgy especially that the faithful are enabled to express in their lives and manifest to others the mystery of Christ and the real nature of the Church" (SC, 2). Because the liturgy is "the summit" toward which the all the Church's activity is directed and "the font from which all her power flows," the sacred liturgy is "the privileged place for catechizing the People of God":

> Liturgical catechesis aims to initiate people into the mystery of Christ... by proceeding from the visible to the invisible, from the sign to the thing signified, from the "sacraments" to the "mysteries".

Because the liturgy serves the entire Church in all the diversity of her rites and cultures, the Catechism presents first what is fundamental and common to the whole Church in the liturgy and as celebration; and then the Seven Sacraments and the sacramentals (nn. 1068-1075).

It is on the harmony of the two Testaments, Old and New, that the Paschal catechesis of the Lord (that of the Apostles and the Fathers of the Church) is built:

> This catechesis unveils what lay hidden under the Letter of the Old Testament: the mystery of Christ. It is called "typological" because it reveals the newness of Christ on the basis of the "figures" (types) which announce him in the deeds, words, and symbols of the first covenant. (n. 1094)

> For this reason the Church... re-reads and re-lives the great events of salvation history in the "today" of her liturgy. But this also demands that catechesis help the faithful to open themselves to this spiritual understanding of the economy of salvation as the Church's liturgy reveals it and enables us to live it. (n. 1095)

"The catechesis of the liturgy entails first of all an understanding of the sacramental economy," revealed in the celebration of the sacraments. A "fundamental catechesis" on the sacramental celebrations responds to the basic questions of What? Who? How? When? and Where?

The Seven Sacraments of the Church. "The seven sacraments touch all the stages and all the important moments of Christian life." The *Catechism* expounds them under three headings: sacraments of Christian initiation;

sacraments of healing; and sacraments at the service of communion, and explains the What, Who, How, When, and Where for each of the seven. Although there are other possible approaches, this order allows one to see "that the sacraments form an organic whole in which each particular sacrament has its own vital place" (nn. 1210-1212).

Besides sacramental liturgy, catechesis must take into account sacramentals and the forms of piety and devotions popular among the faithful. Sacramentals—sacred signs that resemble the sacraments—are instituted by the Church. They sanctify "a great variety of circumstances in Christian life." Popular devotions and other forms of piety are in some way derived from the liturgical life of the Church but they do not replace it (nn. 1667-1668; 1674-1675):

> Pastoral discernment is needed to sustain and support popular piety and, if necessary, to purify and correct the religious sense which underlies these devotions so that the faithful may advance in knowledge of the mystery of Christ. (n. 1676)

Part Three – Life in Christ

The *Catechism* speaks of "two ways:" the way of Christ that leads to life, and a contrary way that leads to destruction. "Catechesis has to reveal in all clarity the joy and demands of the way of Christ." The beginning of Part Three outlines the elements of a catechesis for "the newness of life" (Rom. 6:4). Such catechesis should be:

- *A catechesis of the Holy Spirit,* the interior Master of life according to Christ, a gentle guest and friend who inspires, guides, corrects, and strengthens this life;
- *A catechesis of grace,* for it is by grace that we are saved and again it is by grace that our works can bear fruit for eternal life;
- *A catechesis of the beatitudes,* for the way of Christ is summed up in the beatitudes, the only path that leads to the eternal beatitude for which the human heart longs;
- *A catechesis of sin and forgiveness,* for unless man acknowledges that he is a sinner he cannot know the truth about himself, which is a condition for acting justly; and without the offer of forgiveness he would not be able to bear this truth;

- *A catechesis of the human virtues* which causes one to grasp the beauty and attraction of right dispositions towards goodness;

- *A catechesis of the Christian virtues* of faith, hope, and charity, generously inspired by the example of the saints;

- *A catechesis of the twofold commandment of charity* set forth in the Decalogue; and

- *An ecclesial catechesis,* for it is through the manifold exchanges of "spiritual goods" in the "communion of saints" that Christian life can grow, develop, and be communicated.

It concludes, "The first and last point of reference of this catechesis will always be Jesus Christ himself, who is 'the way, and the truth, and the life' (Jn. 14:6)" (nn. 1698-1698).

Part Three has two major sections. The first considers "Man's Vocation: Life in The Spirit." It describes the communal character of the human vocation, and explains how humans, wounded by sin, stand in need of salvation from God. Section Two interprets the Ten Commandments in light "of the twofold, yet single commandment of love," love of God and neighbor (n. 2055).

The *Catechism* notes that since the time of St. Augustine, "the Ten Commandments have occupied a predominant place in the catechesis of baptismal candidates and the faith." Even today catechisms often expound Christian morality by following the order of the Ten Commandments. The first three concern love of God, and the other seven, love of neighbor (nn. 2065, 2067). The fourth commandment, expressed in positive terms:

> … introduces the subsequent commandments which are concerned with particular respect for life, marriage, early goods, and speech. It constitutes one of the foundations of the social doctrine of the Church. (n. 2198)

The home is the natural environment where humans are initiated into communal responsibilities. "Family catechesis precedes, accompanies, and enriches other forms of instruction in the faith" (nn. 2224, 2226).

Part Four – Christian Prayer

The frontispiece, a miniature painting from Constantinople, captures the theme of Part Four. It pictures Christ turned in prayer towards the Father (n. 2599). St. Peter stands at a distance with the other apostles pointing to him, the Master and Way of Christian Prayer (n. 2607): "Lord, teach us to pray" (Lk. 11:1).

In prayer God calls us first; our own first step is always a response. Part Four describes prayer as "a covenant drama" that unfolds though the whole history of salvation (nn. 2566-2567) under three headings: prayer in the Old Testament, "in the fullness of time," and "in the age of the Church."

Prayer is more than a spontaneous outpouring of an interior impulse, "nor is it enough to know what the Scriptures reveal about prayer: one must learn to pray" (n. 2650):

> In the living tradition of prayer, each Church proposes to its faithful, according to its historic, social, and cultural context, a language for prayer: words, melodies, gestures, iconography. The Magisterium of the Church has the task of discerning the fidelity of these ways of praying to the tradition of apostolic faith; it is for pastors and catechists to explain their meaning, always in relation to Jesus Christ. (n. 2663)

The saints witness to the living tradition of prayer by the example of their lives, the transmission of their writings, and their intercession for us (n. 2685):

> The *catechesis* of children, young people, and adults aims at teaching them to meditate on The Word of God in personal prayer, practicing it in liturgical prayer, and internalizing it at all times in order to bear fruit in a new life. Catechesis is also a time for the discernment and education of popular piety. The memorization of basic prayers offers an essential support to the life of prayer, but it is important to help learners savor their meaning. (n. 2688)

Part Four of the *Catechism* ends with a reflection on the Lord's Prayer which, in the words of Tertullian, is "the summary of the whole gospel"

(n. 2761), and "is essentially rooted in liturgical prayer " (n. 2768). The "handing on" (*traditio*) of the Lord's Prayer to catechumens and neophytes in Baptism signifies new birth into the divine life (n. 2769). In the Eucharist it reveals the eschatological character of its petitions. The petitions addressed to "our Father" rely on the mystery of salvation already accomplished, once and for all, in Christ crucified and risen:

> From this unshakeable faith springs forth the hope that sustains each of the seven petitions, which express the groanings of the present age, this time of patience and expectation during which "it does not yet appear what we shall be." The Eucharist and the Lord's Prayer look eagerly for the Lord's return, "until he comes." (n. 2771)

Compendium of the Catechism of the Catholic Church

In the *motu proprio* that prefaces the *Compendium*, Pope Benedict XVI describes it as "a faithful and sure synthesis of the *Catechism of the Catholic Church*" that "contains in concise form, all the essential and fundamental elements of the Church's faith,... a kind of *vademecum* which allows believers and non-believers alike to behold the entire panorama of the Catholic faith."

Writing a few months earlier (March, 2005) as President of the Special Commission that composed it, Cardinal Ratzinger in the Introduction noted "three principal characteristics" of the *Compendium*: its close reliance on the *Catechism of the Catholic Church*; the dialogical format; and the use of *artistic images* in the catechesis. Here are some of the specifics about the *Compendium*:

- The C-CCC does not stand alone: It relies on the four-part structure, development, and contents of the *Catechism*, and makes constant reference to the *Catechism* by means of numbers in the margins. Quotations from liturgical and hagiographical sources, set off in small print in the CCC, are printed in green ink in the United States edition.

- The C-CCC has an additional feature not found in the *Catechism*: An Appendix at the end gives the text of many common prayers and lists "formulas" of Catholic doctrine.

• The C-CCC presents the material through a series of 583 questions and answers using a "dialogical format."

The *artistic images* used are drawn from "the rich patrimony of Christian iconography," and can express more than what words convey. Living as we do today "in a culture of images," sacred images can "be an extremely effective and dynamic way of communicating the Gospel message." In all, there are thirteen pages of four-color prints chosen to illustrate the theme of each part.

Compendium of the Social Doctrine of the Church

The *Compendium of the Social Doctrine of the Church* (C-SD) is an important catechetical document that deserves study. As the *General Directory for Catechesis* (1997) states that in the context of moral education, catechesis is to present Christian social morality as a demand, consequence, and fulfillment of the great commandment of love (n. 104). In the section "Social Doctrine of the Church," the CCC links the demands of justice and peace to Christian revelation about human dignity and vocation (nn. 2419-2422). For Pope John Paul II, "the teaching and spreading of her social doctrine are part of the Church's evangelizing mission," and to make "this doctrine known constitutes a genuine pastoral priority" (C-SD, n. 7). This compendium of the Church's social doctrine, expanding as it does on Part Three of the Catechism, is an indispensable companion to the CCC.

The three parts of C-SD organize the Church's teaching systematically under the headings:

1. God's Plan of Love for Humanity
2. The Family, the Vital Cell of Society
3. Social Doctrine and Ecclesial Action

The 583 paragraphs are numbered and specific topics are easily accessed through a comprehensive analytical index that runs 163 pages.

Part One – God's Plan of Love for Humanity (Chapters 1-4)

Part One explains the foundation, principles, and values of the Church's social doctrine. It finds its essential foundation in "the revelation in Christ of the mystery of God as Trinitarian love [that] is at the same time the revelation of the vocation of the human person to love" (n. 34). Citing Pope John XXIII's encyclical letter *Mater et Magister* the C-SD states, "*The whole of the Church's social doctrine, in fact, develops from the principle that affirms the inviolable dignity of the human person*" (n. 107).

The human creature possesses the dignity of a person capable of self-knowledge, self-possession, of entering into communion with other persons, and is called by grace to a covenant with his Creator. Citing the Catechism, the C-SD states that "Man and woman have the same dignity and are of equal value, not only because they are both, in their differences, created in the image of God, but even more profoundly because the dynamic of reciprocity that gives life to the 'we' in the human couple, is an image of God" (n. 111). Humans are at the center and summit of the created order, but "their dominion over the world requires the exercise of responsibility [and] is not a freedom of arbitrary and selfish exploitation" (n. 113).

The value and dignity of the human person is afflicted by the mystery of original sin, a wound present in man's inmost self, "that is at the root of personal and social divisions" (nn. 115-116). Although every sin is "an act of the person," every sin is also social so that "by virtue of human solidarity which is as mysterious and intangible as it is real and concrete, each individual's sin in some way affects others" (n. 117). The doctrine of original sin as well as "Christian realism" teaches the universality of sin: it "must not be separated from the consciousness of the universality of salvation in Jesus Christ" (nn.120-121).

In opposition to various "reductionist conceptions... still dramatically present on the stage of modern history," the Church's social doctrine affirms the following indispensable dimensions of the human person:

- The unity of body and soul whereby the person is the subject of moral acts;
- Openness to transcendence and the uniqueness of the person;
- The freedom of the human person;
- The equal dignity of all people; and
- The social nature of human beings.

The ultimate source of human rights is not found in the mere will of human beings, in the reality of the State, or in public powers, but in man himself and in God his Creator (n. 153). By reason of her religious mission the Church promotes human rights and denounces violations of these rights (n. 159).

The dignity of the human person is the foundation of other "permanent principles" of the Church's social teaching that include the common good; subsidiarity; and solidarity (n. 160). Beside the principles that guide the building of a society, the Church also emphasizes social values inherent in the dignity of the human person: truth, freedom, justice, and love (n. 197). Together the principles and values "constitute the indispensable point of reference for public authorities, called to carry out 'substantial reforms of economic, political, cultural, and technological structures and the necessary changes in institutions'" (n. 197). In the concrete circumstances of society, love of neighbor transcends "the mere level of relationships between individuals." To love one's neighbor on the social level means "to make use of social mediations to improve his life or to remove social factors that cause his indigence" (n. 208).

Part Two – The Family, the Vital Cell of Society (Chapters 5-11)

Sacred Scripture repeatedly emphasizes the importance and centrality of the family with regard to the person and society. It is in the family that humans experience community, "the first natural society" (n. 213). Marriage is the foundation of the family. No power can abolish the natural right to marriage and society must safeguard against any attempt to undermine it. The compendium on social doctrine singles out certain characteristics of marriage: the total giving of spouses to one another that implies unity, indissolubility, and fidelity. Although the procreation and education of children is not the sole purpose of marriage (nn. 217-218):

> … conjugal love is by its nature open to the acceptance of life…. Procreation expresses the social subjectivity of the family and sets in motion a dynamism of love and solidarity between the generations upon which society is founded (n. 230).

The *Compendium* speaks of "motivations" that should guide responsible parenthood, but it rejects such methods as artificial contraception, sterilization, and abortion, which it describes as "a horrendous crime… a sad phenomenon that contributes seriously to spreading a mentality against life" (nn. 232-234).

However, the desire for children does not justify recourse to such reproductive techniques as artificial insemination, in vitro fertilization and other means of so-called "assisted procreation" (n. 235). Similarly, the Church rejects human cloning, "an issue of particular social and cultural significance today," because it is "contrary to the dignity of human procreation" and "takes place in total absence of personal love between spouses" (n. 236). Finally, the *Compendium* speaks of the work of education. "Parents are the first educators, [but] not the only educators of their children" (n. 240). They have the responsibility and right to found and cooperate with public educational institutions. Their responsibility in the area of sex education includes the obligation to see that educational institutions deal properly with "such an important and delicate topic" (nn. 241, 243).

The relationship that exists between the family and economic life is particularly significant. A family afflicted by unemployment risks not fully achieving its end. The need for a wage sufficient to allow the family to live decently must be appreciated and safeguarded, and particular attention must be given to the work of women. The importance of housekeeping for the quality of life in which men as fathers have a role "must be socially recognized and valued" (nn. 248-251). Society's service to the family becomes concrete in recognizing, respecting, and promoting the rights of the family (n. 253).

The other chapters in Part Two spell out in a general way the responsibility of humans to care for the resources of the earth and the responsibility of social institutions. Each begins with a biblical reflection:

Chapter Six details the dignity and rights of workers.

Chapter Seven outlines the moral responsibility of economic and business institutions.

Chapter Eight describes the foundation of the political authority and its responsibility to safeguard the freedom and civil rights of individuals and social institutions.

Chapter Nine speaks of the value of international organizations, including the Holy See, in the fight against poverty.

Chapter Ten emphasizes the common responsibility of all to safeguard the environment.

Chapter Eleven wraps up Part Two with some observations on peace and war; peace being the fruit of justice and love, and war, its failure. It ends by highlighting the contribution of the Church to peace, stating that true peace is made possible only through forgiveness and reconciliation. (n. 517)

Part Three – Social Doctrine and Ecclesial Action (Chapter 12)

The Church contributes to the building of the human community by bringing out the social significance of the Gospel. The human development of the person is the moral basis of all social action, creating the conditions that allow every person to achieve his/her integral vocation (nn. 521-522). In light of a rift between the Gospel and a secularized vision of salvation, the C-SD, citing *Christifideles laici*, says "the Church must take a giant step forward in her evangelization effort, and enter into a new stage of history in her missionary dynamism" (n. 523). The following "fundamental criteria" for pastoral action in the area of social activity [namely] are identified: proclaiming the Gospel; placing the Gospel message in context of social realities; planning actions aimed at the renewal of these realities; and conforming them to the demands of Christian morality (n. 526).

The documents state that while the Church's social doctrine is an indispensable reference point for a totally integrated Christian formation "it is neither taught nor known sufficiently." Citing the 1997 *General Directory for Catechesis*, C-SD insists that the Church's social teaching receive more attention and that the history, content, and methodology of the social Magisterium be fully presented in all catechesis: it must be the basis of an intense and constant work of formation, especially of the lay faithful, that helps them meet the cultural, social, economic and political realities in their daily lives and develop a sensitivity for the common good.

At another level the Church's social teaching is to prepare lay Christians who have a talent for "the difficult yet noble art of politics" to engage in political activity. Catholic educational institutions must dedicate themselves in a particular way to the inculturation of the Christian message, that is to say, to the productive encounter between the Gospel and the various branches of knowledge (nn. 528-532).

Although C-SD states that the entire people of God—bishops, priests, seminarians, religious men and women—must be well schooled in the Church's social mission (nn. 533, 538-540), the third part seems to put greater emphasis on the role and commitment of the lay faithful. At the end it outlines in some detail how they must cultivate and nourish an authentic spirituality (nn. 541-548), moral sense for service in social (nn. 549-553), cultural (nn. 554-562), economic (nn. 563-564), and political (nn. 565-574) spheres.

Conclusion

These three documents, the Catechism and the two compendiums, provide a compilation of the Church's authentic teaching that is to shape and guide all that takes place in catechesis. They do not provide the totality of what is to be addressed in catechesis, but they do establish the foundational content that would be required in a life-long process of faith formation. The documents that guide the specifics of catechesis, especially the *General Directory for Catechesis* and the *National Directory for Catechesis* (to be discussed in the next two chapters) flow from these documents.

8. Evangelizing Catechesis

General Directory for Catechesis

Much happened in the thirty-year period between the conclusion of Vatican II and the threshold of the third millennium. On the positive side there was the formation of specialists [*periti*] and the promotion of catechetical research. The *Rite of Christian Initiation of Adults* (1972) had proven especially useful for catechetical renewal. The reflections of the General Assembly of the Synod of Bishops and the post-synodal Apostolic Exhortations, especially *Evangelii nuntiandi* (1975) and *Catechesi tradendae* (1979), fully locate catechesis within the context of evangelization. A number of papal documents issued by Pope John Paul II were of special importance; in particular, *Redemptoris missio* (1990) which re-affirmed the Church's missionary mandate. These magisterial documents together with the publication of the *Catechism of the Catholic Church* (1992) "necessitated a revision of the *General Catechetical Directory* so as to adapt this valuable theologico-pastoral instrument to new situations and needs" (n. 7).

The new edition of the *General Directory for Catechesis* (GDC, 1997) seeks to balance two principal requirements: (1) the contextualization of catechesis in evangelization as envisaged by *Evangelii nuntiandi;* and (2) the appropriation of the content of the faith as presented in the Catechism. As in most Roman documents, the paragraphs are numbered for ease of reference; the paragraphs in the Preface are numbers 1-13. While retaining the basic structure of the 1971 Directory, the new edition has, in addition, an Introduction and Conclusion: five parts, each subdivided into chapters:

1. Catechesis: The Church's Mission of Evangelization
2. The Gospel Message
3. The Pedagogy of the Faith
4. Those to be Catechized
5. Catechesis in the Particular Church

The basic intention of the GDC was (and remains) to offer reflections and principles and not to suggest applications or practical directives. Defects and errors in catechetical material can be avoided only if the nature and end of catechesis, as well as the truths and values that must be transmitted, are correctly understood (n. 9). The parts of the GDC that deal with Divine Revelation, the nature of catechesis, and the criteria governing the proclamation of the Gospel message are universally valid. The parts that refer to present circumstances, methodology, and the manner of adapting catechesis to diverse age groups and cultural contexts are suggestions or guidelines. The immediate end of the GDC is to assist in the composition of catechetical directories and catechisms (n. 11).

Inroduction – Preaching the Gospel in the Contemporary World

The Introduction begins with the parable of the sower (Mk 4:3-8). The Church continues to sow the Gospel in the most diverse social situations. Catechesis must initiate those to be catechized into a "theological reading of modern problems," that is to say, a world-view that sees that (1) every human event—all reality—is marked by the creative activity of God; (2) the power of sin limits and numbs human beings; and (3) the dynamism of the Resurrection of Christ, the seed of renewal, is the hope of a definitive fulfillment.

The Field that is the World (nn. 17-23). Catechesis gives due emphasis to the Church's social teaching. Analyzing "the soil of the world," the Church is acutely conscious of everything that injures the dignity of the human person, and her evangelizing activity has as its objective the task of revealing the inviolable dignity of every human person. Catechesis must prepare the lay faithful for this task.

The sower knows that the seed falls on specific soils. With inculturation, evangelization encounters one of its greatest challenges. The Church must appropriate all the positive value of culture and cultures, but the question of Vatican II is still valid: what is to be done to prevent the exchange between cultures from disturbing the life of communities, overthrowing traditional wisdom, and endangering the character proper to each people? The widespread influence of the media often imposes a vision of life that does not respect the cultural distinctiveness of peoples.

The religious and moral factors are of particular interest to the sower. Contemporary culture is not without ambiguity, religious indifference, and atheism versus a return to the sacred and a thirst for the transcendent. The growth of sects and "fundamentalism" are of serious concern to the Church. The obscuring of the "ontological truth of the human person" contributes to the rise of an "ethical relativism".

The Church in the World (nn. 24-31). The disciples of Jesus are not immune from the influences of human situations. The Church is obliged to take into account the extent to which Christians have been shaped by the climate of secularism and ethical relativism, and the mass of non-practicing Christians. Then there are the simple people who express their faith in "popular devotions" but know little of its fundamental principles, and the highly educated whose religious formation is solely what they received in childhood. Others fail to give explicit and courageous witness to their faith in Jesus Christ. These concrete situations call for a *new evangelization* and for missionary proclamation and catechesis of both the young and adults.

It is important to consider the life of the ecclesial community: How has the Second Vatican Council been accepted? How have its four constitutions borne fruit? (Has liturgy become the source and summit of Church life? Is there a keener awareness of the "common priesthood," the universal call to holiness and a livelier sense of service? Is there a greater appreciation of and meditation on the Sacred Scripture as the Word of God? Are the demands of evangelization linked to dialogue with the world, human development, and the urgent quest for Christian unity?) Difficulties and differences in accepting the Council have led to divisions that impede evangelization. "It is urgent that an authentic "ecclesiology of communion" be promoted and deepened in order to arouse in Christians a deep ecclesial spirituality."

The vitality of catechesis is demonstrated by many positive aspects: the great number of people who devote themselves to catechesis; the missionary character of contemporary catechesis; the awareness that catechesis must have a catechumenal style emphasizing integral formation rather than mere information; the expanding role of adult catechesis; and the priority given it in pastoral planning.

It is necessary, however, to examine some problems so as to identify solutions:

- Catechists do not fully understand that "catechesis is a school of faith, an initiation and apprenticeship in Christian life."
- In much catechesis "the inter-relation of Sacred Scripture, Tradition, and the Magisterium does not enrich the transmission of the faith."
- Catechesis needs to maintain a "balanced presentation" of the divinity and humanity Christ.
- There are certain *lacunae* about God and man; sin and grace; and eschatology.
- There is need for a more solid moral formation, better presentations of Church history, and greater importance on the Church's social teaching.
- The selective tendencies and emphases in some catechisms and texts damage the unity of the faith.
- Frequently catechesis gives limited attention to liturgical symbols and sources, the liturgical year, and marginalizes liturgical celebrations.
- Over-emphasis on a "content-method" dualism often results in a pedagogy without the requisite theological discernment.
- It is difficult "within the cultural horizons of the people" to proclaim the Gospel in such a way that it is really perceived as Good News.
- Education for missionary activity *ad gentes* still seems weak, and catechesis gives only marginal attention to the missions.

The Sowing of the Gospel (nn. 31-33). The sower sends out workers to proclaim the Gospel through all the world and teaches them to read the "signs of the times." The Church uses human sciences, always in the light of faith, to discover the meaning of the present situation. In order to be efficacious, catechesis today needs: to continue to address children, adolescent, young people, and adults; to form, as in the patristic era, the personality of the believer and become a true school of Christian pedagogy; and to promote the Trinitarian experience of life in Christ as the center of the life of faith; to consider its primary task the preparation and formation of catechists.

Part One – Catechesis in the Church's Mission of Evangelization

The first part, divided into three chapters, "defines the proper character of catechesis." The term has undergone a "semantic evolution" in the course the Church's history. The concept of catechesis in the Directory is based on Magisterial documents, principally *Evangelii nuntiandi, Catechesi tradendae,* and *Redemptoris missio.* One's concept of catechesis profoundly conditions the selection and organization of its contents, identifies its addressees, and defines the pedagogy it employs in accomplishing its objectives (n. 35).

Chapter One – Revelation and its Transmission Through Evangelization (nn. 36-59). God uses a pedagogy to reveal himself. He uses the events of salvation history that accompany them to communicate his salvific plan progressively and in stages. Evangelization, which transmits Revelation to the world, is at once testimony and proclamation, word and sacrament, teaching and task. Catechesis for its part proclaims and narrates the words and deeds of Revelation and makes clear the profound mysteries they contain. Catechesis recalls the marvels worked by God in the past, and in the light of Revelation interprets the signs of the times and the human condition for it is in these that God's salvific plan is realized.

The ministry of the word must always give prominence to the entrance of the Son of God into human history that brings about the new and definitive covenant between God and man. It is the task of catechesis to show that Jesus Christ is the fullness of Revelation and to present the Christian faith as the following of his person. Consequently it must be based on the Gospels which "are at the heart of all the Scriptures." The mystery of Christ is the center from which all other elements are structured and illuminated.

In virtue of God's universal salvific will and that Revelation be transmitted to all peoples, Jesus Christ founded the Church, "the universal sacrament of salvation." Born of the Holy Spirit and built on the Apostles the Church "exists in order to evangelize." Proclamation, witness, teaching sacraments, love of neighbor, constitute closely connected essential elements of evangelization, but the tendency to identify them with evangelization itself impoverishes and even distorts it. The process of evangelization is structured in stages or "essential moments:" missionary activity directed toward non-believers and the indifferent; initial catechetical activity directed toward those who need to complete their initiation; pastoral activity directed toward the mature faithful in the Christian community.

The ministry of the word is fundamental to evangelization. The principal functions and forms of this ministry are: the first announcement or missionary preaching; pre- and post-baptismal catechesis, the liturgical form, most important form being the homily; the theological function that develops understanding—*fides quaerens intellectum*. At times forms of ministry of the word assume more than one function. Catechesis, for example, frequently has to discharge tasks of mission, the homily, can assume both the functions of convocation and integral initiation.

Evangelization invites men and women to faith and conversion. Faith is above all, conversion to Jesus Christ and sincere adherence to his person and the decision to walk in his footsteps. In saying "yes" to Jesus Christ, made possible by the action of the Holy Spirit, the disciple's response is twofold: a trustful abandonment to Jesus' person and to the truth God has revealed in him. Faith involves *metanoia*, a conversion that profoundly transforms one's life at every level. Faith and conversion arise from the heart, that is from the very depths of the human person. Faith sets in motion a process of continuing conversion that lasts a life time. Like a new born child, the person grows in faith little by little until reaching maturity in the fullness of Christ. The ministry of the word is at the service of this continuing conversion: the first proclamation of the Gospel is the call to faith; catechesis provides Christian life with a basic structure; on-going education in the faith, "in which the homily must be underlined," is the nourishment for baptized adults that they need to live.

The evangelization of the world takes place today in three diverse and changing situations: (a) Socio-cultural contexts in which Christ and his Gospel are not known. This situation requires a "mission *ad gentes*" directed to non-Christians inviting them to to conversion. Catechesis is usually developed within the baptismal catechumenate; (b) Situations where communities made up of people of profound Christian outlook are well established. In such contexts it is vital that well articulated catechetical programs be developed so that children, adolescents and young people arrive at adulthood with mature faith that makes them evangelizers. In these situations adults need different types of Christian formation; and (c) Intermediate-situations exist in places where entire groups have lost a living sense of faith or no longer consider themselves members of the Church. Such situations require "a new evangelization" directed towards the baptized of all ages. Here missionary proclamation and basic catechesis are priorities.

Today local churches are obliged to address a panorama of these religious situations. The boundaries between pastoral care of the faithful, new evangelization and specific missionary activity are not clearly definable, but it is useful to remember:

- Mission *ad gentes* is the paradigm and primary missionary activity and cannot be supplanted by a new evangelization;
- The model of all catechesis is the baptismal catechumenate; and
- Catechesis for adults is the chief form of catechesis and all other forms are in some way ordered to it.

Chapter Two – Catechesis in the Process of Evangelization (nn. 60-76). Chapter Two describes the relationship of catechesis to other elements of evangelization.

Primary or first proclamation and catechesis, though distinct, are complementary. The first calls non-believers and those living in religious indifference to conversion; catechesis promotes and matures this initial conversion, educates in the faith and incorporates the believer into the Christian community. In practice it is not always easy to define the boundaries of these activities. In the *missio ad gentes* the first step is a "pre-catechumenate" to insure conversion. In the context of new evangelization, a "kerygmatic catechesis" (sometimes called "pre-catechesis") calls one to conversion. Only by starting with conversion can catechesis, strictly speaking, fulfill its proper task of education in the faith.

Initiatory catechesis is the link between missionary activity which calls people to faith and pastoral activity which nourishes the Christian community. Catechesis is a priority in evangelization because the inner growth of the Church depends on it. It is closely connected with the sacraments of initiation, especially Baptism. The aim of catechetical activity is to encourage a living, explicit and fruitful profession of faith, and in order to achieve it, the Church transmits to catechumens and those being catechized her living experience of the Gospel. Initiatory catechesis cannot be reduced to the circumstantial or the occasional. As an "essential moment" in evangelization, catechesis:

- Presents a comprehensive and systematic formation in the faith that includes more than instruction;

- Is an apprenticeship of the Christian life that implies education in knowledge and the life of faith in such a manner that the entire person is enriched by the word of God; and

- Lays a basic foundation for more solid nurture in the life of the Christian community through a formation centered on the nucleus of Christian experience, the fundamental certainties of the faith and the essential evangelical values.

Continuing or on-going education in the faith follows upon and presupposes basic catechesis. It serves the process of continuing conversion and is sustained by a community of faith. The Christian community nourishes disciples of Jesus Christ at a twofold table: the Word of God and Body of Christ. Continuing formation is directed not only to the individual but also to the Christian community, as such, so that it may mature in its interior life as well as in its openness to the world as a missionary community.

Among the forms of catechesis used in continuing education in the faith are:

- The study and exploration of Sacred Scripture, including the *lectio divina;*

- The study of the Church's social teaching;

- Liturgical catechesis;

- Occasional catechesis that interprets circumstances of personal, family, ecclesial or social life;

- Spiritual initiatives that reinforce conviction, open new perspectives, and encourage perseverance; and

- Systematic theological instruction that deepens one's understanding of the Christian message and equips the Christian for giving the reason for his hope. "It is appropriate to call such instruction *perfective catechesis.*

It is important the catechesis of children, young people, and adults complement one another.

Religious instruction in schools and its relationship with the catechesis of children and young people merits special consideration. Religious instruction in schools has an evangelizing character in that it is called on to make the Gospel present in a particular area of culture and help to relate it to other areas of knowledge. It is necessary that religious instruction in schools appear as a scholastic discipline with the same systematic demands and rigor as other disciplines. Through inter-disciplinary dialogue religious instruction underpins, develops and completes the educational activity of the school.

Religious instruction depends on legal and organizational circumstances, educational theories, and the personal outlook of individual teachers, students and their family. It is not possible to identify all the forms of religious instruction but students have the right to learn with truth and certainty the religion to which they belong. In the context of the Catholic school, religious instruction is part of and completed by other forms of the ministry of the word (catechesis, homilies, liturgical celebrations, etc.). In the context of state or non-confessional schools religious instruction will have a more ecumenical character and a more inter-religious awareness. In circumstances where it has an extensive cultural character, especially if presented by teachers with a sincere respect for the Christian religion, religious instruction maintains a true dimension of "evangelic preparation".

Religious instruction should be cognizant of the fact that the life and faith of students are characterized by continuous change. In the case of students who are believers, religious instruction assists them to understand better the Christian message by relating it to existential concerns common to all religions and every human being. Students who are searching or who have doubts find in religious instruction the possible answers that faith in Jesus Christ and the Church makes to their questions. In the case of non-believers religious instruction assumes the character of a missionary proclamation.

Christian education in the family, catechesis and religious instruction in schools are closely related. The local Church and the Episcopal Conference shall establish guidelines for various situations and foster distinct but complementary activities.

Chapter Three – The Nature, Object and the Duties of Catechesis (nn. 77-91). Chapter Three examines catechesis in relation to its ecclesial nature; the fundamental objective of catechesis; the tasks whereby the objective is achieved; and the gradual nature of the catechetical process. This chapter examines further the character of catechesis, already described in Chapter Two, through an analysis of its relationship with other ecclesial activities.

Catechesis is an ecclesial act. The Church transmits the faith she herself lives to catechumens and those to be catechized. The catechumenate becomes a center of deepening catholicity and a ferment of ecclesial renewal. The Church is at the same time mother and teacher. Through catechesis she feeds her children with her own faith and incorporates them into the ecclesial family.

The aim of catechesis is to bring people into communion and intimacy with Jesus Christ. The object of catechesis is expressed in the profession of faith in the one God: Father, Son and Holy Spirit. Catechesis has its origins in the confession of faith and leads to a confession of faith that is complete only in reference to the Church. Although no action is more personal than to proclaim "I believe," the baptized recite the Creed in the Church and through the Church: *Credo* and *Credimus* necessarily imply each other.

Catechesis' objective is realized by diverse, interrelated tasks that correspond to education of the different dimensions of faith. In virtue of the internal dynamic of faith catechesis has the fundamental tasks of helping the faithful know, celebrate, live and contemplate the mystery of Christ:

- *Promoting knowledge of the faith.* Catechesis leads gradually to the whole truth about the plan revealed by the Father by introducing the disciples of Jesus to a knowledge of Tradition and Scripture, and equips them to explain it to the world. The meaning of the Creed, a compendium of Scripture and the faith of the Church, is the realization of this task.

- *Liturgical education.* Communion with Jesus Christ leads to the celebration of his salvific presence in the sacraments, especially in the Eucharist. Catechesis must educate the disciples for prayer, for thanksgiving, for repentance, for praying with confidence, for community spirit, and for understanding correctly the meaning of the creeds in order that they be brought to that full, conscious and active participation which is required by the very nature of the liturgy.

- *Moral formation.* Catechesis assists the disciples on the journey of interior transformation, whereby participating in the paschal mystery of the Lord, "they pass from the old man to the new man who has been perfect in Christ." The Sermon on the Mount is an indispensable point of reference for the moral formation necessary today. The lived witness, prepared for by catechesis, must demonstrate the social consequences of the demands of the Gospel.

- *Teaching to pray.* Communion with Jesus leads the disciples to learn to pray with the same sentiments with which he turned to the Father: adoration, praise, thanksgiving, filial confidence, supplication and awe. All these sentiments are reflected in the Our Father, the model of all Christian prayer. When catechesis is permeated by a climate of prayer, the assimilation of the entire Christian life reaches its summit.

Other fundamental tasks of catechesis are education for community life and for mission:

- *Community life* is not realized spontaneously. Catechesis has the task of inculcating the teaching on community life recounted in Matthew's Gospel: the spirit of simplicity and humility; solicitude for the least of the brethren; particular care for the alienated; fraternal correction; common prayer; and mutual forgiveness. Catechesis takes special note of ecumenical dimension of community life and encourages fraternal attitudes towards members of other Christian churches and ecclesial communities.

- *Missionary initiation.* Catechesis nourishes the evangelical attitudes Jesus taught his disciples when he sent them on mission. It seeks to equip the lay faithful to be present as Christians in secular society through their professional, cultural and social lives and to lend their cooperation to ecclesial services according to their proper vocation. In educating the faithful for this missionary task, catechesis must prepare them for interreligious dialogue. It shows that the link between the Church and non-Christian religions is, in the first place, the common origin and end of the human race. On the other hand, dialogue does not dispense from evangelization.

"It is opportune to make some observations" on these varied tasks that constitute catechesis, all these tasks are necessary; when catechesis omits one, the Christian faith does not attain its full development. Although each task realizes in its own way the object of catechesis, they are interdependent. Each great catechetical theme—catechesis of God the Father, for example—has a cognitive dimension as well implications for moral formation, sacramental life, and prayer. To fulfill its tasks catechesis employs two principal means: the transmission of the Gospel message and experience of Christian life. Every dimension of the faith like faith as a whole is rooted in human experience.

Catechesis, at the service of maturation in faith, is a gradual process. In the baptismal catechumenate formation develops in four stages inspired by the Church's practice in the patristic period:

1. The *pre-catechumenate*, leading to conversion, when the kerygma is explained;

2. The *catechumenate*, properly speaking, is the context of integral catechesis beginning with "the handing on of the Gospels";

3. An intense time of *purification and illumination* in preparation for the sacraments of initiation when the handing on of the Creed and the Lord's Prayer take place; and

4. A time of *mystagogy* when sacraments and entry into the community are experienced.

Post-baptismal catechesis, recognizing that those being catechized have already been initiated into the Church, nonetheless, does well to draw inspiration from some of the elements of the baptismal catecheumenate without slavishly imitating its structures:

• The baptismal catechumenate is the responsibility of the entire Christian community;

• The baptismal catechumenate is permeated by the *mystery of Christ's Passover* with its spirituality focused on the liturgy of the Easter Vigil;

• The baptismal catechumenate receives catechumens with their cultural ties and thus becomes an initial locus of inculturation; and

• The baptismal catechumenate is characterized by comprehensiveness and integrity of formation; its gradual character; its connection with meaningful rites, symbols, biblical and liturgical signs; and its constant reference to the Christian community.

Part Two – The Gospel Message

Although the two aspects of Christian faith—*fides qua* and *fides quae*—cannot be separated, for methodological purposes Part Two focuses on *fides quae*. The first chapter sets out the norms and criteria which catechesis must follow in presenting the Gospel message; the second chapter examines the content of faith as it is presented in the *Catechism of the Catholic Church*, the doctrinal point of reference for all catechesis, and offers some observations that may help locate it within the catechetical activity of the Church. In addition, it sets out some criteria to assist particular Churches in compiling local catechisms (nn. 92-93).

Chapter One – Norms and criteria for presenting the Gospel message in catechesis (nn. 94-118). Catechesis draws its content from the living word of God transmitted in Tradition and the Scriptures that together make up a single "deposit of faith" entrusted to the Church. Although the GDC speaks both of the *source* and the *sources* of catechesis, the former is used to underline the oneness of the word of God, while the latter is used to denote the concrete loci from which catechesis draws its message (see GDC, Part Two, Chapter One, n. 7). Tradition, Scripture and the Magisterium are closely connected and "each account to its own way," are the principal sources of catechesis. Each of the subsidiary *sources* has its own proper language that has been shaped by a rich variety of documents of faith: biblical excerpts, liturgical texts, patristic writings, formulations of the Magisterium, creeds, testimonies of the saints, and theological reflections.

The criteria for presenting the Gospel message are closely inter-connected with each other because they spring from the same source. Although they are valid for the entire ministry of the word, the GDC develops them in relation to catechesis.

The Christocentricity of the Gospel message. The Christocentricity of the Gospel message means that (1) the fundamental task of catechesis is to present Christ, the Word of God, and everything in relationship to him; (2) Christ is the center, the final event toward which all salvation history converges; (3) catechesis is to transmit faithfully what Jesus teaches about God, man, happiness, the moral life, death, etc. The four Gospels occupy a central place in catechesis because Christ Jesus is the center. They are themselves endowed with a "catechetical character" in that they express the teaching of the first Christian communities.

The Trinitarian Christocentricity of the Gospel message. The Trinitarian Christocentricity of the Gospel message is the central mystery of Christian faith and life: the confession of faith in God, Father, Son and Holy Spirit. Catechesis must, therefore, emphasize the following points: (1) "Through Christ to the Father in the Holy Spirit." (2) The salvific works of God reveal his inner Being much as people reveal themselves by their actions, and the more deeply we know them, the better we understand what they do. (3) To confess belief in the one God revealed by Jesus has vital implications for human beings: one's personal freedom should never be subject in an absolute manner to any earthly power; humanity, made in the image of God who is a "communion of persons," is called to be a fraternal society with every one equal in personal dignity.

A message proclaiming salvation. Central to Jesus' preaching was the proclamation of the Kingdom of God with a transforming power equal and even superior to the creation of the world. It is the task of catechesis to transmit this proclamation, develop its implicit consequences and manifest its repercussions for humanity and the world by underlining the following basic aspects: God is a Father who is present among his creatures and whose power is love; the Kingdom offers the gift of salvation that is at once immanent and eschatological beginning in this life and achieving its consummation in eternity; the Gospel is a call to conversion and we shall all be judged in light of the Kingdom of justice and peace; here on earth the Kingdom is mysteriously present and when the Lord comes, it will enter into its perfection; the Church, the community of his disciples, is on earth the seed and the beginning of the Kingdom; man's pilgrimage towards the Father's house is already a taste of the world to come.

A message of liberation. An important part of the Church's mission is to proclaim the liberation of the millions of people, "since many of them are her children," oppressed by "hunger, epidemics, illiteracy, poverty, injustice, economic and cultural neo-colonialism." To prepare Christians for this task catechesis must connect the economic, political, social, and doctrinal messages of liberation with the religious objective of evangelization because it embraces the whole man extending even to his relationship to God. Catechesis, moreover, shall present Christian social morality as the fulfillment of the commandment of love and a consequence of the work of Christ who has liberated and continues to liberate the world. At the same time catechesis shall arouse "a preferential option for the poor" according to each individual's role, vocation and circumstances.

The ecclesial nature of the Gospel message. Catechesis originates in the Church's confession of faith. It is the process of transmitting the Gospel as the Christian community has received it, understands it, celebrates it, lives it, and communicates it. Hence there is present in catechesis the faith of the Apostles, the martyrs, the saints, the doctors of the Church, and all who, under the action of the Holy Spirit, have witnessed to it throughout the course of history. Although catechesis transmits the faith in many different cultural idioms, the Gospel that is handed on is one.

The historical character of the mystery of salvation. The Church interprets the present events of human history where the Spirit of God is continually renewing the face of the earth and she awaits with faith the Lord's coming. The historical character of the Christian message requires that catechesis makes known the great stages of the Old Testament, the deeds and words by which God revealed himself, the life of Jesus whose actions and teachings brought Revelation to completion, and the history of the Church that transmits Revelation. In explaining the Creed and the content of Christian morality doctrinal catechesis should illuminate the "today" of the history of salvation and interpret the signs of the times and things of this world in light of God's salvific plan. It is essential for mystagogical catechesis to show how, by means of the sacraments, the Church re-lives the great events of salvation history in the "today" of her liturgy. Catechesis helps to make the passage from sign to mystery (see GDC, Part Two, Chapter One, no. 67): from the history of the Church to the mystery of the Church as the "sacrament of salvation"; from the "signs of the times" to traces of God's presence in history.

Inculturation of the Gospel message. The Incarnation, the original "inculturation" of the word of God, is the model of all evangelization by the Church. Inculturation means that the Gospel penetrates the very center and roots of culture, purifying and transforming it; discerning modes of thought and life-styles that are contrary to Kingdom of God, and those that are compatible with the Gospel and communion with the universal Church. In this inculturation of the faith, the catechist who represents the ecclesial community must possess a profound religious sense, a social conscience, and deep roots in the cultural environment. Local catechisms must explain the Gospel in relation to the hopes, questions, and problems presented by the culture. The catechumenate and catechetical institutes must incorporate, with discernment, the language, symbols, and values of the culture. Those being catechized must be prepared to give reasons "for their hope" in pagan or post-Christian cultures. "Effective apologetics to assist the faith-culture dialogue is indispensable today."

The integrity of the Gospel message. A fundamental principle of catechesis is that of safeguarding the integrity of the message and avoiding any partial or distorted presentation. Catechesis accomplishes this by following the example of the divine pedagogy with which God revealed himself progressively and gradually and by explaining it in a manner adapted to the capacity of those being catechized. The complex relationship between inculturation and safeguarding the integrity of the Gospel message maintain a missionary openness to truly human and religious values without falling into facile accommodations that enfeeble the Gospel and secularize the Church.

A comprehensive and hierarchical message. The Gospel message transmitted by catechesis is organized around the mystery of the Holy Trinity, the source of all the other mysteries of faith and the starting point of a "hierarchy of truths" that connect these mysteries in a harmonious whole. This hierarchy means that some truths are based on others as of a higher priority and are illumined by them. All aspects of the Christian message—the Apostles' Creed, the sacraments, the twofold commandment of love, and the Our Father—participate in this hierarchical system. The preparation for the Gospel in the Old Testament, the fullness of Revelation in Jesus Christ and the time of the Church provide the structure of all salvation history of which creation and eschatology are the beginning and the end.

A meaningful message for the human person. In presenting the Christian message catechesis not only reveals God and his saving plan but, as Jesus himself did, reveals man to man and makes him aware of his sublime vocation. Catechesis seeks to teach humans to think like Jesus, to act like him, and to love like him. Catechesis is eminently Christological and should, therefore, be concerned with making people attentive to their more significant experiences, both personal and social. It should examine, in the light of the Gospel, the questions that arise from those experiences so that individuals are moved by a desire to transform their way of life. The first evangelization shall always show how the Gospel satisfies the aspirations of the human heart. Biblical catechesis helps to interpret present-day life in light of the experiences of the people of Israel and the ecclesial community in which the Spirit continually lives and works. In explaining the Creed, catechesis shows how the great themes of faith (creation, original sin, Incarnation, Easter, Pentecost, eschatology) are sources of life and light for the human being. Moral catechesis roots the Beatitudes and the spirit of the Decalogue in the human virtues present in the human heart. Liturgical catechesis makes constant reference to the great human experiences represented by the signs and symbols of liturgical actions.

Methodological principle for the presentation of the message. Although the norms and criteria indicated in this chapter must be applied in the various forms of catechesis, the selection of a particular order for presenting the message is conditioned by circumstances, and by the faith level of those to be catechized. Care must be taken in deciding which pedagogical method is most appropriate to a particular ecclesial community and to whom catechesis is addressed. Bishops are to draw up particular norms by means of catechetical directories and catechisms for different ages and cultural conditions.

Chapter Two – "This is our faith, this is the faith of the Church" (nn. 119-136). This chapter reflects on the content of catechesis. The Church has always used short formulations to express the essentials of what she believes and lives: New Testament texts, creeds, liturgical formulas, Eucharistic prayers. Over time, many local churches compiled more ample explicitations of the faith in the form of catechisms. In "two historical moments" (after the Council of Trent and in our own time) the Church found it opportune to furnish a comprehensive presentation of the faith in a catechism that would serve as a reference point for catechesis throughout the Church. The present chapter situates these official instruments in the Church's overall catechetical activity, and explains how the *General Directory for Catechesis* (GDC) relates first to the *Catechism of the Catholic Church* (CCC) promulgated by Pope John Paul II and then to local catechisms that adapt the content of faith to different circumstances and cultures.

The *Catechism* is a statement of the Church's faith and Catholic doctrine; the GDC provides pastoral principles taken from the Church's Magisterium, especially the Second Vatican Council, that govern and guide the ministry of the word. The CCC, issued by the pope in virtue of his apostolic authority, is a normative reference for the presentation of the content of faith. The GDC is an official aid issued by the Holy See for the transmission of the Gospel message, the whole of catechetical activity. These two instruments are complementary in nature, which explains why the GDC does not devote a chapter to the contents of the faith as was the case in the 1971 *General Catechetical Directory*. The GDC seeks to facilitate a better understanding and use of the Catechism.

The Catechism of the Catholic Church. The Prologue to the Catechism describes its *nature* and *purpose*. It is a comprehensive synthesis of Catholic doctrine as regards both faith and morals in light of the Second Vatican Council and Church Tradition. It promotes the bond of ecclesial union by helping the disciples of Jesus Christ to make "the profession of one faith received from the Apostles." It is an obligatory point of reference for teaching Catholic doctrine and for the other forms of the ministry of the word. Rather than replacing local catechisms, its intent is to encourage and assist in their writing.

The *Catechism* is *structured around the "four pillars"* of catechesis: the Creed (Part One), the Sacraments (Part Two), the Decalogue (Part Three), and the Lord's Prayer (Part Four). The structure derives from the unity of Christian life as it refers to the faith as it is believed, celebrated, lived and prayed, and maintains the explicit interrelation between *lex orandi, lex credendi* and *lex vivendi*. It does not, however, impose a predetermined configuration on one or the other because "the best structure for catechesis must be one which is suitable to particular concrete circumstances." Fidelity to Catholic doctrine is compatible with a rich diversity of presentation.

Centered on Jesus Christ the *Catechism* is *oriented in two directions*: toward the mystery of the Triune God that runs through the entire work, and toward the human person contemplated in the light of the humanity of Jesus. The doctrine of the *Catechism* is distilled in the remark of the Council, "Jesus Christ, by revealing the mystery of the Father and of his life, fully reveals man to himself and brings to light his most high calling."

It is important to understand the *literary genre* of the *Catechism* in order to understand its authority and its role in the catechetical ministry in our time: the *Catechism* is an official text of the Church's Magisterium that constitutes the basic reference for catechesis; it presents all that is fundamental and common to Christian life avoiding interpretations that are only private opinions or the views of some theological school; universal in scope it is offered to the entire Church. It presents the doctrine of the Second Vatican Council as well as the religious and moral concerns of our times, but leaves the adaptation of catechetical methods required by the differences of culture, age, spiritual maturity and social and ecclesial conditions to local catechisms and, "even more," to those who instruct the faithful.

The *Catechism* provides a service by insuring that the *deposit of faith*—the proclamation of the Gospel and the teaching of the Church—be transmitted in all its truth and purity. It is not the only source of catechesis:

1. The Church desires that Sacred Scripture have a pre-eminent position in the ministry of the word. In concrete terms, catechesis should be an authentic introduction to *lectio divina*, and that it imbibe biblical and evangelical thought, spirit and attitudes by constant contact with the Scriptures. Sacred Scripture and the Catechism, as a significant contemporary expression of the Church's Tradition, are sure norms for teaching the faith, and each in its own way nourishes catechesis.

2. The Fathers of the Church witness to the life-giving presence of Church's Tradition which together with Scripture is contained in the deposit of faith. They attribute a decisive importance to the baptismal catechumenate in the building up of the particular churches because it was modeled on the divine pedagogy that took the people of Israel by gradual and progressive stages through a journey to arrive at the promised land. The catechumenal process began with a narration of the history of salvation; as Lent advanced, it proceeded to the handing over of the Creed and the Our Father with their moral implications; and finally helped the people to interiorize the sacraments of initiation and to savor the experience of Christ.

The *Catechism of the Catholic Church*, for its part, brings together the richness of patristic catechesis as well "the great tradition of catechisms" that constantly remind the Church of the need of the faithful to have an organic knowledge of the faith and an education in the faith that embraces all the different dimensions of faith profession, celebration, life, and prayer. These traditions bring together seven basic elements that are characteristic of catechesis: the three phases in the narration of salvation history (OT, the life of Jesus, and the history of the Church); and the four pillars (Creed, Sacraments, Decalogue, and Our Father).

Catechisms in the Local Churches. The CCC is meant to encourage and assist Episcopal Conferences to prepare local catechisms faithful to the essential content of Revelation, up to date in method, and capable of educating future generations in a study of the faith. They are to be invaluable instruments for communicating the Gospel as the "Good News" of salvation to the very heart of culture and cultures.

Three principal traits characterize a catechism prepared by a local church: (1) Its official character distinguishes it from textbooks, unofficial catechisms, and other catechetical instruments; (2) Its organic structure presents a synthesis of the fundamental events and basic truths of the Christian mystery with regard to the hierarchy of truths; and (3) It is offered, along with Sacred Scripture, as a reference point for catechesis. Being an instrument of catechetical activity, that is to say, an act of communication, the local catechism reflects a certain pedagogical inspiration and "must always make apparent, in its own way, the divine pedagogy."

The Second Vatican Council affirms the need to adapt the Gospel Message and the *Catechism of the Catholic Church* indicates ways the local catechism must adapt to the differences of culture, age, spiritual maturity and social and ecclesial conditions. These catechisms will:

- Incorporate original expressions of life and thought and the fruits of the inculturation of the local church.
- Present the Christian message in a way that is meaningful to the psychology and mentality of the people and refer to the fundamental experiences of their lives.
- Be attentive to whether society is indifferent to religion or

profoundly religious, and take great care in treating the relationship between belief and science.

- Draw inspiration from the social teaching of the Church so that it can address problems arising from social conditions, especially those affecting economic, political and family life.
- Make reference to the concrete ecclesial situation that provides the context of evangelization.

A "catechism that adapts the Christian message to different ages, situations and cultures" is different from a catechism that is "mere summary of the *Catechism of the Catholic Church* and serves as an introduction to its study." Local catechisms may be diocesan, regional or national. Although the CCC is a point of doctrinal reference, it does not impose a determined structure on other catechisms that may be organized differently. Without sacrificing its essential truths local catechisms must transpose the Christian message into an idiom that will be understood by the people they are intended to serve. The *Catechism of the Catholic Church* and local catechisms together create a "symphony of faith" that has an important theological significance: they manifest the catholicity of the cultural richness and make visible the unity of the Church; they clearly express the reality of episcopal collegiality; the communion of bishops who, with the Successor of Peter, have the greatest responsibility for catechesis. By contemplating the unity and diversity of the catechisms the disciples of Christ can say in truth, "This is our faith, this is the faith the Church."

Part Three – The Pedagogy of the Faith

In Jesus Christ, Lord and Teacher, the Church finds transcendent grace, permanent inspiration and convincing model for all communication of the faith. The transmission of the Gospel is the work of the Holy Spirit, but the Spirit works through people whose experience and competence form part of the pedagogy of faith. Chapter One explains that Revelation is a fundamental witness and norm for the transmission of the Gospel, and Chapter Two addresses a series of questions that are concerned with catechetical activity, its sources, its methods, its recipients and the process of inculturation.

Chapter One – Pedagogy of God, source and model of the pedagogy of the faith (nn. 139-147). Scripture reveals God as a merciful Father, teacher and sage. As with human pedagogy the pedagogy of God assumes the cultural patterns and characteristics of individuals and communities. As a creative and insightful teacher God transforms events in the life of his people into lessons of wisdom, adapting himself to the diverse ages and cultural situations. He liberates his people from the bonds of evil and attracts them to himself by bonds of love, and causes them to grow progressively toward the maturity of free children, faithful and obedient to his word. The task of catechesis is to emphasize the relationship people have with God so that they allow themselves to be guided by him.

The Incarnation and redemptive mission of Jesus Christ continued the pedagogy of God. The Gospels record how the disciples had direct experience of the pedagogy of Jesus: how he proclaimed the Kingdom of God to the poor, the little ones and sinners; how he used all the resources of interpersonal communication: word, silence, metaphor, image, example, signs. In passing on this pedagogy of faith, he made them sharers in his actions and destiny.

From her beginning the Church has lived the mission as a continuation of the pedagogy of the Father and of the Son. The Christian community proclaims, celebrates, works, and is in herself a living and primary *locus* of catechesis. The Church has produced an incomparable treasure of pedagogy in the faith: the witness of saints and catechists; variety of life-styles and forms of catechetical institutions and services. These and other examples form part of the history of catechesis and have a rightful place in the memory of the community and the praxis of catechists.

The pedagogy of God is completed when the disciple, thanks to the gift of the Holy Spirit, becomes "the perfect Man, fully mature with the fullness of Christ himself" (Eph. 4:13). For this reason only those who are convinced and faithful disciples of Christ and his Church can be teachers of the faith.

Catechesis encourages a true experience of faith, that is to say, a filial encounter with God. Thus catechesis:

- Is a pedagogy that serves as a "dialogue of salvation" between God and the person; with regard to God, it underlines the divine initiative and respect for our liberty; with regard to us, it highlights the dignity of the gift and the demand to grow continually therein;

- Accepts the principle of the progressiveness of Revelation, the transcendence of the word of God and its adaptation to different persons and cultures;

- Recognizes the centrality of Jesus Christ through whom the Gospel is to be proposed for and in the life of people;

- Values the community experience of faith proper to the Church;

- Rooted in inter-personal relations, it makes its own the process of dialogue;

- Conducts a pedagogy of signs, where words and deed, teaching and experience are interlinked; and

- Draws its power to witness to the truth from the inexhaustible divine love, which is the Holy Spirit.

Thus catechesis takes the form of a journey, following the Christ of the Gospel in the Spirit towards the Father.

Catechesis neither confuses nor separates the divine salvific action of God and human pedagogy. It seeks dialogue with people in accordance with the directions offered by the Church's Magisterium. The following objectives inspire its choice of methodology and carry out a complete work of initiation, education, and teaching:

- To promote a progressive synthesis between full adherence of man to God (*fides qua*) and the content of the Christian message (*fides quae*);

- To convey the dimensions of faith as it is known, celebrated, lived, and prayed;

- To move the person to abandon intelligence, will, heart, and memory to God; and

- To help the person discern the vocation to which the Lord calls him/her.

Genuine catechesis helps one perceive the action of God throughout the formative journey. By encouraging listening, thanksgiving, and prayer, it invites a free response and promotes active participation on the part of those to be catechized. Catechesis has the never-ending task of finding a language capable of communicating the whole word of God and the creed of the Church in the concrete existence of people. It does so in a manner that penetrates and transforms intelligence, conscience, liberty, and action after the example of Christ. The catechist appreciates and avails him/herself of the contribution of the educational sciences, understood always in a Christian sense.

Chapter Two – Elements of Methodology (nn. 148-162). Catechetical methodology has the simple objective of education in the faith. The Church's history confirms that she has employed a great variety of methods in the service of the Gospel. The variety of methods is a sign of life and richness as well as an indication of the respect for age, degree of spiritual maturity, and personal circumstances of those to whom catechesis is addressed.

The catechist knows there is a necessary correlation and interaction between method and content and content cannot be indifferently subjected to any method. Catechesis requires a process of transmission that is adequate to the nature of the message, to its sources and language, to the concrete circumstances of ecclesial communities and the faithful to whom it is addressed. Because of their importance in tradition and present day catechesis, mention must be made of the methods of approaching the Bible, the Creed, liturgical and ecclesial signs, and the methods proper to the mass media.

The communication of the faith in catechesis, an event of grace in which a person encounters the word of God, is expressed in sensible signs and is ultimately open to mystery. It can happen in ways not always known to us. Reference to inductive and deductive methods is common. The former has many advantages because it conforms to the economy of Revelation and knowledge of the faith that comes by way of sensible signs. It presents biblical events, liturgical acts, events in the Church's life as well as in daily life so as to discern the meaning they might have in divine Revelation. The inductive method required does not exclude the deductive method but in fact requires that it explain and describe facts by proceeding from their causes. The deductive synthesis is fully effective when the inductive process is completed. In practice the one is called the "kerygmatic" (*descending*) approach; it begins with the proclamation of the message, expressed in the principal documents of the faith and applies them to life. The other is called the "existential" (*ascending*) approach; it moves from human conditions and enlightens them with the word of God. Both are legitimate approaches.

Because experience has different functions in catechesis it must be continuously and duly evaluated. Experience arouses interests, questions, hopes, anxieties, reflections and judgments that converge to bring a person to desire to transform his/her existence. Just as Jesus used human experiences and situations to point to the eschatological and transcendent, experience is a necessary medium for exploring and assimilating the truths that constitute the content of Revelation. The catechist must teach the person to read his/her own lived experience so as to accept the invitation of the Holy to conversion, to commitment, to hope, and to discover God's plan for him/her. Experience assumed by faith becomes in a certain manner a *locus* for the manifestation and realization of salvation. Interpreting and illuminating experience with the data of faith, even though difficult, is a constant task of catechetical pedagogy.

Memorization has formed a constitutive aspect of the pedagogy of the faith since the beginning. Particular consideration should be given to memorizing the principal formulae that insure a precise exposition of the faith and guarantee a common doctrinal, cultural, and linguistic patrimony. They should include texts of the Bible, dogma and liturgy as well as common prayers. To overcome the risk of mechanical memorization, mnemonic learning should allow for spontaneous reaction and reflection, moments of dialogue and silence, as well as oral and written work. The texts must be gradually understood in depth in order that they become a source of Christian life on the personal and community levels. Even more importantly, the learning of the formulae and their profession must be understood in the context of the *traditio* and *redditio*; this corresponds in catechesis to the handing on of the faith and the response of the recipient. This process encourages participation in received truth.

The role of the catechist is indispensable in every phase of the catechetical process. Only the human and Christian qualities of the catechist guarantee a good use of texts and methods. The catechist facilitates between the people and the mystery of God, between subjects among themselves and with the community. His/her cultural vision, social condition, and lifestyle help to create the most advantageous conditions for deepening the Christian message. He/she does not forget that belief is a fruit of grace and liberty. Finally, the personal relationship of the catechist with the subject is of crucial importance.

The call of believers to respond to the gift of God assumes those being catechized participate actively in the formation process through prayer, the sacraments, works of charity, etc. In catechesis the subjects, especially if they are adults, can contribute by pointing out the most effective ways of "learning while doing," by employing research and dialogue, by exchanging challenging points of view.

The Christian community as the visible place of faith-witness is the source, the *locus*, and means of catechesis. It receives members as the family of God and constitutes itself as the living and permanent environment for growth in the faith. Person-to-person contact is indispensable. The gift of the Holy Spirit comes from one living person to another and the power of persuasion becomes more effective.

Groups play an important function in the catechetical process. For children they foster well-rounded sociability, and for young people, they are vital for personality formation. For adults, they promote dialogue and sharing as well as a sense of Christian co-responsibility. Catechists who participate in such groups act in the name of the Church, witnessing to the Gospel and sharing with others the fruits of their mature faith. Apart from the didactic aspect the Christian group provides an experience and a form of participation in ecclesial life that is more fully manifested in the Eucharistic community.

The means of social communication have become powerful instruments of information and education. The media, which is constantly being developed and perfected, has become essential for evangelization and catechesis. All kinds of electronic media provide the Church with a new and more effective forum from which she can address the multitudes. Audio-visuals and other such aids cannot be absent from well-planned catechesis. Reciprocal assistance is encouraged among churches to help to defray the high cost of acquiring such aids.

To make good use of the media, catechists should be committed and trained in its use. It is not enough, however, to use the media to spread the Christian message. Only by integrating it into the "new culture" created by modern communications with it new languages, techniques, and psychology, can the Gospel message penetrate everyone's consciousness and obtain a personal commitment.

Catechists should focus their efforts on people who work in and with the mass media: media professionals to whom they can point out the Gospel as a great horizon of truth, responsibility and inspiration; families who are exposed to the influence of the media; and the younger generations who are users and creative subjects of mass media. The use of the instruments of mass communications and their reception by the public demand both education in a critical sense animated by a passion for truth, and respect for the liberty and dignity of individuals as well as peoples' authentic culture.

Part Four – Those to Be Catechized

Jesus proclaimed the Kingdom of God and made himself a *catechist* for people of every walk of life, great and small, rich and poor, healthy and sick, Jews and pagans, men and women, individuals and groups. He concluded his earthly life by sending his disciples to do the same. Throughout its history the Church, prompted by the Holy Spirit, has acquired an immense variety of experience in proclamation and catechesis, and has articulated the characteristics of a pedagogy of faith. Attention to the diverse life situations of peoples moves catechesis to employ different approaches and to adapt the Christian message to their needs. Because it is impossible to deal with every type of catechesis, Part Four focuses on aspects of catechesis that are important in any situation:

- General aspects of catechetical adaptation (chapter 1);
- Catechesis based on age (chapter 2);
- Catechesis for those in special circumstances (chapter 3);
- Catechesis in various socio-religious contexts (chapter 4); and
- Catechesis in the socio-cultural context (chapter 5).

Chapter One – Adaptation to those to be catechized: general aspects

(nn. 167-170). All the baptized because they are called to maturity of faith have a need for and right to adequate catechesis and the Church has a responsibility to respond. Recipients of catechesis cannot remain silent and passive but must be active, conscious, and co-responsible in the catechetical process. In giving attention to individuals it should not be overlooked that the whole Christian community is the recipient of catechesis: the adaptation of the Gospel concerns and involves the community as a community.

The theological motivation for this adaptation is the Incarnation. It corresponds to the elementary demands of human communications that takes into account diversity of circumstances and cultures while maintaining the unity in the one, saving Word. Catechesis does not stop with exterior elements of a situation but is always mindful of the interior world of the person: questions, aspirations and needs. (A note explains why both the terms *adaptation* and *inculturation* are used: the first applies mainly to persons, while the second is applied to cultural contexts.)

Chapter Two – Catechesis according to age (nn. 171-188). Providing catechesis based on different age groups is an essential task of the Christian community. Such catechesis pays attention to the anthropological-evolutionary, theological-pastoral, and up-to-date scientific data and pedagogical methods. The various stages in the journey of faith must be integrated so that successive phases harmoniously complete catechesis received in childhood. This chapter sets out general elements by way of example and leaves further details to the catechetical directories of particular Churches and episcopal conferences.

The Catechesis of Adults. The GDC starts first with a focus on adult faith formation. It notes that the discourse of faith with adults must take serious account of their experience and the challenges they have encountered in life. Such ongoing formation is needed for all adults, whether they live their faith and desire to deepen it; were baptized but not sufficiently catechized or who have fallen away so they may be called "quasi catechumens"; come from other Christian confessions; or have never been baptized.

The role and identity of the catechists who are responsible for the formation of adults in the community are vitally important. Adult catechesis must systematically propose the Christian faith in its entirety in accordance with the Church's understanding. To this end, the *Catechism of the Catholic Church* and the catechisms of the particular Churches based on it provide a fundamental service. In particular the tasks of adult catechesis are:

- To promote formation in the Risen Christ by means the sacraments, retreats, spiritual direction, etc;
- To educate toward an evaluation of the socio-cultural changes in societies in the light of faith;
- To clarify current religious and moral questions, e.g., public

and private morality with regard to social issues and the education of future generations;

- To clarify the relationship between temporal actions and ecclesial action, and to this end included the social doctrine of the Church as an integral part of adult catechesis;

- To develop the rational foundation of the faith and thereby promote the pastoral aim of Christian thought that helps overcome forms of fundamentalism as well as subjective and arbitrary interpretations; and

- To encourage adults to exercise responsibility for the Church's mission and to be able to give Christian witness in society.

Certain situations require special forms of catechesis: the catechumenate/RCIA for Christian initiation; traditional forms duly adapted to the liturgical year and in the extraordinary form of missions; on-going forms for catechists and those involved in the lay apostolate; and catechesis for significant events in life (e.g. Marriage), critical times during youth, in sickness; for events such as beginning work, military service, emigration, etc.; at the beginning of holidays and travel.

Catechesis for events in the life of the Church and society and many other forms of special catechesis complement but do not replace the ongoing, systematic, catechetical courses which every ecclesial community must provide for all adults.

The Catechesis of Infants and Young Children. Christ wants the child to be a privileged member of the Kingdom of God. Catechesis must always be available to Christian children who today more than in the past demand help in their spiritual and human growth. Those who have given them life and enriched them with the gift of Baptism have the duty continually to nourish it.

The catechesis of children, the work of various but complementary agents, is linked with their particular situations and conditions:

- Infancy and childhood are times of primary socialization as Christian education takes place in the family, school, and the Church. These are foundational moments for subsequent stages of faith.

- Childhood is normally the time when the reception of the sacraments of Christian initiation, inaugurated with Baptism, is completed.

- The catechetical process in infancy establishes the anthropological basis for a life of faith, a sense of trust, freedom, self-giving, appeal, and joyful participation. Central are training in prayer and introduction to Sacred Scripture.

- The family and the school are two vital educational *loci*. Nothing replaces family catechesis because of its positive and receptive environment, the example of adults, and the first explicit experience of the faith.

- School introduces the child to a wider society with the possibility of greater development of intellectual, affective, and behavioral capacities. Often the school offers religious instruction. Catechists must co-operate with parents and school teachers. Pastors should remember that by helping parents and educators to fulfill their mission, the Church is being built up and provides an occasion for adult catechesis.

There are many disadvantaged children who lack adequate support in the family or who do not attend school or who are victims of dysfunctional social conditions and other environmental factors. Many are not even baptized; others do not bring to completion the journey to initiation. It is the responsibility of the Christian community to address their situation by proposing appropriate forms of education and providing catechesis proportionate to their needs.

Catechesis of Young People. The Church should proclaim the Gospel to youth with courage and creativity because the young are the first victims of the spiritual and cultural crisis griping the world and because any commitment to the betterment of society finds its hopes in them.

Experience suggests that it is useful in catechesis to distinguish between pre-adolescence, adolescence, and young adulthood. In developed regions, the question of pre-adolescence is of particular concern. Insufficient attention is given to their difficulties, needs, and human and spiritual resources. The fact that after receiving the sacrament of Confirmation adolescents very often abandon the practice of faith is a matter of serious concern which requires specific pastoral action.

Even though it is difficult to distinguish between adolescence and young adulthood, taken together they are the period of life that precedes the taking up of responsibilities proper to adults. Youth catechesis must be profoundly revised and revitalized. Young people are at once the hope and the challenge for the future of the Church. The many rapid and tumultuous socio-cultural changes all contribute to make of young a world in waiting, a world of disenchantment, boredom, angst, and marginalization. Alienation from the Church or at least diffidence to it often reflects lack of spiritual and moral support in the family, and weakness in the catechesis that they have received. However, many are driven to find meaning, solidarity, social commitment, and even religious experience.

Catechesis must note the contrasts in the condition of youth as found concretely in various regions and environments. The explicit proposal of Christ to the young man in the Gospel is a direct proposal to all young people with an understanding of their problems. Young people must be active in their own catechesis and protagonists of evangelization and artisans of social renewal.

The catechetical directories of particular Churches and episcopal conferences must determine suitable measures for their areas, but some general directions are indicated:

- Catechesis is most successful when it is given in the context of wider pastoral care and addresses the problems that affect the lives of young people.

- Group action, youth associations, and personal accompaniment of young people are useful approaches for effective catechesis. Spiritual direction is also an important element.

Among diverse forms of youth catechesis are the catechumenate during school years, catechesis for Christian initiation, catechesis on specific themes as well as occasional and informal meetings.

Youth catechesis should be proposed in new ways that are open to their sensibilities and problems. In particular, they should emphasize education in truth and liberty as understood by the Gospel, to the formation of conscience, education for love, vocational discernment, and on missionary responsibility in the world. Contemporary evangelization often demands that the apostolate among young people adopt a missionary (rather than a strictly catechumenal) dimension as a first step to bringing to maturity those dispositions favorable to the strictly catechetical moment. Very often it is useful to intensify pre-catechumenal activity.

One difficulty to be addressed and resolved is the question of the "language" (mentality, sensibility, tastes, style, vocabulary) of young people. Adaptation of catechesis to their language is necessary in order to translate the message of Jesus into their terms.

Catechesis for the Aged. The growing number of old people represents a new pastoral challenge for the Church. In the light of faith they must be seen as a gift of God to the Church and society. In catechesis, they have the same rights and duties as all Christians. It must pay attention to the diversity of personal, family, and social conditions, and in particular to such factors as isolation and the risk of marginalization. The proclamation of the faith takes place best in the family, but the caring presence of the catechist and the community of believers is also important. The aged should participate fully in the catechetical journey of the community.

Catechesis for the aged who are solid in faith brings an attitude of thanksgiving and hopeful expectation. Catechesis for others whose faith is weakened by poor Christian practice becomes a moment of new light and religious experience. Catechesis can help those who have reached old age wounded in body and soul to live in an attitude of prayer, forgiveness, and inner peace. The condition of the old calls for a catechesis of hope derived from the certainty of finally meeting God. The Christian community in turn benefits and is enriched when the old bear witness to a faith that grows more resplendent as they approach meeting the Lord.

In the Bible the old man is symbolic of a person rich in wisdom and fear of God and a repository of experience that makes him a natural "catechist" in the community. He is a witness to the tradition of faith, a teacher of life, and worker of charity. Catechesis helps the aged to discover the riches within themselves and to assume the role of catechists among children, young people and adults, and thus promote a dialogue between generations within the family and community.

Chapter Three – Catechesis for special situations, mentalities and environments (nn. 189-192). Individuals, especially children, who suffer handicaps, physical or mental, are particularly beloved of the Lord. Every person, however limited, is capable of growth in holiness. Progress in social and ecclesial consciousness along with specialized pedagogy makes it possible for family and others to provide adequate catechesis for them. Education in the faith, which should take into account the findings of pedagogical research, is most effectively carried out in the context of the integral education of the person. It is necessary that the community be made aware of this specialized catechesis and be involved in it. The particular demands of this catechesis, moreover, require a special competence from catechists.

The catechesis of the marginalized—immigrants, refugees, the chronically ill, drug addicts, prisoners—must be considered within the same perspective. The strength of catechesis is measured by its capacity to identify different situations, to meet everyone's needs, to stress personal contact and sometimes to turn to indirect and occasional forms. The Christian community supports those catechists who dedicate themselves to this service.

Special programs are required for workers, for professionals, for artists, for scientists and for university students. All these sectors demand a competent approach and language adapted to those being catechized while always maintaining fidelity to the message.

The service of faith takes careful note of the environment and habitats where persons live. It is here that they are influenced and exercise influence and responsibility. Two major environments—rural and urban—call for different forms of catechesis. The needs of country people are often linked with poverty, sometimes with fear and superstition, but often they are also rich in simplicity, trust, a sense of solidarity, faith in God, and fidelity to religious traditions. Urban catechesis must take account of a variety of social conditions extending from great prosperity to pockets of poverty. Stress can dominate the rhythm of life. There are many temptations to escapism and irresponsibility; anonymity and loneliness are widespread. For both of these environments the service of the faith requires planning, trained catechists, and familiarity with the resources of the mass media.

Chapter Four – Catechesis in the socio-religious context (nn. 193-201). In a secularized world unbelief and religious indifference may be encountered together with expressions of religious and cultural pluralism. In the face of spurious forms of religion and dubious adherence to the faith some Christians become incapable of knowing how to confront situations or to judge the messages they receive. Their faith is exposed to trials and risks being extinguished altogether unless it is constantly nourished and sustained.

In these circumstances a catechesis of evangelization becomes indispensable: a catechesis impregnated with the Gospel and imparted in language adapted to the times and hearers. Such catechesis educates Christians in a sense of their identity as baptized, as believers, as members of the Church, who are open to dialogue with the world. It reminds them of the fundamental elements of faith, stimulates a real process of conversion, and deepens the Christian message in the face of theoretical and practical objections. Catechesis of evangelization helps them to live out the Gospel in everyday life, gives reasons for the hope that is theirs, and encourages their missionary vocation by witness, dialogue, and proclamation.

"Popular piety" is a vital dimension in Catholic life. Popular piety requires a catechesis that is quick to appreciate its desirable qualities and is zealous to direct it so that the dangers of errors or fanaticism, superstition, syncretism, or religious ignorance may be avoided. When properly directed, popular piety can contribute toward bringing the masses of our people into contact with God in Jesus Christ.

Every Christian community is moved by the Spirit to recognize its ecumenical vocation by participating in dialogue and initiatives to foster the unity of Christians. Catechesis is called on to assume an ecumenical dimension (1) by an exposition of Revelation conserved in the Catholic Church while respecting the hierarchy of truths; (2) by explaining the divisions among Christians and the steps being taken to overcome them; (3) by nourishing a desire for unity, particularly with the love of Sacred Scripture; and (4) by having children, young people and adults cultivate their own Catholic identity and by respecting the faith of others.

Catechesis needs to give specific attention to the religion of the Jewish people "the first to hear the word of God." Religious instruction, catechesis, and preaching should be a preparation for understanding and dialogue. Both traditions are too closely related to ignore each other, and a reciprocal consciousness should be encouraged at all levels. In particular, an objective of catechesis should be to overcome every form of anti-semitism.

For the most part Christians live in multi-religious contexts. The GDC calls for catechesis to be offered to assist us to live richly in these situations. Such catechesis would assist Christians to understand and live more fully with Muslims and for all of those who practice many other forms of religion.

Chapter Five – Catechesis in the socio-cultural context (nn. 202-214). Along with evangelization in general, catechesis is called to bring the Gospel into the heart of culture and cultures. The history of catechesis, particularly in the patristic period, is the history of inculturation of the faith and, as such, merits careful study. This chapter expounds some methodological directions concerning this demanding task, ever open to the risks of syncretism and other misunderstandings. Because of the importance of inculturation there exists today a need for systematic reflection on the catechetical experience.

The tasks of inculturation of the faith form an organic whole. Briefly stated they are:

- To know the culture in depth and to what extent it has penetrated people's lives;
- To recognize the cultural dimensions of the Gospel itself while recognizing it is not grounded in some human culture;
- To proclaim the Gospel as a profound force for transforming culture;
- To witness to the Gospel's transcendence, while at the same time discerning the seeds of the Gospel which may be present in culture;
- To promote a new expression of the Gospel looking for a common language of the faith and thus a fundamental element of communion; and
- To maintain the integrity of the faith and explain traditional formulations of doctrine while taking into account the cultural and historical circumstances of those being instructed.

Catechesis proposes the Gospel by going to the very roots of culture by an interactive process consisting of various elements: listening and discerning in the culture of the people for what has an authentic Gospel value and purifying it from marks of sin or human frailty; and impacting on people through stimulating a radical conversion to God, dialogue, and of patient interior maturation.

In attempts at inculturation the catechetical process must be attentive lest it be infiltrated by syncretistic elements. In positive terms, catechesis inspires not only intellectual assimilation of the faith but also touches the heart and transforms conduct. Catechesis bridges the gap between belief and life, between the Christian message and cultural context, and brings forth fruits of true holiness.

Inculturation must involve the whole People of God since the people reflect the authentic *sensu fidei*. It must be an expression of the community's life and not be exclusively the result of erudite research. The incarnation of the Gospel requires the cooperation of clergy, pastoral workers (catechists), and laity.

Catechesis of the young and adults are most apt to inculturate the faith because of the possibilities they offer of relating faith and life. The Christian initiation of children also has important cultural implications in acquiring new motivations in life, education of conscience, biblical and sacramental language, and knowledge of Christian history. Liturgical catechesis is a privileged means because of its richness of signs and accessibility to the People of God: the Sunday homily, the lectionary and the liturgical year along with marriages, funerals, visits to the sick, etc. The care of the family is the primary agent of an incarnate transmission of the faith. Catechesis emphasizes multi-ethnic and multi-cultural situations because they can lead to a discovery of resources whereby diverse groups receive and express the faith.

To say that inculturation of the faith is a linguistic task implies that catechesis respects and values the language proper to the message, especially biblical language, as well as the traditional language of creed, liturgy, and doctrine. It also implies that catechesis must enter into dialogue with forms and terms proper to the culture in which the Gospel has been planted and demonstrate its existential importance. Similarly, catechesis must speak a language suited to children and young people in general as well as to other groups: intellectuals, scientists, illiterate people, the handicapped, and the like.

Intrinsically connected with the question of language is the use of mass media and realizing the importance of balancing image with word, of safeguarding of the genuine religious meaning of the latter, of promoting critical discernment as to what is received from the media, and of producing catechetical aids. The catechism is central to inculturation, above all the *Catechism of the Catholic Church* expressly calls for preparation of local catechisms incorporating adaptations required by difference of culture, age, social and ecclesial situations, etc.

The Gospel seeks a catechesis which is open, generous and courageous. It is important, therefore, for catechesis to discern and penetrate environments where elementary cultural exchanges take place: the family, school, work environment, and free time. There are many cultural areas that need to be enlightened with the light of the Gospel, "modern *areopagi*" like campaigns for peace, development of peoples, the protection of creation, defense of human rights, scientific research, and international relations.

In the process of inculturation, catechesis confronts different concrete situations. In the first place, it is necessary to distinguish the situation in countries of recent Christian origin from that in countries of long Christian tradition that need a new evangelization. Second, there are situations open to conflict and tension because of ethnic and religious pluralism, social and economic differences, and secular versus religious influences. Finally, cultural differences divide social and professional strata, workers and youth, the marginalized, and disabled. Attention should be paid to the diverse cultures that co-exist in one nation.

Inculturation is a task for local churches precisely because it takes place in concrete and specific circumstances. To this end, episcopal conferences propose catechetical directories, catechisms, workshops, centers of formation, and research. "In light of what has been expressed in the present Directory, an updating and revision of local directories become necessary."

The importance of the matter as well as research and experimentation require pastors to:

- Promote widespread catechesis that permits dialogue and direct involvement of persons who indicate effective ways of proclaiming the Gospel;

- Carry out pilot-schemes of inculturation; the adult catechumenate assumes a particularly influential role in this respect;

- Translate guides and directories; and promotion by way of catechetical centers a homogenous catechetical ministry for linguistic and ethnic groups; and

- Encourage dialogue between the Churches and between these and the Holy See that allows for the certification of experiences, criteria, programs, tools and for an up-to-date inculturation.

Part Five – Catechesis in the Particular Church

Part Five presents the more important pastoral elements of the catechetical ministry in the particular Church:

- The agents of catechesis—bishops, priests, deacons, religious and laity (chapter 1);
- The formation of catechists (chapter 2);
- The *loci* where catechesis is realized (chapter 3); and
- Organization, structures, coordination and some specific tasks (chapter 4).

The directives and suggestions in Part Five cannot find immediate application in all parts of the Church but they offer a series of goals to be achieved gradually.

Chapter One – The ministry of catechesis in the particular Churches and its agents (nn. 217-232). The particular Church is constituted by the community of Christ's disciples in a definite socio-cultural space. Each particular Church makes the universal Church present with all its essential elements. Built around two pillars—the proclamation of the Gospel and Eucharist—the particular Church, like the universal Church, exists for evangelization, a part of which involves catechesis. By means of catechesis the diocese provides a formative process within a particular cultural horizon that permits the disciples of Christ to confess and proclaim the faith—the goal of catechesis—in their own tongue.

Although catechesis has an important role in all the ministries and services by which the particular Church carries out its mission of evangelization, the following should be underlined:

- In the diocese, catechesis is a unique service performed by the entire Christian community in communion with the Bishop. Although priests, deacons, religious, and laity have a common responsibility, they exercise catechesis in different ways according to their particular condition in the Church.
- Catechesis is a fundamental ecclesial service indispensable for the growth of the Church. The catechetical ministry acts in the name of the Church and cannot be realized on a private basis or by purely individual initiative.
- The catechetical ministry has a proper character derived from its specific role in the evangelization process. The task of catechists, as educators in the faith, differs from that of other pastoral agents, even though they always act in coordination with them.

- In order to be fruitful catechetical ministry needs to involve other agents who support and sustain catechesis by the formation of catechists, the production of catechetical materials, reflection, organization, and planning. These agents together with catechists serve a single diocesan catechetical ministry.

Catechesis is a responsibility of the entire Christian community. Every member has a responsibility for Christian initiation and continuing education in the faith so that catechumens and those being catechized—children, young people and adults—are actively incorporated into the community's life. At the end of the catechetical process it is the Christian community that welcomes the catechized in a fraternal environment. The Christian community also receives much from new converts who bring religious and human wealth. Catechesis brings to maturity the faith of individuals and brings the community itself to maturity.

The Church calls some members of the community to be catechists and confers on them the ecclesial mandate and the delicate task of organically transmitting the faith.

Missionary proclamation and catechesis are two closely united aspects of the prophetic ministry of bishops. The bishops, endowed with "the charism of truth" more than anyone else, are the ones primarily responsible for catechesis and catechists. Saintly bishops whose writings and initiatives mark the richest period of the catechumenate regarded catechesis as a fundamental task of their ministry. The bishop in assuming the overall direction of catechesis in the particular Church ensures an active and fruitful catechesis by engaging the necessary personnel, and providing them with the resources they need to succeed. Bishops are to be vigilant with regard to the authenticity of the faith as well as the quality of texts and instruments being used in catechesis. Bishops are also called to bring about a real passion for catechesis in the diocese and ensure that catechesis is held in high esteem.

The ministry of priests is to form the Christian community and coordinate and strengthen charisms. As educators of the faith, priests see that the faithful are properly formed and reach true Christian maturity. Conscious that their "ministerial priesthood" is at the service of the "common priesthood of the faithful," they foster the vocation and work of catechists and assist them in carrying out a function which springs from Baptism and a mission entrusted to them by the Church. The quality of catechesis in a community depends largely on the presence and activity of the priest.

The catechetical activity of the laity also has a proper character. They engage in catechesis on the basis of their insertion into the ordinary circumstances of the world. Sharing the same form of life as those whom they catechize, lay catechists have a special sensitivity for incarnating the Gospel in the life of men and women. Catechumens and those receiving catechesis can find in them a Christian model for their future as believers.

Through the sacraments of Baptism and Confirmation the laity are called to participate in the priestly, prophetic, and kingly ministry of Christ. In addition to this common vocation, some lay people feel called to assume the service of catechist; the Church discerns this divine vocation and confers on them the mission to catechize. The personal call of Jesus and its relationship to him are the true moving forces of catechetical activity. Even when the catechist gives limited time or on an occasional basis it is always a valuable service and a worthy collaboration. The importance of the ministry suggests that there should be a number of religious and laity publicly recognized and permanently dedicated to catechesis who, in communion with the priests and bishop, give to the diocesan service the ecclesial form which is proper to it.

Just as the needs of catechesis are varied according to circumstances so are the types of catechists. The title applies in a special way to catechists in missionary countries. In addition to their specific responsibility for catechesis, catechists collaborate with other forms of the apostolate. In countries where there is a shortage of clergy, the role of catechists is analogous to those in missionary countries. It involves the animation of small rural communities deprived of the constant presence of a priest and a missionary presence in large urban areas. In countries that require a new evangelization, the catechist is indispensable in promoting initiatory catechesis and providing continuing catechesis. In such tasks the role of the priest is equally fundamental. The catechist has the delicate mission of giving children and adolescents the first notions of catechism and preparation for the sacraments of Penance, First Communion, and Confirmation, especially where they do not receive adequate religious formation within the family. Catechists must also be formed "for pre-sacramental encounter," for adults on occasions such as the Baptism or First Communion of their children, or celebration of the sacrament of

Matrimony. Specifically, it comprises the welcoming of the faithful, of primary proclamation and accompanying them on the journey of faith.

There is an urgent need for catechists for the elderly, handicapped or disabled, migrants and the marginalized, who require a special pedagogy, in addition to their total integration into the community. The local Church by analyzing her own cultural and religious situation may find that other types of catechists may be advisable. The organization and orientation of the formation of catechists is a fundamental responsibility.

Chapter Two – Formation for the service of catechesis (nn. 233-252). Catechists are fundamental to adequate pastoral care in the catechetical ministry and, therefore, efforts must be made:

- To encourage in parishes and Christian communities the *vocation* for catechesis and promote catechists with specializations to meet the varied needs in today's communities;

- To provide a number of *full time* catechists in addition to *part time* catechists;

- To distribute catechists among the various groups (adults, young people) and to establish a greater balance in relation to the number of catechists who work with children and adolescents;

- To foster animators of catechetical activity at diocesan, regional, and parish levels;

- To organize the formation of catechists both in relation to basic training and continuing formation;

- To attend to the personal and spiritual needs of [individual] catechists as well as to catechists as a group. (Priests and Christian communities are principally responsible for this activity.); and

- To coordinate catechists with other pastoral workers so that the work of evangelization is consistent and to insure that catechesis will not be isolated from the life of the community.

The quality of any form of pastoral activity is at risk if it does not rely on competent and trained personnel. Consequently dioceses must give absolute priority to the formation of catechists. And bishops are called upon to insure the catechetical formation of priests ("a fundamentally decisive element") both in seminary and at the level of continuing formation.

The purpose of formation is to assist catechists in acquiring an aptitude and ability to communicate the Gospel message. The Christocentric purpose which permeates all aspects of the formation of catechists aims at leading catechists to know how to animate a catechetical journey through the necessary stages: namely, the proclamation of Jesus Christ; setting his life in the context of salvation history; explaining the mystery of the Son of God, made man for us; and finally, to help the catechumen and those being catechized to identify with Jesus Christ through the sacraments of initiation. Continuing catechesis deepens these basic elements. The identity of catechists is to be read in this Christocentric light and built around a familiarity with Christ and the Father, in the Spirit.

Because catechists act in the name of the Church, their formation is to assist them in identifying with the living and the actual awareness that the Church has of the Gospel. The Church like a spouse "keeps pure and intact the faith of the Spouse," and like a "mother and teacher" desires to transmit the Gospel by adapting it to all cultures, ages, and situations. This ecclesial quality of the transmission of the Gospel permeates the entire formation of catechists and gives it its true nature.

Certain criteria must always inspire and shape the formation of catechists:

- In order to evangelize in the present historical context with its values, challenges, and disappointments, catechists must have a deep faith, a clear Christian and ecclesial identity, and a social sensitivity.

- Catechists must be able to transmit not only a teaching but also an integral Christian formation by becoming teachers, educators, and witnesses to the faith.

The present catechetical moment in the Church requires catechists who are capable of overcoming "unilateral divergent tendencies" by linking the truth and meaning of faith, orthodoxy and orthopraxis, the ecclesial and social.

- The apostolic training of the laity acquires a special character from the secular nature of their state and from its peculiar type of spirituality. The lay state in the Church has a specific character that is not merely a synthesis of the mission received by priests and religious.

- The pedagogy used in formation is of fundamental importance. Unless there is a coherence between it and the pedagogy proper to the catechetical process, it will be very difficult for the catechist to improvise a style and sensibility to which they had not been introduced during their own formation.

The formation of catechists includes being, knowing, and *savoir-faire*. The first and deepest refers to the very being of the catechists, to their human and Christian dimension because formation, above all else, must help them to mature as persons, believers, and apostles. The second, knowing, is permeated by the double commitment catechists have to the message and to those to whom they transmit it. And thirdly, *savoir-faire* presumes knowledge of the social context in which the recipients live and of knowing how to transmit the message so it is an act of communication.

Human and Christian maturity allows catechists, by constant evaluation, to grow in a critical outlook, integrity, the ability to relate, to promote dialogue, to be constructive, and to engage in group work. It will cause them to grow in respect and love for those being catechized. Formation fosters and nourishes the exercise of catechesis which in turn nourishes their spirituality so that their activity springs from their own witness of life. Every theme covered by formation should feed the faith of the catechist. Catechists catechize others by first catechizing themselves. Formation nourishes the apostolic consciousness of catechists, that is, their sense of being evangelizers. They should be aware of the evangelizing efforts in the diocese and parish and harmonize their own efforts with them. The best way to feed this apostolic awareness is by identifying with the figure of Jesus Christ. Beginning with the exercise of catechesis, the apostolic vocation of catechists, constantly fostered by continuing formation, will progressively mature.

Besides being witnesses, catechists must also be teachers of the faith and, therefore, formation must afford them an organic awareness of the Christian message structured around the central mystery of the faith, Jesus Christ. This doctrinal formation should be drawn from the areas that constitute every catechetical program, namely, the three great eras in the history of salvation: the Old Testament, the life of Christ, and the history of the Church; and the great nuclei of the Christian message: the Creed, the Liturgy, the moral life and prayer. Sacred Scripture should be the very heart of formation while the

Catechism of the Catholic Church remains the fundamental doctrinal reference together with the catechism proper to the particular Church.
The biblico-theological formation:

1. Should be of a summary nature. The various elements of the Christian faith should be presented in a structured and harmonious way that respect the "hierarchy of truths."

2. Should be such as to help catechists mature in their own faith and, in view of today's grave and difficult problems, enable them to offer a reason for their own hope.

3. Must be close to human experience and capable of correlating the Christian message with life. While remaining theological it must in some fashion adopt a catechetical style.

4. Will not only communicate the Gospel message accurately but will also enable those being taught to receive it actively and to discern what in their spiritual journey agrees with the faith.

The Second Vatican Council emphasizes the use not only of the principles but also the findings of secular sciences, especially in the field of psychology and sociology as a way of bringing the faithful to a more mature living of the faith. Catechists must have some knowledge of the fundamentals of psychology as they touch on the dynamics that motivate people and open them to the mystery of the sacred, personality structure, the phases of the human life-cycle, etc. The formation of catechists should include social sciences that provide analysis of the religious situation as well as the sociological, cultural, and economic conditions which influence the success of evangelization. Other secular sciences recommended by the Council that should be included in catechetical formation are education and communication.

Together with being and knowledge, the formation of catechists must also cultivate *savoir faire*—technique. Because catechists are educators who facilitate maturation of the faith account must taken of concerning the original pedagogy of faith. It is God who implants faith in human hearts; it is the responsibility of catechists to cultivate this gift by nourishing it and helping it to grow. A mature educational capacity implies an ability to be attentive to people, to organize learning activities, and to lead groups toward maturity. Most importantly, catechists should acquire their own style by adapting the general principles of catechetical pedagogy to their own personalities.

Concretely, catechetical formation must enable catechists, particularly full-time catechists, to organize educational activity by carefully considering the circumstances, by elaborating a realistic plan, and by knowing how to evaluate it critically. The educational activity must be capable of animating a group by applying with discernment techniques of group dynamics. This "know-how," along with the knowledge, attitudes, and techniques it involves can best be acquired if they are taught simultaneously while the apostolic lessons of catechesis are being prepared and tested. Catechists should be protagonists of their own learning by being creative in formation and not by just applying external rules. One starts with praxis to be able to arrive at praxis.

It is within their own Christian communities that catechists are best formed and their vocations tested and their apostolic awareness nourished. The figure of the priest is fundamental in assuring their maturation as believers and witnesses. A Christian community can develop various types of formation activities for their catechists: (1) keeping alive an awareness of being sent by the Church; (2) insure that catechists have a mature faith; (3) group preparation activities with immediate feedback; and (4) courses, retreats, and experiences at important liturgical times; conferences on pressing themes; and systematic doctrinal formation using the *Catechism of the Catholic Church*.

9. Catechesis in the American Context

National Directory for Catechesis

The 1972 Catechetical Directory developed by the Bishops of the United States, *Sharing the Light of Faith*, (SLF) anticipating that the methods and cultural context of catechesis were likely to change and that new Church documents would be published, called for its own revision: it was to be "reviewed periodically for updating and improvement" (n. 7). The bishops newly formed subcommittee on catechesis (a subcommittee of the Committee on Education) began to consider this revision in 1992, but was told by the Holy See's Congregation for the Clergy to stop its work until the new *General Directory for Catechesis* (GDC) could be published, which occurred in 1997.

The immediate purpose of the new GDC, like it's predecessor, the original *General Catechetical Directory* in 1972, was to assist in the composition of directories and catechisms for the use of local Churches. It was this call for local directories and catechisms that led the U.S. Bishops to begin again its revision of *Sharing the Light of Faith*. This revision was developed by the USCCB's subcommittee on Catechesis under the authority of the Committee on Education and was approved by the bishops at their General Meeting in June, 2003. The revised document was submitted to the Holy See for the necessary *recognitio* in September of that year. The letter of recognition was granted in December of 2004 and the text was published in May, 2005. It should be noted that of the 18 changes requested in the document by the Congregation for the Clergy, most of them were concerned with protecting the prerogative of bishops and pastors on specific matters. The Holy See also requested that most references to Eastern Catholic practices be removed: the Holy See wanted to make sure that there was no confusion that this directory was for the Latin Church only—the Eastern Churches have the right to create their own catechetical directory if they wish to do so.

The NDC, created from two broad, nation-wide consultations and two additional consultations with bishops and their consultants, runs 314 pages in length, including an introduction, ten chapters, and a subject index. A user-friendly Table of Contents outlines the subject matter and numbers the principal sections in each chapter. The Introduction cites "more than a dozen documents" as evidence of the bishops' commitment to the catechetical ministry in the United States. These documents—*Catholic Higher Education and the Pastoral Mission of the Church; A Vision of Evangelization; Empowered by the Spirit; Statement in Support of Catholic Elementary and Secondary Schools; Guidelines for Doctrinally Sound Catechetical Materials; The Teaching Ministry of the Diocesan Bishop; Go and Make Disciples: A National Plan and Strategy for Catholic Evangelization in the United States; Renewing the Vision; Statement in Support of Catechetical Ministry; Sharing Catholic Social Teaching;* and *Our Hearts Were Burning Within Us*—are all available from the publications office of the United States Conference of Catholic Bishops, Washington, DC.

The Introduction makes it clear that the National Directory, following the *Catechism of the Catholic Church*, is based on the premise that catechesis is an "essential ministry of the Church" that embraces "the totality of the Church's efforts to make disciples, to help men believe that Jesus is the Son of God so that believing they might have life in his name..." It "includes especially the teaching of Christian doctrine imparted, generally speaking, in an organic and systematic way, with a view to initiating the hearers into the fullness of life." Following the lead of the *General Directory for Catechesis*, the NDC lists both a number of developments as "signs of remarkable vitality" (pp. 8-12), and a number of "challenges" to the catechetical ministry in the United States. Among the latter are social and cultural conditions; and the need to present "the complete and authentic content of the faith;" (pp. 13-17). The stated purpose of the NDC is: (1) to provide fundamental theological and pastoral principles; (2) to offer guidelines for applying them "in order to continue a renewal of catechesis"; and (3) "to set forth the nature, purpose, object, tasks, basic content, and various methodologies" (p. 17).

Chapter One – Proclaiming the Gospel in the United States

Chapter One expands on the social and cultural conditions that challenge the catechetical ministry. It identifies some general characteristics of U.S.

culture, among them religious and economic freedom, interest in science and technology, and mobility. It explains how ethnic, religious, and regional diversity exists in the U.S. and in places fosters anti-Catholicism. The NDC describes "salient elements" and, in broad strokes, sketches the diverse pastoral settings and personnel in Catholic parishes. (It is "more ethnically diverse than a similarly sized Catholic population in any other country in the world" p. 34.) "Family life continues to be a cornerstone of social life in the United States," but the divorce rate even among Catholic and organized efforts to re-define "marriage" indicate an "erosion" of some fundamental values. ("The Church has a distinctly Christian vision of marriage and family that is rooted in natural law and to which Sacred Scripture and Tradition testify.")

Chapter Two – Catechesis Within the Church's Mission of Evangelization

Chapter Two describes how catechesis "is an indispensable stage in the rich, complex, and dynamic reality" of the Church's fundamental mission of evangelization. The chapter begins (see, n. 16) with a word on the ways that God reveals himself in creation and the person of Jesus Christ and how Revelation is intended for all humanity because God "wills everyone to be saved and to come to knowledge of the truth" (1 Tm 2:4). The response of human beings has "two integral dimensions": the content of Divine Revelation *which* one believes, and the grace, a gift, *by which* an individual is moved to give assent of the intellect and will to it.

The purpose of evangelization (see, n. 17) is to bring about faith and conversion that involves a profound change of mind and heart, a change of life, a *metanoia*. It embraces the totality of the Church's efforts to bring the Gospel to every people and nation so that "it finds a home in every culture." Evangelization is a complex process that often begins with a kind of pre-evangelization that builds on basic human needs and shows how they include a desire for God and his word. Ministry of the word is a fundamental element in every stage because it involves the proclamation of Jesus Christ, the eternal Word of God. It progresses through a number of stages: *missionary preaching, initial catechesis, mystagogical* or *post-baptismal catechesis, permanent* or *continuing catechesis.*

The NDC also identifies two other forms of catechesis. The first, *liturgical catechesis,* has several dimensions: it prepares individuals and communities for celebration of the sacraments; the homily within the celebration of the sacraments; and catechesis that is part of and integral to the sacred rites themselves, especially the Eucharist. The second, *theological catechesis*, is the systematic treatment of the truths of faith that helps Christians engage with "philosophical forms of thought, various forms of humanism, and the human sciences."

In the United States the Church's evangelizing and catechetical activity takes place in diverse social and religious contexts whose boundaries are not always clearly definable and the various stages are not entirely distinct from one another. Dioceses and parishes are encouraged to study, reflect on the pastoral principles, and adopt the goals of *Go and Make Disciples: A National Plan and Strategy for Catholic Evangelization*. They should pursue the following "fundamental objectives":

1. To foster in the heart of every believer an experience of personal conversion to Jesus Christ that leads to a personal renewal and greater participation in the Christian life in the Church;

2. To encourage a greater knowledge of the Holy Scriptures and Sacred Tradition of the Church;

3. To focus their efforts and resources on the conversion and renewal of every parish, especially through the implementation of the *Rite of Christian Initiation of Adults;*

4. To rededicate themselves to a liturgical renewal that develops a greater appreciation for the presence and power of Christ in the Word of God and the sacraments of the Church, especially the Eucharist;

5. To make the evangelical and social justice dimensions of the Sunday Eucharist more explicit;

6. To call their people to a more effective integration of daily prayer in their lives, especially... the Psalms and the Church's Liturgy of the Hours... the Rosary... adoration of the Blessed Sacrament; and

7. To insure that all Catholic institutions, especially parishes, are accessible and welcoming.

These and other pastoral directives outlined in subsequent chapters give catechesis in the United States "a missionary dynamic that encourages us to continue to evangelize the culture, affirming what is compatible and challenging what is not" (p. 52).

The principal source of catechesis (see, n. 18) is the word of God in Sacred Scripture and Sacred Tradition. This means it must be based on the thought, spirit, and perspective of the Old and New Testaments within the Church's two-thousand-year experience of faith and life. Catechesis is also nourished by the liturgy and enriched when the word of God shines forth in the lives of the saints and in the Christian witness of the faithful.

Catechesis aims (see, n. 19) to bring about an ever more mature faith in Jesus Christ, a deeper knowledge and love of his person and message, and a firm commitment to follow him for in Christ the whole of God's eternal plan is revealed. "Jesus Christ is always the first and last point of reference in catechesis..."

"Catechesis is an essentially ecclesial act." It is bound up with the whole of the Church's life, her geographic expansion and her inner growth. Catechesis springs from the Church and the Church is both its *locus* and its goal. It is the natural environment, where men and women are invited to conversion and discipleship, where they celebrate the sacraments and are motivated to apostolic witness. Catechesis also has the Church as its goal in that it aims to build up the Body of Christ and strengthens her internal life as a community of believers and her external activity as a missionary Church. In some situations initial catechesis precedes Baptism, while in others it follows Baptism, but in all situations the profession of faith is its goal. The whole Catholic community has the responsibility to foster continuing conversion and ongoing catechesis that nurtures mature faith in its members.

The fundamental task of catechesis is the formation of disciples of Jesus Christ. Just as Jesus formed his disciples, by instructing them, praying with them, showing them how to live, and sending them on mission, catechesis accomplishes its work by diverse yet complementary tasks. The *Directory* describes six, each of which is related to an aspect of faith in Christ:

1. Catechesis promotes knowledge of faith.
2. Catechesis promotes a knowledge of the meaning of the Liturgy and the sacraments.

3. Catechesis promotes moral formation in Jesus Christ.
4. Catechesis teaches the Christian how to pray with Christ.
5. Catechesis prepares the Christian to live in community and to participate actively in the life and mission of the Church.
6. Catechesis promotes a missionary spirit that prepares the faithful to be present as Christians in society.

Together these tasks constitute a unified whole. They are interdependent and all are necessary to attain the full development of the Christian faith.

It is not enough to evangelize individuals. The Good News, the word of God proclaimed to the nations, must be inculturated in the life situation of the hearers. In his apostolic letter, *The Church in America*, Pope John Paul II wrote, "The new evangelization calls for a clearly conceived, serious and well organized effort to evangelize culture" (EA, 70). The inculturation of the Gospel message in the United States, an urgent mission, has several specific tasks:

- To discover the seeds of the Gospel that may be present in the culture;
- To know and respect the essential elements and basic expressions of the culture of the persons to whom it is addressed;
- To recognize that the Gospel message is both transcendent and immanent... yet it has a cultural dimension, that in which Jesus of Nazareth lived;
- To proclaim the transforming and regenerating force that the Gospel works in everyday culture;
- To promote a new enthusiasm for the Gospel in accordance with evangelized culture;
- To use the language and culture of the people as a foundation to express the common faith of the Church; and
- To maintain the integral content of faith and avoid obscuring the content of the Christian message by adaptations that compromise or diminish the deposit of faith.

The catechist, an important instrument of inculturation, needs to be alert to these tasks. Catechesis loses much of its effectiveness when it does not take into consideration the language and culture of the people to whom it is addressed. In the United States "Heralds of the Gospel" must learn as much as possible about mass media and how best to employ the media to serve the Christian message. The faithful must learn how to be discriminating in their use of the media, especially in their homes.

In conclusion (see, n. 22), Chapter Three makes the point that catechesis is so central to evangelization that without it discipleship in Christ would not mature.

Chapter Three – This is Our Faith; This is the Faith of the Church

Chapter Three, "provides criteria for the authentic presentation of the Christian message in the United States at this time in history." It begins by identifying the "normative instruments of catechesis," (n. 24) their relationship and dependence on each other: Sacred Scripture, "the starting point, foundation, and norm of catechetical teaching;" the *Catechism of the Catholic Church*, the *General Directory for Catechesis*, and the *National Directory for Catechesis*. It makes no mention of the *United States Catholic Catechism for Adults* because it had not yet been published, but it does make explicit mention of *Our Hearts Were Burning Within Us*, that gives a "plan and strategies for development of an effective ministry of adult faith formation in parish life."

The NDC does not attempt to summarize the content of the *Catechism of the Catholic Church*. Rather, it seeks to facilitate a better understanding of the *Catechism* and its use in the United States. The *Catechism* does not impose a predetermined format for the presentation of doctrine, but by design it leaves to local catechisms and, "even more," to those who instruct the faith to make "indispensable adaptations" required by the culture, age, spiritual maturity, and social and ecclesial condition of those being catechized.

Catechesis must be permeated with biblical and evangelical thought, spirit and attitudes through constant reference to the Scriptures and Sacred Tradition. In addition to being a "true vehicle" for mediating the word of God the *Catechism* retrieves important aspects of the catechetical tradition of the Church Fathers, who placed a high priority on the baptismal catechumenate.

The NDC describes in some detail nine "criteria for the authentic presentation of the Christian message" (n. 25):

1. Catechesis presents the history of salvation with reference to **the person of Jesus Christ**. It promotes a personal relationship with Christ and presents his teaching "about God, man,

happiness, the moral life, death, etc. without in any way changing his thought."

2. Catechesis must emphasize the **Trinitarian character of the Christian message** by presenting God's plan of loving kindness, conceived by the Father, fulfilled in the Son, and directed by the Holy Spirit in the life of the Church.

3. Catechesis helps the Christian faithful to situate **Christ's proclamation of salvation and liberation from sin** at the center of the Good News. It presents Christian social morality as a consequence of the great commandment of love, and arouses a "love of preference for the poor."

4. Catechesis owes its **ecclesial character** to the fact that it originates in the Church's confession of faith and leads to the profession of faith on the part of individuals and nourishes the Body of Christ. It witnesses to the "one Lord, one faith, one baptism; one God and Father of all" that binds members of the community of Jesus' disciples as one wherever they may be.

5. Catechesis stresses the **distinctly historical character** of the Christian message. It presents salvation history in the Old Testament; the fulfillment of Revelation in the life and teaching of Jesus; and the history of the Church as it transmits the message to future generations. Catechesis helps to interpret the "signs of the times" in light of events of salvation history and Revelation. In the light of ecumenical developments, it contributes to a healing of past animosities.

6. The **inculturation of the Christian message** is a process whereby the transforming power of the Gospel touches persons in their hearts and cultures at their deepest levels. Its success depends on catechists who have a profound religious sense, a social conscience, and are well grounded in their cultural environment. Catechesis must use culturally appropriate methods and resources as well employ popular devotions.

7. The presentation of the Christian message requires that its **hierarchical character** be organized around its central truths. It does not mean that some truths pertain to faith less than others, but rather some truths enjoy priority (e.g. the mystery

of the Most Holy Trinity, "the source of all the other mysteries of faith," and the Incarnation) and others are illumined
by them.

8. Catechesis explains that the desire for God is written in the
    human heart and that the Christian message **communicates
    to human beings the profound truth about their own true
    nature and their eternal destiny**. A "catechesis of the beati-
    tudes" illumines the path to the eternal beatitude for which
    the human heart longs. Liturgical catechesis relates the signs
    and symbols of the sacraments and sacred rites to human
    experiences. Ecumenical catechesis calls all the faithful to
    commit themselves to promoting communion with other
    Christians.

9. Catechesis should foster **a common language of the faith** so
    that it may be proclaimed, celebrated, lived, and prayed in
    words familiar to all the faithful. Catechesis values the tradi-
    tional language of the Scriptures and the Church—the creed,
    liturgy, and dogmatic formulations as means of handing on
    the faith to future generations.

Chapter Four – Divine and Human Methodology

Chapter Four describes how God's self-revelation in Christ and through
the Spirit is the norm for all catechetical methodology. It outlines the elements
of methodology for effective catechesis and the impact of communication
technology on the proclamation of the Gospel.

(See, n. 28) God's self-revelation is realized in creation and gradually
through his actions and words transmitted in Sacred Scripture and Tradition.
It is most fully achieved in Jesus Christ, the Word made flesh. The whole of
Christ's life was a continual teaching and the fulfillment of revelation. The
Holy Spirit unfolds the divine plan of salvation within the Church and under
the guidance of the Spirit the Church continues God's own methodology in
a living catechesis. The Church's proclamation of the Gospel is both progressive
and patient, respecting the freedom of individuals and taking into consideration
their "slowness to believe."

Catechetical methods must exhibit a two-fold fidelity and harmonize
the content of the Christian message and the personal adherence of the believer

to God by respecting the liberty and promoting the active participation of those being catechized. Genuine catechesis employs methodology that:

- Emphasizes God's loving initiative and the person's free response;
- Accepts the progressive nature of Revelation, the transcendence and mysterious nature of the word of God, and the word's adaptation to different persons and cultures;
- Recognizes the centrality of Jesus Christ;
- Is rooted in interpersonal relations and makes its own the process of dialogue;
- Utilizes signs, which link words and deeds, teaching and experience; and
- Draws its power of truth, and its task to bear witness to the truth, from the Holy Spirit.

(See, n. 29) Using the divine pedagogy as a reference point, the Church chooses a variety of methods to ensure that the Gospel is proclaimed "to all the nations." The personal circumstances of the people to be addressed—their age, intellectual development, degree of ecclesial and spiritual maturity—are integral to the successful transmission of the Gospel. Content and method interact and harmonize the communication of the faith.

Catechesis uses two approaches identified with *inductive* and *deductive* methods. The first consists in presenting facts (biblical events, liturgical acts, events in the Church's life as well as events from daily life) so as to discern the meaning they might have in Divine Revelation. The latter corresponds to the *kerygmatic* approach. It begins with the proclamation of the faith as expressed in the principal documents of the faith and applies it to concrete human experiences. Both are legitimate approaches. Though distinct they are complementary methods for communicating the faith. It lists the following:

A. Jesus consistently used ordinary experiences of daily life to form and teach his disciples. Catechesis links human experience to the revealed word of God, enabling people to explore, interpret, and judge their basic experiences in light of the Gospel and helping them ascribe Christian meaning to their existence.

B. "An integral element in catechesis is learning by disciple-ship." By learning from Christ's example, his disciples become aware that there are dimensions of Christian life that come to full expression only in imitating him. Mary is the first disciple and the model for all disciples. Children are capable of being formed as disciples of the Lord from an early age. God's grace often develops within them a deep spirituality that continues to grow as they mature. Children with cognitive disabilities often have an intuitive understanding of the sacred.

C. The effectiveness of catechesis depends to a great extent on the vitality of the Christian community in which it is given. Because of this, the parish and its leadership have the responsibility of seeing that the community is a clear living, and authentic sacrament of Christ.

D. The Christian family is the primary environment for growth in faith. Parents are the primary educators in the faith, but all the family members, even members of the extended family, contribute to the basic environment in which a sense of God's loving presence is awakened and lived. It is within the family that the members begin to pray and have their consciences formed.

E. The witness of the catechist is pivotal. Catechists exercise a powerful influence by their proclamation of the Gospel and the transparent example of their Christian lives.

F. The learning by heart of basic prayers as well as key biblical, liturgical, and doctrinal formulations ensure an accurate exposition of the faith and foster a common language that can be understood within the Church's cultural diversity. Among the formulations that should be memorized are (1) Prayers, (2) Factual information contributing to an appreciation of the place of the word of God in the Church and life of the Christian, (3) Formulas providing factual information regarding the Church, worship, the Church year, and major practices in the devotional life of Christians, (4) Formulas and practices dealing with the moral life of Christians. The texts that are memorized must at the same time be gradually understood in order to become a source of Christian life on the personal and community levels.

G. An essential component of catechetical methodology is learning by living. Adults especially learn through active participation in their in their own formation. Both the private practice and the public witness of knowledge and committed Christians are a responsibility to which all the baptized are called.

H. Catechesis includes more than instruction. Learning by apprenticeship links an experienced Christian believer, or mentor, with one who seeks a deeper relationship with Christ and the Church. It is a guided encounter with the entire Christian life, a journey toward conversion to Christ.

(See, n. 30) Catechetical methodology must be considered in the context of the revolution in communications technology—Internet, satellites, cable systems, etc. Catechists must be knowledgeable about the culture created by the mass media and learn how to use the new technology to bring people to Christ. They must learn the language, the techniques, and the psychology necessary integrate the Christian message into the new culture. They must also develop a critical sense with which to evaluate the media and be able to recognize its "shadow side" which at times promotes secularism, consumerism, materialism, dehumanization, and lack of concern for the poor.

While catechists rightly employ a variety of methods and techniques in the transmission of the faith, God's own methodology—the Father's self-revelation in Jesus Christ and through the Holy Spirit—remains the model for all human methodologies.

Chapter Five – Catechesis in a Worshiping Community

Chapter Five is the longest chapter in the *Directory*. (The writing committee considered splitting it into two separate chapters, one focusing on the Mass and the sacraments and one focusing on prayer, sacramentals, and other devotions, but chose to keep it intact.) After explaining that the rites of the Church are identified with the Paschal Mystery of Christ, the chapters describe the relationship between catechesis and liturgy; personal and liturgical prayer; catechesis for the sacramental life; sacred time and space, sacramentals, popular piety, and popular devotions.

(See, n. 33) Catechesis both precedes the liturgy and springs from it. It prepares people for a full, conscious, and active participation in the liturgy by helping them understand its nature, rites, and symbols. Catechesis stems from the liturgy insofar as it helps people to reflect and come to know the Paschal Mystery ever more intimately and experientially.

(See, n. 34) Prayer expresses one's vital and personal relationship with the living and true God. Personal prayer permeates the daily life of Christians and disposes them toward liturgical, communal, and public prayer. Catechesis for prayer emphasizes the major purposes for prayer—adoration, thanksgiving, petition, and contrition. It includes various prayer forms: communal prayer, private prayer, traditional prayer, spontaneous prayer, gesture, song, meditation, and contemplation. From infancy children should be inculturated into the life of daily prayer in the family: morning and evening prayer, prayer before and after meals; prayer at special moments in the life of the family.

(See, n. 35) There are two sections on sacramental catechesis. The first deals with general principles for sacramental catechesis, guidelines for the celebration of sacraments, and the baptismal catechumenate: "the inspiration for all catechesis." The general principles direct that sacramental catechesis:

- Integrates knowledge of the faith with living the faith;
- Presents Christian life as a lifelong journey into the life of the Triune God;
- Is appropriate for the age, maturity, and circumstances of the catechized;
- Takes place within and involves the whole Christian community;
- Involves parents;
- Is integrated into a comprehensive catechetical program;
- Focuses on the symbols, rituals, and prayers in the rites; and
- Implements a *mystagogia* that reflects on the meaning of the sacramental celebration.

The norms and guidelines found in introductions to the *Rite of Christian Initiation of Adults*, the *Directory for Masses with Children*, and other official documents "are essential tools for sacramental catechesis."

The baptismal catechumenate is a fruitful blend of instruction and formation in the faith. It progresses through four stages: (1) the pre-catechumenate that coincides with the first evangelization; (2) the catechumenate proper begins the period of systematic catechesis accompanied by the handing on of the Gospels; (3) the period of "purification and enlightenment" accompanied by the handing-over of the Creed and Lord's Prayer and immediate preparation for the sacraments of initiation; and (4) mystagogy or post-baptismal catechesis when the neophyte enters fully into the life of the community. The baptismal catechumenate reflects the gradual nature of catechesis, provides a model for the whole of the Church's catechetical efforts, and emphasizes the need for lifelong catechesis.

(See, n. 36) The second section of Chapter Five deals with catechesis for the sacraments of initiation, of healing and sacraments at the service of the community.

A. Sacraments of Initiation.

Baptism. The process outlined in the *Rite of Christian Initiation of Adults* is to be followed for all catechumens, including children who have reached the age of reason, and by the parents and godparents to be baptized. The preparation of infants and children for baptism presents an important opportunity for the parents and godparents to examine the meaning of the Christian message in their own lives. An infant should be baptized within the first weeks after birth. If baptism is deferred because there is no assurance that the child's faith will be nurtured, the parish should reach out to evangelize the families of these children. Christian initiation is to be an apprenticeship for the Christian life.

Confirmation. Because the age set for Confirmation differs from diocese to diocese, only general guidelines are offered. Catechesis for Confirmation teaches that the sacrament increases the grace of Baptism; bonds the Confirmed more strongly with Holy Spirit and deepens their relationship with Christ; associates them more closely with the Church and its mission; and increases the gifts of the Holy Spirit. Parents and sponsors should be involved in preparation for the sacrament. The instruction should explain the basic symbols of the rite and that the bishop is the ordinary minister of the sacrament.

Eucharist. Because the Eucharist is the "source and summit of the Christian life," catechesis for the sacrament is lifelong and comprehensive. In the Mass, the Eucharist constitutes the principal liturgical celebration of the Paschal Mystery, and the ritual memorial is our communion in that mystery. Catechesis for the Eucharist teaches that Christ is present whole and entire and in a unique way under the species of bread and wine; that Christ is also present in his word, in the body of the faithful gathered in his name, and in the person of the priest who acts in the person of Christ, the Head of his Body the Church. Catechesis helps the People of God understand that, through the power of the Holy Spirit, the Eucharist forms the Church and is the preeminent sign of Church unity. While teaching that Catholics must receive Holy Communion during the Easter season, catechesis encourages the faithful to receive Communion whenever they participate in the celebration of the Eucharist. Catechesis includes instruction regarding Eucharistic devotions, proper conduct in Church, the Eucharistic fast and the guidelines for Eucharistic sharing set forth by the bishops of the United States.

Children's preparation for first reception of the Eucharist begins in the home. When they attend Mass with their family they gradually learn to join in the Eucharistic assembly. Parents together with the pastor determine a child's readiness to receive First Communion. The *Directory for Masses with Children* provides a framework for catechizing children for Eucharistic celebration. Catechesis on the Mass is an indispensable part of the preparation of children for their first reception of the Eucharist. In some Eastern Churches where it occurs in conjunction with Baptism and Chrismation, the child's first reception of the Eucharist is the culmination of the rite of initiation. Catechesis follows later and supports the young Christian's growth into the life of the Church.

Special Groups. The Sunday Eucharist provides the opportunity for everyone to move beyond their particular circles to celebrate in common the sacrament of unity. Occasionally, however, Mass may be celebrated with groups who share special ties or a particular need. In those instances clearly indicated in the *Roman Missal* the celebrant may choose from the options provided. Catechists who are called upon to assist in planning these Masses and in preparing groups to participate in them should have adequate liturgical preparation. Liturgical diversity can be a source of enrichment, but it must not diminish the unity of the Church. Liturgical adaptation, however, must not distort the prescriptions of the universal laws of the Church.

The *Directory for Masses with Children* is the normative reference for the preparation and celebration with young children who may have difficulty understanding the words, symbols, and actions of the Eucharist. It leads them to the celebration of Masses at which the Christian community comes together on Sundays. (The adaptations authorized in this *Directory* do not apply to Masses with adolescents or other special groups.)

All forms of the liturgy and the design of parish buildings should be completely accessible to persons with disabilities who should, as much as possible, be invited to take an active role. *Guidelines for the Celebration of the Sacraments with Persons with Disabilities* provides directions for the celebration of the Eucharist and other sacraments.

B. Sacraments of Healing. Christ's healing and reconciling ministry is carried on principally through the Sacraments of Penance/Reconciliation and Anointing of the Sick.

Penance. Catechesis for the Sacrament of Penance depends on the acknowledgment of God's desire to save everyone, one's sinfulness, and the Church's power to reconcile the sinner with God. Catechesis reveals a merciful God whose love is more powerful than sin. It challenges individuals and the community to recognize evil in society, to evaluate it in light of the Gospel, and to accept responsibility for it, and encourages Christians to seek forgiveness from others and to offer forgiveness when necessary.

With regard to children catechesis must respect their natural disposition, ability, age, and circumstances. Catechesis for the Sacrament of Penance/ Reconciliation is to precede First Communion and must be kept distinct by a clear and unhurried separation. Because conversion is a lifelong process, children have a right to a fuller catechesis each year. Parents should be involved with the preparation of their children for this sacrament.

Anointing of the Sick. Jesus charged his disciples and with them the whole Church to "cure the sick". In the Latin Church the *Rite of Anointing and Pastoral Care of the Sick* sets the norm for catechesis that examines the meaning of human suffering, sickness, aging, healing, and death in light of the Christian faith; explains the basic symbols and ministers of the sacrament; teaches the liturgical and communal character of the Anointing; explains who it is for, and explores the effects of the sacrament.

Integral to the rites with which the Church fortifies her faithful in their last hours is the Eucharist as viaticum, the Body and Blood of Christ, that accompanies the dying person on the way from this life to the next. Catechesis should instruct the faithful to arrange for *viaticum* to be brought while the dying person is able to receive the Eucharist.

C. Sacraments at the Service of Communion. The sacraments at the service of communion are the sacraments of Holy Orders and Matrimony that "confer a particular mission in the Church and serve to build up the People of God." Eastern Catholic Churches call them "Mysteries of Vocation".

Catechesis should teach that while the whole Church is a priestly people, and all the faithful share in the priesthood of Christ through Baptism, some are consecrated through the Sacrament of Holy Orders to minister (in the midst of the community) in the name and in the person of Christ. Although they differ in essence from one another, the ministerial priesthood and the common priesthood of the faithful each participate in the priesthood of Christ and are ordered to each other. Catechesis should explain the specific roles and tasks of bishops, priests, and deacons, representing the three degrees of the ordained ministry, who are empowered to serve in the name of Christ and the Church. In addition, catechesis for the Sacraments of Holy Orders should explain the various aspects of the sacrament, who may receive it, and what the sacrament confers.

Catechesis should also provide instruction on the value and importance of religious life, which is distinguished by its liturgical character, public commitment to the evangelical counsels—poverty, chastity, and obedience—and community life. Catechesis should also include instruction on secular institutes, societies of apostolic life, and other forms of consecrated life recognized by the Church.

Catechesis on Christian marriage should emphasize the covenant that develops between a baptized man and woman by which they establish a partnership for the whole of life, ordered by its nature to the good of the spouses and the procreation and education of offspring. The self-giving love of husband and wife represents the mutual love of Christ for his bride the Church and the love of the Church for her bridegroom, Christ. It gives permanent witness to fidelity of love so that when consummated, the marriage bond can never be dissolved. Catechesis for the Sacrament of Matrimony is addressed directly to couples intending to marry and through all stages of married life. Catechesis on Christian marriage and family values should be given to the whole community; children should begin learning the meaning of married love at a very early age from the example of their parents as well as through formal instruction. This catechesis should stress marriage as a distinct vocation in the Church, and that it is in the love and struggles of marriage that a couple attains holiness. It should also teach that marriage is founded on an equal personal dignity and expressed in an unreserved mutuality of self-giving. Finally, this catechesis should address all other aspects of the sacrament.

Dioceses and parishes should have great care and concern for those who have suffered the trauma of divorce by making them and their children feel welcome in the Christian community. Catechesis should make clear what is and isn't part of the Church's teaching concerning divorce and remarriage.

(See, n. 37) The third section of Chapter Five is titled "The Sacred: Time (Liturgical Year) and Space (Art)." It begins with the liturgical year and explains how the Church's calendar is divided into seasons that correspond to the major events in the history of salvation in Christ. The *Commentary on the Revised Liturgical Year* and the *General Norms for the Liturgical Year and the Calendar* establish the basis for catechesis on the liturgical year. The customs and traditions of the diverse ethnic groups in the United States offer many opportunities for recognizing God's presence in time and for keeping time holy.

Sacred art has both a liturgical and catechetical purpose. It expresses the reverence for the sacred, conveys faith, and leads to prayer. In the Eastern Churches, liturgical icons have a special place in catechesis and spirituality. The sacred images lead the faithful to contemplate the mysteries they depict, and to meditate on the Word of God. Catechesis on sacred art should:

- Introduce the tradition of religious art in both the Eastern and Latin Churches;
- Use music, stained glass windows, paintings, mosaics, and sculpture as teaching tools;

- Encourage the placement of the crucifix, statues, and sacred images of Christ, the Virgin Mary, and the saints in the home; and

- Reflect on the purpose, symbolism, and functions of Church architecture.

Similarly sacred music has both a liturgical and catechetical purpose. It is an integral part of the Church's worship, enhancing the solemnity of the liturgical celebrations, encouraging the active participation of the people, and expressing the common faith and shared love of the assembly.

(See, n. 38) The fourth and final section of Chapter Five deals with sacramentals and popular devotions. Sacramentals include a variety of blessings, sacred signs, and objects that bear a certain resemblance to the sacraments. They signify spiritual effects obtained through the prayers of the Church. The church building, the altar, holy oils and holy water, sacred vessels and vestments, crosses and crucifixes, rosaries, candles, and medals are all examples of sacramentals. Catechesis on sacramentals should relate them to faith in Christ's Paschal sacrifice, to their function in the Church, and in the lives of individual Christians.

The number and great diversity of popular devotions brought to the United States by immigrants requires careful attention. They provide many opportunities for evangelization and catechesis expressed in the native languages and spiritual traditions of Hispanics/Latinos, African-Americans, and Asians. In the Eastern Catholic communities various forms of prayer services, devotions to the Blessed Virgin Mary, reverence for icons, are important forms of popular devotion.

Various forms of devotion to the Blessed Virgin Mary reflect the different cultures and popular sensibilities of Catholics in the United States. Here, as elsewhere in the world where the Rosary holds a place of honor, catechesis should explain how the mysteries lead the faithful to a true encounter with Jesus Christ. Catechesis promotes Marian devotion that clearly expresses its "intrinsic Trinitarian, Christological, and ecclesiological aspects." As with other manifestations of popular piety, catechesis discovers the authentic spiritual values in Marian devotion and the ways it enriches Catholic doctrine so that it might lead to sincere conversion and a practical exercise of charity.

Chapter Six – Catechesis for Life in Christ

Chapter Six describes the new life in Christ witnessed by individuals and the community of faith, and presents catechetical principles and guidelines for both and personal and social moral formation.

(See, n. 40) Catechesis for life in Christ reveals both the joy and demands of the way of Christ. It is a catechesis of the Holy Spirit who inspires, corrects, and strengthens us on the journey to the Father in Christ. It is a catechesis of grace, the love of God, and good works, a catechesis of the Beatitudes, a catechesis about sin and forgiveness, and virtues, both human and Christian. It is a catechesis about the twofold commandment to love God and neighbor. And it is a catechesis of the Church in which the Christian life is received, nourished, and perfected in Christ. It always begins and ends in Christ who is the "the way and the truth and the life."

(See, n. 41) Human beings, created in the image and likeness of God, are destined for eternal happiness. Every human person has an inalienable right to exercise freedom, especially in moral and religious matters. "In fact, action is human action insofar as it is free."

Life in the United States today poses serious challenges to the Church's catechetical mission. The dominant secular culture often contradicts the values on which this nation was established. The inherent dignity and incomparable value of human life is being threatened. The gradual erosion of the principles on which this country was founded contributes to secularism, materialism, and an ethical relativism. To address these challenges, catechesis must:

- Uphold the right to life from conception to natural death;
- Present the distinctively Christian understanding of human freedom and that freedom reaches its authentic goal in love of the weak and in defending their rights;
- Promote the public expression of faith in the formation of social policy;
- Encourage concern for and action on behalf of the poor, the disabled, and the sick;
- Help the faithful make practical moral decisions in light of the Gospel; and

- Teach that power, wealth, utility, and productivity must be guided by higher moral values.

(See, n. 42) Moral formation presents the integration of Christian moral principles in the lived experience of individuals and community. It must always demonstrate the social consequences of the Gospel. Human beings are wounded by sin and need divine grace to lead morally good lives. The gift of grace can take the form of the cardinal virtues (prudence, justice, fortitude, and temperance) as well as the form of the theological virtues of faith, hope, and charity. By the grace of the Holy Spirit, the virtuous person consistently practices the good, seeks communion with God, and becomes like God.

The moral conscience reflects God's law written in the human heart. Nonetheless, it needs to be rightly formed and informed by the Word of God. The formation of conscience, influenced by many human factors, is a lifelong task. When a poorly formed or ignorant conscience is the result of personal neglect, the individual is culpable for the choices that are made.

Sin is an offense that turns the human heart away from God's love, wounds human nature, and injures human solidarity. Because original sin weakens human nature one cannot consistently avoid personal sin. Mortal sin is a person's deliberate choice made knowingly to do something seriously contrary to divine law. It places the sinner in danger of eternal separation from God and everlasting death. Though venial sin is less serious, it still impairs a person's relationship with God. Our sinfulness is the object of God's great mercy, for which the Church continually prays.

In order to communicate the fundamental moral teachings, catechesis must help the faithful (1) restore a sense of the sacred and transcendent in life and reassure them that God offers grace to everyone; (2) live in harmony with God and the created order; and (3) assist them in developing their capacity to discern God's will and in deepening their personal relationship with Christ. This catechesis will (a) form their consciences through careful consideration of the life of Christ and the Church, the advice of competent people, and the help of the Holy Spirit; and (b) identify the effects of original, personal, and social sin, and help people understand the idea of sins of commission and sins of omission. Catechesis will prepare people to make moral judgments, persevere in the pursuit of virtues, and reach out in love to people who seem not to respond.

(See, n. 43) The fact that human beings are social by nature forms a fundamental tenet of Catholic social doctrine. The Church's social teachings are based on indispensable components of life in Christ, and are deeply integrated in her vision of Christian morality. They cannot be treated as if they are peripheral or optional. The American Bishops identify seven key themes that form the heart of Catholic social doctrine: (1) life and dignity of the human person; (2) call to family, community, and participation; (3) rights and responsibilities; (4) the option for the poor and the vulnerable; (5) the dignity of work and the rights of workers; (6) solidarity; and (7) care for God's creation.

The effects of sin over time have created structures that by analogy are referred to as "social sin." It resembles original sin in that it exists in society and is sometimes the inheritance of families and communities. Sinful structures set up social relationships that in turn cause systematic denial or abuse of the rights of groups or individuals. Organized social injustice, institutionalized racism, systemic economic exploitation, and the destruction of the environment are examples of the social consequences of sin. Social injustice can be so deeply ingrained into the life of a society that it is very difficult to hold individuals accountable for it, but they should work to change those structures and systems that cause evil.

(See, n. 44) The Ten Commandments and the Beatitudes are named as the primary reference points for the application of Christian moral principles. The Decalogue, the expression of God's covenant with his people, is a privileged expression of the natural law that sums up love of God and neighbor. In the Beatitudes, Jesus teaches the attributes and virtues that should be cultivated by those who follow him. Those being catechized should understand how the spirit of the Beatitudes permeates the Decalogue. Other reference points are the spiritual and corporal works of mercy, the theological and moral virtues, the seven capital sins, and the laws of the Church. Scripture and the lives of the saints provide concrete examples of Christian moral living.

(See, n. 45) Catechesis should present the teaching of the *Catechism of the Catholic Church* on the Decalogue in light of the Sermon on the Mount. The *Directory* gives specific guidelines highlighting the principal points of each Commandment as well as the outlining principles for catechesis on the Beatitudes.

(See, n. 46) By way of conclusion the *Directory* emphasizes life in Christ is a way of being, a way of loving. Life in Christ provides new vital principles for human activity.

Chapter Seven – Catechizing the People of God in Diverse Settings

Chapter Seven reiterates the point that the Church is both the principal agent and the primary recipient of catechesis. It describes the conditions involved in the catechetical process and gives principles and guidelines for presenting the Gospel to different age groups, to persons with disabilities, and for catechesis in the context of ecumenical and interreligious dialogue.

(See, n. 48) Growth in faith is related to human development and passes through stages. Catechesis must take into consideration all the human factors in a particular age level in order to present the Gospel message in a compelling way.

A. Catechesis for Adults. This is the principal form of catechesis and all other forms—catechesis of childhood, adolescence, and old age—are oriented to it. Adult catechesis has three major goals: (1) the acquisition of an attitude of on-going conversion; (2) the fostering of active participation in the Christian community; (3) Christian discipleship in the world, evangelizing, working for justice, promoting Christian unity, and bearing witness to salvation won by Christ for all. The major tasks of catechesis, including the development of an informed moral conscience and the rational foundations of faith, are related to these goals. Sacred Scripture and Tradition form the basic content for adult catechesis and the *Catechism of the Catholic Church* is the normative reference text. A full treatment of the content of adult catechesis is contained in *Our Hearts Were Burning Within Us* (1999).

Effective adult catechesis relates the content of the faith to life experience. It enables the Christian to read the signs of the times in light of the Gospel. Adult catechesis requires a comprehensive, multifaceted, and coordinated approach and a variety of learning activities. Adults themselves should be involved in the process so that they can teach and learn from one another. Among the special forms of catechesis for adults are Christian initiation (see, the RCIA), catechesis for catechists and teachers, and catechesis for special moments (e.g. sickness, bereavement).

B. Catechesis for Older Adults. The growing number of elderly in the United States represents a new pastoral challenge. The catechesis of the elderly takes into account the diversity of their personal, family, and social conditions. Older people need a mix of activities that connect them with each other as well as the larger faith community which in turn should be concerned about the physical, emotional, mental, and social well being of the elderly as well as their spiritual needs. Intergenerational dialogue adds a significant dimension to the proclamation of the Gospel within the family and community of faith.

C. Catechesis for Young Adults. Young adults are college and university students, workers, professionals, and in the military. They are single, married, divorced, and widowed. Catechesis for young adults takes its inspiration from Christ's invitation: "Come follow me." Many who are looking for opportunities to grow in faith, explore moral decisions, and make career choices, need a non-threatening place where they can freely express their questions, doubts, and even disagreements with the Church. Effective catechesis will assist them in examining their lives and engaging in dialogue about questions they face. Marriage preparation and baptism of their children offer important opportunities to evangelize young adults and draw them closer to Christ and the Church.

Parish and diocesan programs should actively seek out young adults, enthusiastically welcome them, and facilitate their homecoming. The goals of a comprehensive program of young adult ministry are to connect them with the Church through: (1) spiritual formation/direction, religious education, and vocation discernment; (2) evangelizing outreach and pastoral care; (3) forming a Christian conscience, educating and working for justice, and developing leadership skills for the Church's mission to the world; and (4) forming faith communities with their peers.

Several important themes need to be emphasized with young adults, including the formation of conscience, education for love, vocational discernment, Christian involvement in society, missionary responsibility, the relationship between faith and reason, the existence of God, the problem of evil, the Church, the objective moral order, the relationship between man and woman, and the social doctrine of the Church.

D. Catechesis for Pre-adolescence and Adolescents. This catechesis should take into account their physical, social, and psychological conditions. Ministry with adolescents is to be integrated into a pastoral program for youth that includes catechesis, community life, evangelization, justice and service, leadership development, pastoral care, and prayer and worship. This catechesis should teach the core contents of the Catholic faith, respond to the age-appropriate needs, interests, and concerns of younger and older adolescents, and integrate knowledge of the faith with liturgical and prayer experiences and develop practical skills for living the faith in today's world in a variety of settings. In addition, this catechesis will:

- Foster a dialogue between the life experiences of the adolescent and the wisdom of the Catholic Church.

- Incorporate a variety of approaches, methods, and activities, including music and media, that keeps the interest of adolescents alive and responds to their different learning styles.

- Involve group participation in a warm, accepting, and caring environment that fosters trust and freedom to search and to express oneself.

- Help them to apply their learning to real-life situations.

- Provide parent education programs and resources, and incorporate a family perspective in catechetical programming.

- Promote Christian attitudes toward human sexuality.

- Recognize and celebrate the Church's multicultural diversity by incorporating stories, songs, feasts, saints, and rituals from the rich heritage of other cultures.

- Explicitly invite young people to explore a personal call to ministry and the beauty of the total gift of self for the sake of the kingdom.

E. Children's Catechesis. Though ordinarily unstructured and spontaneous, nothing replaces catechesis within the family. The role of parent is irreplaceable in the forming of Christian values in their children. School-age children should also receive formal and systematic catechesis in a structured catechetical program that presents the content of faith and the experience of Christian life authentically and completely. Catechists of children should:

- Understand them, be sensitive to their circumstances and current values.
- Recognize their importance not only for what they will be but for what they are.
- Use catechetical materials adapted to cultural, racial, and ethnic pluralism, and persons with special needs.
- Present religious truths in greater depth as their capacity for understanding increases.
- Provide experiences that enable them to apply the message of salvation to real-life situations; encourage the use of imagination as well as intelligence and memory.
- Provide experience that link catechesis to liturgy and promote an appreciation for the community celebration of the Eucharist.
- Stimulate a prayerful response from the heart.
- Foster a sense of community that is an important part of education for social life.

Catechesis for older children should:

- Assist them in ascribing a Christian meaning to their lives and in learning to act according to the norms of faith and love.
- Emphasize the desire for a deeper, more mature knowledge of the truths of faith.
- Present private prayer as a means of personal communication with God.

(See, n. 49) All persons with disabilities or special needs should be welcome in the Church. However limited, they are capable of growth in holiness. They have a right to adequate catechesis and deserve the means to develop a relationship to God. Persons with disabilities should be integrated as much as possible into ordinary catechetical programs. For some the involvement of their families is indispensable. The Church's pastoral response is to learn about the disability, offer support to the family, and welcome the disabled. Parishes should not assume that the parents will serve as the primary catechists of the disabled. Catechesis for persons with special needs should: (1) be adapted in content and method to their particular situations; (2) be interpreted, with the help of specialized catechists, the meaning of their lives and give witness to

Christ's presence in the local community in ways they can understand and appreciate; and (3) take care not to isolate any individual and to take care that programs for persons with disabilities be integrated, insofar as possible, with the normal catechetical activities of the parish. Diocesan staffs and parish committees that promote catechetical efforts should include persons with disabilities. Dioceses and parishes need to provide adequate funding.

(See, n. 50) The community of the baptized comprises different groups of believers all of whom have a right to sound and adequate catechesis and some of whom may need programs specially adapted to their needs, e.g., professional people, artists, migrants/refugees, divorced, widowed, homosexual persons. The most effective catechesis for persons in special situations is integrated into a comprehensive pastoral ministry for and with them.

(See, n. 51) Charity is the fundamental bond of the Church's unity. It is expressed in the profession of the one faith received from the apostles, the common celebration of the sacraments, and apostolic succession. The unity of the Church is a dimension of her catholicity, characterized by the great diversity that comes from the variety of God's gifts and multiplicity of peoples and cultures gathered together. The Church must continue to pray and work to maintain, reinforce, and perfect the unity that Christ wills for her.

Ecumenism. Catechesis should aim to foster ecumenism and form a genuine ecumenical attitude in those being catechized. It does this by: (1) enabling Catholics to give an accurate account of her teaching and discipline; (2) engendering an authentic desire for unity; (3) presenting the Church's doctrine clearly and unambiguously with due regard to the hierarchy of truths; (4) presenting the teachings of other churches, ecclesial communities, and religions correctly and honestly; and (5) preparing Catholics for living in contact with others.

Catechists need specialized training in ecumenism, shaped by the *Directory for the Application of Principles and Norms on Ecumenism.* Key elements in ecumenical formation include careful study of Sacred Scripture and the Church's living Tradition, familiarity with the biblical foundations of ecumenism, familiarity with Catholic principles and knowledge of ecumenism, training in ecumenical collaboration and dialogue. This can be done in many ways, including visits to other churches, informal exchanges, joint study days, and common prayer, participating in ecumenical collaboration and dialogue, and becoming familiar with fundamental ecumenical issues

Relationship with the Jews. Special care should be given to catechesis in relation to the Jewish religion. Precise, objective, and accurate teaching uncovers the link between the Church and the Jews and Judaism. Its objective should be to overcome caricatures, stereotypes, and every form of anti-Semitism. *God's Mercy Endures Forever: Guidelines on the Presentation of Jews and Judaism in Catholic Preaching,* issued by the USCCB's Committee on the Liturgy (1988), contains principles that can be adapted for catechists. Catechists are encouraged to:

- Affirm the value of the whole Bible and recognize the special meaning of the Old Testament for the Jewish people, its original audience;
- Show both the independence and the interconnectedness of the Old and New Testaments;
- Emphasize the Jewishness of Jesus and his teachings;
- Respect the continuing existence of God's covenant with the Jewish people and their faithful response to God's call; and
- Show that Christians and Jews together look to the Ten Commandments as a foundation of morality.

Other Religions and Groups. In a religiously pluralistic society, catechesis should deepen and strengthen the identity of Catholics who encounter adherents of other religions and help Catholics grow in respect for them. Catechesis must clearly teach that Jesus Christ is the unique and universal savior of the human family and that his Church is the universal sacrament of salvation. The goodness and truth found in other faiths is a preparation for the Gospel.

The growing number of adherents of Islam in the United States makes it imperative for Catholics to be acquainted with their beliefs and to be familiar with the history of conflicts between Christians and Muslim. Well-informed catechists, indispensable for the task of promoting respectful relations with all non-Christian religions, are encouraged to: (1) present the essential elements of traditional non-Christian beliefs; (2) develop an appreciation of the insights in other religions and their contributions to humanity; (3) foster a missionary spirit among those being catechized and bear a lively witness to the faith.

Catechists should accurately describe the beliefs and practices in the new religious and spiritual movements, sects, and cults that have proliferated in the United States. Some derive from Christian traditions, some from Far Eastern, non-Christian traditions, and others from obscure origins. They have a certain appeal and reveal a hunger among many to find a source of transcendent meaning in their lives. These movements form an important group for the Church to evangelize.

Chapter Eight – Those Who Catechize

Chapter Eight describes the roles and responsibilities of all who participate in the Church's catechetical mission. It provides principles and criteria to guide their formation as catechists (see, n. 54).

A. Bishops. Catechesis is a collaborative effort under the direction of the bishop who has the primary responsibility for catechesis in the diocese. The bishop supervises the catechetical mission in the diocese and ensures that it receives the support of competent personnel and adequate financial resources. He makes certain that the texts and other instruments used in catechesis transmit the faith completely and authentically and that catechists are adequately prepared for their task. The bishop is also to adopt a catechetical plan that is integrated into the overall diocesan pastoral plan and coordinated with the United States Conference of Catholic Bishops.

B. Pastors and Priests. Pastors are the bishop's closest collaborators in ensuring that the goals of the diocesan mission are achieved. The pastor is to see to it that a parish plan for catechesis is developed and implemented in consultation with the parish council and parish catechetical leadership. He has the primary responsibility to see that the catechetical needs, goals, and priorities of the parish are met. He should ensure catechesis for all language groups and age-appropriate formation for adults, youth, and children. It is his responsibility to see that the baptismal catechumenate is a vital component in the parish organization. In parishes where there is no resident pastor, pastoral administrators have the same obligation.

Parish priests assist catechists in carrying out their responsibilities in a variety of ways. Before ordination, as seminarians, they need to acquire a clear understanding of the nature, goals, and methods of catechesis as well as the roles they will have in catechetical programs. In order to enrich their own ministry as catechists, they are to continue their education and spiritual formation after ordination. Similarly, the formation of permanent deacons who may serve as catechetical leaders, should include studies and supervised catechetical experience.

C. Consecrated Persons. The catechesis offered by consecrated persons has a distinctive character because of their public witness and singular commitment to the mission of the Church. Some religious institutes were founded for the specific purpose of providing catechetical formation and the history of catechesis in the United States is a chronicle of their dedication and leadership. With appropriate training, women and men religious are particularly suited to served as parish or diocesan leaders.

D. Parish Catechetical Leaders. "The single most critical factor in an effective parish catechetical program is the leadership of a professionally trained parish catechetical leader" (p. 224). Although the position is known by various titles, the main responsibilities of catechetical leaders ordinarily includes the overall direction of the parish catechetical programs for adults, youth, and children, and the planning, implementation, and evaluation of the entire parish catechetical program. These catechetical leaders also have responsibility for recruiting, forming, and evaluating catechists, and implementing diocesan and parish catechetical policies and guidelines, including catechist certification and supervision, and administrative policies regarding the safety and protection of minors. Collaborating closely with pastors, other parish ministers, and appropriate committees, these leaders help to shape the life of the parish.

Preparation for service as a parish catechetical leader should include advanced studies in theology, Scripture, liturgy, catechesis and catechetical methodology, educational psychology and theory, and administration, as well as practical catechetical experience. A comprehensive knowledge of the *General Directory for Catechesis* and the *Catechism of the Catholic Church* is essential. The need for systematic training and study should not be minimized.

E. Youth Ministers. Coordinators of youth ministry have specific catechetical responsibilities that should be fulfilled in collaboration with pastors and parish catechetical leaders. A comprehensive youth ministry program includes structured or formal catechesis. Youth ministers should be models of Christian living and have the ability to speak credibly about their personal faith experience. Training for youth ministry should employ principles of sound adult faith formation. At a minimum it should include emphasis on the Church's mission of evangelization, catechesis in general, and youth catechesis in particular. Coordinators of youth ministry should be provided compensation and benefits appropriate to full-time or part-time work.

F. Campus Ministers. The apostolic service of campus ministers includes giving Christian witness within the academic world. They prepare students to bring the Gospel into the ordinary situation of everyday life and, duly appointed by the bishop, form a faith community that is a genuine sign and instrument of the kingdom. The university campus provides campus ministers who are theologically qualified and professionally competent with a prime opportunity for catechesis. The college years are a time of both challenge and opportunity to grow in knowledge and practice of the faith. Campus ministry programs should also serve faculty and administrators. They should work for responsible governance and evaluate the institution's programs, policies, and research in the light of Catholic social doctrine.

G. Catechists. Catechists need to be Catholics who participate fully in the communal worship and life of the Church and who have been prepared for their ministry by appropriate training. Their commissioning by the Church is a participation in the divine calling to teach as Jesus did. Because of their ministry and mission, their call to holiness—shared by all the faithful—has a particular urgency. Lay catechists have a special sensitivity to the needs of those whom they catechize because they share their experiences of everyday life and are able to incarnate the Gospel into ordinary circumstances. Catechists must adapt their methods to the needs of particular groups because they serve a wide variety of persons and the message of the Gospel must be proclaimed in such a way they can understand it. To this end, catechist formation must ensure that catechists receive help in developing their knowledge of the faith and how to transmit the message.

H. Catholic Schools. The Catholic school is an effective vehicle of total Christian formation. It is a center for evangelization and, thus, its catechetical program is essential to its distinctly Catholic identity and character. The principal of a Catholic school is called to recognize that all members of the faculty and staff are an integral part of religious education, and to design a curriculum that supports the school's catechetical goals. Catechetical instruction, based on the *Catechism of the Catholic Church*, should be thoroughly integrated into the curriculum and objectives of the school. All teachers in Catholic schools share in the catechetical ministry but the teacher of religion is the key, a vital component of the Catholic school's effectiveness as a community of faith and center for evangelization and catechesis. While all teachers, insofar as possible, should be practicing Catholics, religion teachers must have a thorough knowledge of the Christian message and the ability to communicate it; they should also meet diocesan standards for certification as catechists.

I. Parents and Families. Parents and families are the most influential agents of catechesis for their children. They catechize primarily by the witness of their Christian lives and their love for the faith. Their participation in the life of the parish, above all in the Sunday Eucharist, their willingness to evangelize and serve others, and their dedication to daily prayer demonstrate the authenticity of their profession of faith. The vibrancy of the parish community, the beauty of worship, and the example of generous love and service of parishioners strengthens parents in faith. Programs that prepare parents whose children will be receiving sacraments should encourage parents to ensure that their children receive formal catechetical instruction in parish programs.

(See, n. 55) Programs of formation should be designed to help catechists to acquire the knowledge and skills they need to hand on the faith to those entrusted to their care and assist them in living as disciples in Christ. The Church entrusts the ministry of catechesis to exemplary followers of Christ with unquestioned personal integrity and moral character. In consultation with the parish catechetical leader, and after careful and prayerful consideration on the part of the candidate, the pastor formally invites the person to begin initial catechetical formation. ("The suggestion that anyone can be a catechist should be scrupulously avoided in all communication involving the recruitment of catechists.") Some form of commissioning ceremony should be planned that expresses the Church's call and recognizes the catechist's generous response.

Catechists are called to continual conversion and growth in their faith. They should be provided with opportunities for spiritual growth. Whether the initial formation of catechists is done at a diocesan center or in the parish, it should be adapted as much as possible to the specific needs of the individual. ("Under no circumstances should the initial formation of new catechists 'be improvised or left to the initiative of the candidates themselves.'") The initial formation should: (1) help them understand the nature and goals of catechesis; (2) familiarize them with available resources and make them aware of the social, cultural, ethnic, demographic, and religious circumstances of the people they will serve; and (3) emphasize the importance of ongoing study, especially of Scripture and the *Catechism of the Catholic Church*. Formation programs for catechists should include a basic presentation of the social sciences, since they provide an awareness of the socio-cultural contexts in which those being catechized live and by which they are strongly influenced.

The ongoing formation of catechists enhances the human, spiritual, and apostolic qualities and catechetical skills they bring to their ministry. The pastoral care of catechists is an essential aspect of the diocese's overall catechetical plan. Ongoing formation helps catechists to harmonize the human, spiritual, doctrinal, and apostolic dimensions of their ministry and to keep abreast of developments (documents) in the life of the Church and of changing social, cultural, ethnic, and religious circumstances. It helps them overcome discouragement and burnout.

The formation of catechists takes place most effectively within the community of faith under the direction of the pastor. Parish-centered programs remind catechists that their calling comes from the Church. Some opportunities for catechist formation are more appropriately provided by diocesan institutes, workshops, and seminars; dioceses are well-advised to develop comprehensive programs that lead to a formal certification of catechists.

Catholic colleges and universities and seminaries are encouraged to collaborate with dioceses in the establishment of opportunities for the advanced study of pastoral catechesis and the ongoing formation of catechetical leaders. Some make productive use of distance learning models. The USCCB's Commission on Certification and Accreditation affirms and verifies the quality and validity of such programs.

Chapter Nine – Organizing Catechetical Ministry

Chapter Nine describes the responsibilities and the need for coordination in catechetical ministry. It gives principles and guidelines for organizing catechesis.

(See, n. 58) The organization for catechesis at every level should be part of an overall pastoral plan that flows from the Church's comprehensive mission. It should be based on a clear statement that explains the principles and goals of catechesis, the measure of accountability and the provision for the communication of information, ensuring the equitable distribution of services, resources, and opportunities and flow from specific catechetical needs. Planning, an essential part of catechetical organization, should include an analysis of the social, cultural, ethnic, and religious situation; an assessment of catechetical needs and resources; identification and prioritization of goals and strategies; and a budget. Evaluation is another essential part of catechetical organization. Norms and criteria for evaluation appear in the following chapter.

(See, n. 59) The organization of catechetical pastoral care has, as its reference point, the bishop and the diocese. The bishop should ensure that necessary structures exist, that programs are implemented, and catechetical endeavors are coordinated. He sees that suitable instruments for catechesis are available, even by preparing a catechism, if it seems opportune.

A plan for catechesis is a key component in a diocesan pastoral plan. This plan is established by the bishop in consultation with catechetical leaders, and sets goals for the diocese. The diocesan commission, committee, or board that has the responsibility of developing policy and providing unified leadership to the catechetical ministry, collaborates closely with the diocesan catechetical office. It should be broadly representative of all the people of the diocese.

Ordinarily, several diocesan offices and agencies share responsibility for the diocesan catechetical mission. Chief among them is the catechetical office that directs and moderates all the catechetical activities of the diocese. The diocesan catechetical office should have sufficient professional personnel to serve as a resource to parishes in all aspects of catechesis, including the needs of persons with disabilities. While catechetical needs and priorities vary from diocese to diocese, the diocesan office, among its other functions, helps develop the diocesan catechetical plan and collaborates with the liturgical office especially for catechumenal and initiatory catechesis. It formulates curriculum guidelines, and recommends and evaluates catechetical textbooks, materials, and other resources. The diocesan office develops processes for the recruiting, certifying, and informing catechetical leaders of important Church documents, and provides recommendations for adequate compensation for catechetical leaders.

The diocesan catechetical office should collaborate with other diocesan offices and agents that have a catechetical dimension, most especially the Catholic school office. The superintendent of Catholic schools is a diocesan catechetical leader who should provide leadership, advocacy, and support for the catechetical mission of Catholic schools. Catholic school office personnel should ensure in-service training for teachers, especially those who have catechetical responsibilities. Other agencies with whom the diocesan catechetical office should collaborate include evangelization, liturgy, youth ministry, continuing education for the clergy, Catholic missions ecumenical and interfaith affairs, family life, social justice, and the office for communications. The efforts of all these offices should be collaborative and not organized as if they were "separate watertight compartments" without any communication between them.

(See, n. 60) The parish is the preeminent place for catechesis, energizing the faithful to carry out Christ's mission by providing spiritual, moral, and material support for the catechetical development of adults, youth, and children. Every parish needs to develop a coherent plan that reflects the priority of adult catechesis, taking into account everyone's needs and the needs of groups with special needs. The plan should be adequately financed and staffed by professionally trained personnel. To assist him with his responsibilities, the pastor may establish a catechetical commission or committee. The commission can take different forms according to the local circumstances but it should be representative of the diverse groups in the parish.

(See, n. 61) A comprehensive parish-based catechesis harmonizes the catechesis of adults, families, parents, youth, and children. As noted in Chapter Seven, adult catechesis is to be seen as primary. All forms of organized family catechesis should flow from and lead back to the parish. They should include prayerful celebration that is closely linked to the liturgical celebration of the parish. Special attention needs to be give to the catechetical needs of inter-church families by including everyone in activities and encouraging everyone to celebrate what is held in common.

Home schooling is a viable option for the general education of children. Parents who choose home-based catechesis (as the NDC calls it) must not feel alone in this task. Pastors and parish catechetical leaders should provide the support and direction that parents need to ensure their children are taught according to diocesan guidelines. Parents who provide catechesis in their homes should participate in the life of the local parish, celebrating the Sunday liturgy there, and involving themselves in its charitable works. Preparing children for the reception of sacraments should always be undertaken in collaboration with the local pastor and catechetical leader.

Parishes are to provide a comprehensive and systematic program of instruction and formation for children who attend public schools or who are schooled at home. Guidelines for this are found in Chapter Seven. The Catholic school is to be an integral part of the total parish catechetical plan, not a separate entity. It should have a clearly defined religion curriculum with specific goals and objectives that are in harmony with the parish catechetical plan and with the diocesan catechetical priorities.

The organization of catechesis for young people should be guided by their need to hear the Gospel proclaimed, to pray and celebrate the Holy Mass, to form a Christian community, to live the Christian life, and to serve the needs of others. It should provide concrete ways by which they can personally experience the demands, excitement, and adventure of being a disciple of Jesus Christ. Programs should reach out to Catholic junior high and high school students who do not regularly participate in the life of the parish.

The baptismal catechumenate is a vital component in the organization of catechesis in the parish. It should be the cornerstone of the parish catechetical plan. Specific information and guidelines regarding the catechumenate are in Chapter Five.

Small Christian communities within parishes provide opportunities for the faithful to experience a more intense communion and are a particularly fruitful climate for adult catechesis. To be authentic, they must live in heartfelt communion with the Church's pastors and the Magisterium, with a commitment to missionary outreach and without yielding to isolationism or ideological exploitation.

While the parish is the primary setting for catechesis, the organizational structure of the Church's catechetical mission encompasses structures that are beyond the boundaries of a single parish. Some Catholic schools, for example, are inter-parochial, regional, diocesan, or private. In these situations each school should work in close collaboration with parishes from which the students come. Other examples include catechetical programs for persons with disabilities and catechetical programs in seminaries and colleges and universities. *Empowered by the Spirit,* a document published by the U.S. bishops, contains specific recommendations regarding campus ministry.

Other structures, whether or not they are under Catholic auspices, provide opportunities for catechesis for people with special needs and in particular settings: daycare, convalescent and nursing homes, residential facilities for persons with physical, mental, or emotional disabilities, etc. Hospitals, professional groups, police and fire departments, fraternities and sororities, and prisons provide settings especially for adult catechesis. As much as possible, the bishop should assign chaplains to such groups so that the opportunities for catechesis can be properly developed and supervised.

(See, n. 62) Regional and interdiocesan cooperation enables dioceses to share their resources, assist one another, and offers the Church the advantage of speaking in a common voice across diocesan boundaries regarding public policy decisions. Diocesan and parish catechetical personnel should be aware of the services and resources offered by national associations and organizations.

(See, n. 63) The United States Conference of Catholic Bishops has within its permanent structure a Committee on Catechesis. Committee and its staff serve the catechetical needs of the country as a whole. Their efforts extend to publications of national importance, national congresses, and relations with the mass media. They serve dioceses and regions by publicizing catechetical ideas and undertakings, by coordinating action, and by assisting dioceses that are less advanced in catechetical matters. The bishops' national office may also coordinate its efforts with other catechetical institutes and cooperate with catechetical activities at the international level.

(See, n. 64) In issues regarding catechesis the Congregation for the Clergy assists the Roman Pontiff in the supreme exercise of his pastoral office. The Congregation promotes and issues norms for the religious education of all the faithful. Together with the Congregation of the Doctrine of the Faith, it grants the prescribed approbation of the Holy See for catechisms and other catechetical writings. Where necessary it lends assistance to catechetical offices and coordinates international initiatives on religious education.

(See, n. 65) National, regional, and parish catechetical structures embody Christ's commission to go, make disciples, baptize, and teach. They are essential if the Church is to be faithful to her mission in the world.

Chapter Ten – Resources for Catechesis

Chapter Ten provides principles, guidelines, and criteria for the production, use, and evaluation of catechisms, textbooks, and other instructional materials.

(See, n. 67) Sacred Scripture provides the starting point, foundation, and norm of catechetical teaching. Catechists should assume the thought and perspective of Scripture and make frequent, direct use of the biblical texts themselves. Catechesis should be an introduction to *lectio divina*, a correct and fruitful reading of the Bible, inspired by the Spirit who dwells in the Church. Catechesis should present persons and events and stories in both the Old and New Testaments in the light of God's overall plan. It should single out the Decalogue and make use of prophetic oracles, the wisdom teaching, and the great discourse in the gospels such as the Sermon on the Mount.

The *Catechism of the Catholic Church* is the authoritative expression of the living Tradition of the Church and a basic source of wisdom for all catechetical activity. It is normative for the composition of all materials and resources used in catechesis. Local catechisms are invaluable instruments of catechesis because they present a synthesis of faith with reference to the particular culture of the people. A local catechism may be prepared by an individual bishop for use within his own diocese. Catechisms published by the conference of bishops for their territory require prior approval of the Holy See.

(See, n. 68) In the United States textbooks for children and young people are ordinarily part of an integrated series prepared for a number of grade levels, usually pre-school through sixth or eighth grade. High school texts address core components of the faith in different formats. Textbooks used in catechesis should present the message of Christ and his Church, adapted to the culture and capacity of the learners, and reflect the real-life situations of those who use them. They should be in conformity with the *Catechism of the Catholic*

Church and be approved by the local bishop. Textbooks should employ a variety of methodologies, be visually attractive, and incorporate examples of Christian art. They should include examples of prayer and opportunities for liturgical experiences, and incorporate Scripture texts for study.

Catechist and teacher manuals are essential components of any sound catechetical series. The manuals should make constant reference to the sources and distinguish clearly between those things that pertain to faith and doctrine and those things that are mere opinions of theologians. Textbook series should also include information and practical tools specifically designed to help parents in their roles as catechists.

Other catechetical materials include guides for program leaders, resources for the baptismal catechumenate, and resources for preparation for marriage and other sacraments. These texts should contain the items that were articulated above in Chapter Five, "Guidelines in a Worshiping Community." All these instructional materials should be artistically sensitive, technically up to date, theologically authentic, ecumenically accurate, methodically sound, and conform to the *Catechism of the Catholic Church*.

(See, n. 69) Developments in communication technology provide a new and effective forum for presenting the Gospel to all nations and all people. Contemporary media not only transmit information; they generate visual, audible, emotional, and, in some cases, entirely virtual experiences. Well-planned catechesis must employ them so that the message of Jesus Christ can be effectively communicated in the real circumstances and culture of those who seek him. The media proceed from fundamental assumptions that often contradict basic premises in anthropology, psychology, and ethics. They raise profound questions about the distinction between the medium and the message, the "how" and "what" of communications.

Catechetical programs should incorporate the use of electronic media. While catechists are not expected to be media specialists, diocesan and parish catechetical leaders should be aware of public service airtime offered to eligible groups. Dioceses or regions should establish media centers to assist catechists in developing the skills to use multimedia resources most effectively. They should be given the criteria with which to evaluate the media and for judging the culture it creates.

The print media, especially Catholic publications of all kinds, remain an important means of evangelization and catechesis in the United States. Catechetical leaders at all levels should provide the press with leads, information, and stories of newsworthy aspects of catechesis. They should be prepared to meet with secular journalists and editors to help them understand the Church and its ministry of evangelization and catechesis. Community-based newspapers, in particular, may be interested in covering catechetical activities of parishes.

The age of the computer has opened the world of cyberspace to catechetical activities via the Internet, along with opportunities for the personal and spiritual development of catechists. Dozens of sites provide immediate access to enriching resources: daily readings from Scripture, liturgical books, Church documents, and the like. The Internet also gives easy access to pornography, hate messages, and damaging misinformation. The anonymity and lack of accountability in cyberspace requires a more sophisticated level of media literacy than has ever been needed in the past. Nevertheless, the Internet's potential to proclaim the Gospel, to invite potential disciples to follow Jesus Christ, is only limited by the imagination of contemporary evangelists and catechists.

The communications media are themselves suitable subject matter for catechesis. Catechetical plans should help people develop their knowledge and skills so that they might develop a critical understanding by which to evaluate the media in light of the Gospel. Parents need to be educated in order to guide their children in the appropriate use of the Internet. Television viewers and Internet users need to know who sponsors and produces programs and websites. They need to be aware of the techniques used by advertisers and others to influence and manipulate their audiences, and be able to distinguish between the image and the reality it represents (or distorts). It is necessary that viewers understand the profit motives of commercial television and the Internet.

(See, n. 70) This *National Directory for Catechesis* gives criteria and guidelines for the production of catechetical textbooks and other materials. Authors, editors, and publishers should be guided by the *Catechism of the Catholic Church* and the *General Directory for Catechesis*. In particular they should adhere to the *Guidelines for Doctrinally Sound Catechetical Materials* set forth by the bishops of the United States, further refined in the *Protocol for Assessing the Conformity of Catechetical Materials with the Catechism of the Catholic Church*. The fundamental criteria that should be their guide derive from the principles of authenticity and completeness. Authentic materials contain nothing contradictory to the *Catechism* while promoting a healthy and vital Catholic identity in such a way that the believer is encouraged to hear the message clearly, live it with conviction, and share it courageously with others. For catechetical materials to be considered complete, they must present the doctrines of the Church as an integrated whole. Specifically they should reflect the four pillars of the *Catechism*.

The preparation of catechetical materials should also be based on sound principles of methodology, and take into account the cultural, racial, ethnic, and ecclesial conditions characteristic of those who will use them. The staff of the USCCB's (now) Catechism subcommittee serves publishers by ensuring their materials are authentic and complete. Before publication, according to the directives of Canon Law, the materials must have the approval of the local ordinary.

By reason of his pastoral responsibility for catechesis, the local bishop should establish a process for the evaluation of catechetical materials used in his diocese. The process should assess both the doctrine presented and the methods employed in the presentation of the doctrine. The bishop should call on his diocesan catechetical staff to coordinate the evaluation process. It is advisable that knowledgeable pastors, Catholic school principals, parish catechetical leaders, teachers, catechists, and parents representing various cultural groups be involved in the selection and evaluation process. The evaluation committee or task force should be familiar with the list of catechetical materials found to be in conformity with the *Catechism*. The committee or task force should devise an instrument that measures the level of effectiveness of the catechetical materials used in the diocese, and determine if they respect the cultural diversity of the diocese. The instrument should be developed directly from the official documents of the universal Church and those of the Catholic Church in the United States. As much as possible the committee should keep the publishers informed of the progress of the evaluation and provide them with the results.

(See, n. 71) No material resources can ever replace the personal witness of the catechist. Nevertheless, catechetical aids that are faithful to God's Revelation and suited to those being catechized can be very effective in the hands of skilled catechists.

Conclusion – A New Millennium, A Renewed Passion for Catechesis

"This *National Directory for Catechesis* provides the fundamental theological and pastoral principles drawn from the Church's teaching and offers guidelines for the application of those principles within the catechetical mission of the Church in the United States. We bishops . . . have developed this directory to be a source of inspiration for the new evangelization and for a renewed catechesis in the dioceses and parishes of this country. It is our hope that this publication fires a new energy and fresh commitment that impels the disciples of this age… to reinvest themselves in catechetical initiatives that ensure the faithful and enthusiastic proclamation of the Gospel."

10. Addressing American Culture

United States Catholic Catechism for Adults

The *Catechism of the Catholic Church*, in the words of Pope John Paul II, was "meant to encourage and assist in the writing of new local catechisms" and, as previously noted, the *General Directory for Catechesis* stressed the need for local catechisms as well. A plan to develop a national catechism for adults was approved by the bishops of the United States in June, 2000. They established an editorial oversight board chaired by Bishop Donald Wuerl of Pittsburgh and engaged the services of Alfred McBride, O.Praem., to begin drafting a text. After a number of drafts and extensive consultation, the final text was approved by the bishops and confirmed by the Holy See in November, 2004. It was published July 31, 2006.

At the outset the bishops determined that a catechism for adults would be an effective means for "preserving the unity of faith and fidelity to Catholic teachings found in the Church's Catechism" (p. v). They intend it for members of both Latin and Eastern Churches ("with the understanding" that the latter may develop catechisms emphasizing their own traditions). They see it as an instrument to be used in the *Rite of Christian Initiation of Adults* (RCIA) to introduce those entering the Church to Catholic teachings. They intend it, according to a press release issued at the time of publication, especially for "young adult Catholics whose education in the faith was inadequate or incomplete in any way."

The *U.S. Catholic Catechism for Adults* (USCCA) has thirty-six chapters, organized like the *Catechism of the Catholic Church* (CCC) according to the basic pattern of the "Four Pillars" of creed, sacraments, moral life, and prayer. All chapters follow much the same outline. They begin with a biographical sketch of a prominent Catholic: some canonized saints, other saintly witnesses who lived out their lives in the United States. The short biography leads into a presentation of Catholic doctrine and practice, followed by a "sidebar" that highlights three questions and answers designed to lead the reader to explore the text of the CCC itself. Other sidebars interspersed throughout the chapters explain specific points. A fourth section reflects on how the Church's teaching relates to contemporary culture and issues in U.S. society. The "questions for discussion" in each chapter encourage readers individually and in groups to explore ways that the chapter's theme applies to themselves and the community. For purposes of review, each chapter has a series of doctrinal statements that summarize its main points. And because "a catechism needs to be more than a summary of teachings" the chapters conclude with a short meditation and prayer drawn from the writings of spiritual masters and the liturgy. Three appendices at the end of the book present (A) a glossary of terms; (B) a selection of common Catholic prayers; and (C) a list of Church documents recommended for further reading. In all, the original edition numbered 637 pages.

The Introduction notes that, "in keeping with cultural practice in the United States," the text uses "inclusive language," so as not to exclude either gender. References to God, however, maintain traditional usage (p. xxiii).

Preface

The Preface (pp. ix - xii) establishes the scope of the *USCCA*. On the one hand it presents "an organic synthesis of the essential and fundamental contents of Catholic doctrine" as found in the CCC, and on the other hand it seeks to be an instrument for evangelizing American culture. By way of introducing "the uniquely American policy of religious freedom"—enshrined in the Declaration of Independence and the Bill of Rights—the Preface describes the life and career of the country's first bishop, John Carroll of Baltimore. He had the task of insuring that the universal practice of the Church was being carried out while, at the same time, addressing the pastoral needs of Catholics in the United States. During the twenty-five years he served (first as bishop and then archbishop of Baltimore), he saw the Church grow and the policy of religious freedom begin to take shape. A sidebar briefly describes the earlier work of the Spanish, French, and Native Americans in building the nascent Catholic community.

Since the USCCA closely follows the structure and outline of the *Catechism* the following "digest" highlights the points in each of the chapters that give it a specifically American flavor.

Part One – The Creed: The Faith Professed

The first four chapters of Part One correspond to the first section of Part One in the CCC. The principal themes are introduced with thumbnail sketches of Mother Elizabeth Ann Seton ("the human quest for God"); Moses ("God reveals a plan of loving goodness"); Pope John XXIII ("the transmission of divine revelation"); and Isaac Hecker ("faith as the human response to God's revelation"):

Chapter One. The interface of Church teaching with issues in American society is a thread that runs through the USCCA and gives it its unique character. The acknowledgment of individual rights and the free exercise of religion are positive elements, but issues such as disbelief, relativism, and differences about morality highlight conflicts between Catholic teaching and American culture. The first chapter, for example, considers how the culture provides support for people seeking a deeper meaning in life—"religious seekers"—while at the same time corrodes the faith in practice.

Chapter Two. The second chapter deals explicitly with the relationship of the Gospel and culture. Culture is not an abstraction. It is the sum of the beliefs, attitudes, and practices of individuals and communities. Despite many elements that allow the free exercise of religion, the *Catechism* says "attitudes and actions in the United States have fostered a 'culture of disbelief'." American society marginalizes religion and causes many to think that faith is strictly a private matter. The Church's response must be to evangelize culture, building on what is positive and changing what is not.

Chapter Three. The Sacred Scriptures transmit God's revelation. Chapter Three explains how biblical scholars assist believers to deepen their understanding of the faith, but it warns against simplistic interpretations of the text. In American circles there are those who interpret the Bible in the strictest literal sense while others deny supernatural aspects of the Gospel.

Chapter Four. Faith, born of our response to God's revelation, is challenged by intellectuals in the United States by a culture born of the Age of Reason that still endures. Many of the founding fathers were Deists who believed that after God created the world he left us to our own devises. Today Deism has given way to an ideological secularism, a belief that we are self-sufficient and that religious faith should not impact on the state or society.

Chapters Five through Thirteen, emphasizing the work of the Holy Trinity, correspond to the second section of the CCC's Part One. Again, lives of outstanding Catholics are cited to illustrate various aspects of the Church's teaching regarding creation, redemption, and sanctification:

- A sketch of Orestes Brownson, described as "an intellectual Catholic," prefaces Chapter Five, which takes up the first article of the Creed, "faith in God as Mystery and Trinity."
- Rose Hawthorne Lathrop, a.k.a. as Mother Alphonsa, O.P., daughter of Nathaniel Hawthorne, was chosen to introduce "the creation of man and woman, the fall and the promise" because "she saw the image of God in the cancerous poor" and "shows us how we, urged by God, can overcome the self-centeredness caused by Original Sin."
- The inspiring story of Haitian-born Pierre Toussaint, is told at the beginning of Chapter Seven which focuses on the mysteries of Christ's life. Toussant's life illustrates how the Incarnation can impact on lives of ordinary Christians.
- The career of African-American Thea Bowman exemplifies the transforming power of the Paschal Mystery. Debilitated by bone-cancer, Sister Thea bore her cross courageously, continued to sing alleluias from her wheelchair, and challenged Christians of every background to break bread together and relive the holy mystery of redemption.
- Blessed Kateri Tekakwitha, the daughter of a Mohawk chief and an Algonquin mother, witnesses to the working of the Holy Spirit in the lives of the baptized. Her story prefaces Chapter Nine subtitled, "The Revelation of the Spirit, Joint Mission of Son and Spirit."
- The introduction to Chapter Ten, "images and mission of the Church," recalls the exchange in Matthew 16 when Jesus says to Simon "You are Peter, and upon this rock I will build my Church."
- The missionary zeal that took Fra Junipero Serra to California exhibited in an extraordinary way how the Church—one, holy, catholic and apostolic—continues to carry the Gospel teachings to all peoples.

216

- The reflection in Chapter Twelve on Mary as "mother of Jesus, mother of God, Mother of the Church" begins with an account of the apparition of Our Lady of Guadalupe to St. Juan Diego. He is in the company of numerous others who were privileged to have a vision of the Virgin Mary, among them St. Bernadette at Lourdes.

- A short account of Philadelphia-born St. Katharine Drexel prefaces the final chapter in Part One, a reflection on "our journey from life through death to the perfection of the Communion of Saints in eternity." The chapter presents the Church's teaching on the "last things: resurrection of the body, death, particular judgment, heaven, purgatory, hell, last judgment, new heavens, and new earth."

Chapter Five. The Bible and the Apostles' Creed begin by affirming that God created "the heavens and earth." For many this affirmation seems to contradict the findings of modern science. In the United States the issue focuses on whether there is a place for God the Creator in Darwinism and theories of evolution.

Chapter Six. "There is a perceptible discomfort in our culture with the notion of sin as an evil for which we must give an account to God, our Creator, Redeemer, and Judge." Linked to this is the popular reliance on self-help programs that run counter to the Church's teaching that sin is not simply a weakness that we can overcome by our own effort but is "a condition from which we need to be saved."

Chapter Seven. Jesus is the Savior of all people of every land, language, and culture. The diversity of cultures in the United States presents a case study in the Church's mission to unite all people in the love of Jesus Christ.

Chapter Eight. The Resurrection makes credible everything Jesus did and taught. When they first heard it even the Apostles thought the report of Jesus' Resurrection seemed like nonsense (Lk. 24:11). In our present culture there are skeptics who support their disbelief by reinterpreting the text of the Scriptures, claiming that Jesus' post-Resurrection appearances were inward spiritual experiences.

Chapter Nine. The secular or worldly nature of American culture notwithstanding, there is seemingly a unique quality that moves millions in the

United States to seek an immediate experience of God. This is most evident in outpourings of faith and charismatic movements that focus on the Holy Spirit.

Chapter Ten. American history recalls the freedom of the frontier, voluntary association and a resistance to institutions. Thus for some there is a tension between the Church as an institution and the Church as a community of believers. "Problems with the institution are not arguments for its removal, but for its renewal."

Chapter Eleven. The mission of the Church is to evangelize: "we have Good News to share with others." Among the approaches to evangelization in the United States, the interpersonal approach is the most effective. Another approach is to address people's four basic fears: failure, rejection, pain, death, and raise questions about existence and future life.

Chapter Twelve. In contemplating Mary's motherhood the Church reflects on her own calling to be mother of the members of Christ's Mystical Body. Although Christians from earliest times have sought Mary's prayers and help, there are some in our culture who are uncomfortable with praying for her help and intercession.

Chapter Thirteen. "Our Eternal Destiny" presents the Christian attitude towards death. This first part of the USCCA concludes with a short excursus on Christian funerals and cremation.

Part Two – The Sacraments: The Faith Celebrated

The second part of the USCCA follows the same pattern as the first. Chapter Fourteen parallels the first section of the *Catechism of the Catholic Church* in that it explains the nature of liturgy and presents general principles. Chapters Fifteen through Twenty-Two correspond to the second section of the CCC, explaining the Seven Sacraments and devotional practices.

The second part begins with a brief description of the efforts of Msgr. Martin Hellriegel, long-time pastor in St. Louis (in the spirit of Pope Pius XII's 1947 encyclical *Mediator Dei*) to open people's hearts to the presence of Jesus in their lives by involving them actively in Christian worship, especially the Sunday Eucharist.

Like the CCC, the USCCA names the Sacraments of Initiation—Baptism, Confirmation, and the Eucharist—as "the foundations of the Christian life." Chapter Fifteen holds up John Boyle O'Reilly, an editor of the *Pilot*, Boston's diocesan paper, as an example of how the laity can live out their baptismal commitment and bring the Gospel to society. St. Frances Cabrini, who tirelessly ministered to Italian immigrants in the United States, South America, and other countries, is offered as an example of someone who "responded generously to the grace of the Sacrament of Confirmation that binds Christians to a deeper identification with the Church and her mission." The *Catechism* describes Carlos Manuel Rodriguez as an "alert Puerto Rican layman [who] showed university students how to base their faith life on the liturgy, especially the Eucharist." He taught them to live the Easter mystery of Christ's dying and rising, especially at the Easter Vigil.

St. Augustine, moved by St. Paul's denunciation of licentiousness, turned from his sinful ways. In his *Confessions* he describes his conversion and praises God for his mercy and forgiveness, "the same mercy and forgiveness" that is available to us today in the Sacrament of Penance, the "Sacrament of Healing," by which we are reconciled to God and the Church. Chapter Nineteen, prefaced by a short account of Cardinal Joseph Bernardin's bout with terminal cancer, describes the other "Sacrament of Healing," the Anointing of the Sick. Cardinal Bernardin wrote, "Uniting our suffering with that of Jesus, we receive strength and courage, a new lease on life, and undaunted hope for the future."

By way of introduction to the Sacrament of Holy Orders, the USCCA briefly describes the work of Philadelphia's St. John Neomucene Neumann and the lesser known Redemptorist, Blessed Francis Xavier Seelos. Their varied ministries in Pennsylvania and Maryland exemplify what priests, by reason of ordination, are called to do. Both Holy Orders and Marriage are called "Sacraments of Communion". St. Thomas More withstood to death the wrath of the King of England to uphold the indissolubility of marriage. Personally, More "continued his quest for virtue and union with Christ while fostering the faith of his [own] family."

No one did more to promote the praying of the rosary, that most popular of popular devotions, than Father Patrick Peyton. The story of his devotion to Mary prefaces an explanation of sacramentals and other popular devotional practices, the last chapter in Part Two.

Chapter Fourteen. It is important to emphasize the link between liturgy and life because of the value that our society puts on being practical. One's liturgical experience provides a unique spiritual vision and strength for making this a better world.

Chapter Fifteen. In Baptism, the Holy Spirit moves us to answer Christ's call to holiness. It involves a life-long commitment to learning about the faith and supporting others in their ongoing of conversion of heart and mind to God.

Chapter Sixteen. The impact of the seven gifts of the Holy Spirit bestowed through the sacrament of Confirmation accompanies us in the various stages of our spiritual development. The gift of Wisdom, for example, "saves us from the illusion that the spirit of the times is our only guide."

Chapter Seventeen. In and through the Eucharist Jesus transforms us into himself, and "then in Christ we become bread for the world's bodily and spiritual hungers."

Chapter Eighteen. Although our sins have been forgiven and we have been reconciled to God and the Church in the Sacrament of Penance, we are still liable to temporal punishment. In the mutual exchange of spiritual goods, particularly the merits of Christ and the saints, the Church attaches an indulgence or pardon, that is, the full or partial remission of temporal punishment, to certain prayers and actions.

Chapter Nineteen. The Sacrament of the Anointing of the Sick has an important community dimension. Communal celebrations can serve the purpose of the Sacrament and at the same time build up the faith of the community itself.

Chapter Twenty. The spiritual life of the priest is dominated by a search for Christ and bringing him to others. An essential element of priestly formation is the prayerful reading of the Word of God so that it becomes "our new basis for judging and evaluating persons and things, events and problems."

Chapter Twenty-One. After presenting the Church's teaching on marriage, the question is asked, "How does the modern, secular view of marriage and the family affect your own family relationships? How do you resist forces that can weaken marriage?"

Chapter Twenty-Two. The second part of the USCCA concludes with a word about popular devotional practices and how they play a crucial role in helping to foster prayer. They do not replace the Church's liturgy; but extend it into daily life.

Part Three – Christian Morality: The Faith Lived

The third part of both the *Catechism of the Catholic Church* and the *United States Catechism for Adults* presents in two sections ways that Christians live out their lives in Christ and the Holy Spirit. Section One expounds the principles of Christian morality based on Church teaching regarding the dignity of the human person, the human community, and God's law and grace as the foundation. It begins with the question asked of Jesus, "Teacher, what good must I do to gain eternal life" (Mt. 19:16). In his answer Jesus emphasizes the fundamental importance of the Ten Commandments, but in the Sermon on the Mount, specifically in the Beatitudes, and elsewhere, Jesus teaches that love is at the heart of all law.

Chapter Twenty-Four begins with an account of Cesar Chavez's efforts to apply the Church's teaching on social justice to the plight of migrant workers in California. It focuses on morality as it pertains to the individual as situated within a community.

Chapter Twenty-Three. Our culture tends to hold traditional rules and norms suspect. However, Christians sometimes lapse into a legalism that leads to unproductive moralizing. Love has to be the essential foundation of the moral life but rules and laws are necessary to show how love may be applied in real life.

Chapter Twenty-Four. The tragedy of September 11, 2001 "dramatized the issues of good and evil and the need to draw moral guidance from the teachings of Christ and the Church." They provide moral guidance on how to respond justly to terrorism in order to reestablish peace and order. Section Two explores these principles in the context of each of the Ten Commandments. The first three Commandments concern our relationship to God; the last seven, our relationship with each other.

Catherine de Hueck Doherty's life witnesses to the meaning of the First Commandment in that she loved the Lord with all her being and because of that, respected and worked for the dignity of every human being.

The story of Job dramatizes the Second Commandment: in every circumstance the character Job kept holy God's name. Despite a series of calamities—loss of family, wealth, and health—nothing could shake Job's faith in God. His wife and friends, seeing his pitiable state, tell him "Curse God and die" (Job 2:9 and *passim*), but Job did not cease to praise God's awesomeness and majesty.

To bring the Mass and the sacraments to widely scattered Catholics in the early days of the country, priests like Eusebio Kino in Arizona and Jacques Marquette in Michigan and Wisconsin established mission stations. The stories of two of these priests, Demetrius Gallitzin and James Fitton, are told to illustrate the premium that Catholics put on Mass attendance as a way of observing the Third Commandment. Father Gallitzin is called "Apostle to the Alleghenies," and Father Fitton established a seminary in Worcester, Massachusetts that grew into the College of the Holy Cross.

Chapter Twenty-Five. The First Commandment is an announcement of the presence of God both in outward creation and within the human soul. Most people in our culture say they believe in God's existence but their lives are filled with many distractions that shut out his voice.

Chapter Twenty-Six. Reverencing the name of God honors him, but public discourse at times displays little respect for his name and matters religious. Reverence for God's name extends to the respect we pay to each other based on our being created as an image of God. What means do you take to eliminate the wrong use of God's name in your family or workplace?

Chapter Twenty-Seven. God built into human nature the rhythm between work and rest. Sunday rest puts our whole life in perspective. It helps us stand back from material concerns and reflect on spiritual values. Unfortunately, Sunday for many is neither a day of rest nor a time for worship because of incessant activity, "so characteristic of a consumer society."

Commandments four through ten focus on relationship and responsibility that humans have for each other and to society as a whole.

In 2001 Pope John Paul II celebrated the anniversary of his Apostolic Exhortation *The Role of the Christian Family in the Modern World* by beatifying Luigi and Maria Quattrocchi, parents of four children. A reflection on their home and family life introduces the Fourth Commandment at the beginning of Chapter Twenty-Eight.

Chapter Twenty-Nine begins with a lengthy quote from a sermon given by New York's Cardinal John O'Connor that focused on the value Dorothy Day placed on human life and how she came to reject the violence of abortion.

Her defense of life and abhorrence of war and crushing poverty makes her story a suitable introduction to the Church's teaching on the Fifth Commandment.

Pope Paul VI guided the Church through the last three sessions of the Second Vatican Council and implemented many reforms recommended by the Council. Pope Paul's clear teaching on family, marriage, and moral issues such as artificial contraception fostered the values and virtues embodied in the Sixth Commandment.

The Seventh Commandment goes beyond ownership and stealing to deal with issues of social justice and human dignity. To illustrate what this means in practice, the USCCA cites the work of Mother Joseph who spent most of her life in the Pacific Northwest building hospitals, orphanages, schools, homes for the aged, and shelters for the mentally ill. Her institutions were open to all who needed help.

In explaining the Eighth Commandment the *Catechism* emphasizes the right of individuals and society to know truth and the corresponding duty of the media and people in public positions to tell the truth. Bishop John Francis Noll, best known as the founder of *Our Sunday Visitor,* spent his lifetime in spreading the truth of the Gospel and defending the Church against anti-Catholic propaganda and lies.

The Ninth Commandment directs us to purify our hearts from evil and disordered desires. The young man who attempted to rape young Maria Goretti shows how carnal desires lead to crime, even murder. St. Maria Goretti's purity of heart gave her the strength to resist his advances even at the cost of her life.

Like the previous Commandment, the Tenth Commandment is concerned with desires of the heart. "Where your treasure is, there also will your heart be." Henriette Delille discovered a treasure in serving the poor: She founded the Sisters of the Holy Family and sold her property to found schools and orphanages for freed slaves and blacks.

Chapter Twenty-Eight. The Fourth Commandment is an invitation to reflect on family life. Couples need regularly to renew their commitment to each other and welcome children. Family members must work at giving love, respect, commitment, and support to and for each other.

Chapter Twenty-Nine. The Fifth Commandment affirms the sanctity of life. In our society moral confusion leads many to support choices and policies that desecrate life: abortion, physician-assisted suicide, capital punishment, war, euthanasia.

Chapter Thirty. The cult of the body in American culture for hedonistic attraction is a prime example of how American culture exploits sexuality for commercial gain. Pope John Paul II offers a theology of the body that provides a healing vision of sexuality, the body, and the human person. He retrieves the nuptial meaning of the body by taking us back to life before the Fall, a time of original innocence.

Chapter Thirty-One. The wealth of our nation notwithstanding, we witness the ravages of poverty: the homeless, destitute families, neglected children. Charity towards the poor is a good way to start living the Church's social teaching.

Chapter Thirty-Two. In our culture where opinions and "a marathon of inconclusive discussions" displace objective truth, how do we observe the mandate of the Eighth Commandment to avoid lying?

Chapter Thirty-Three. The virtue of modesty is difficult to maintain in a sexually permissive culture. The environment of indecency challenges people of faith to witness to modesty as a method for healing a culture that has strayed from God's plan for sexuality and marriage.

Chapter Thirty-Four. The financial scandals that periodically occur in our culture are a reminder that greed is a constant threat to moral behavior. The Tenth Commandment warns against the interior attitudes of greed and envy that lead people to steal and act unjustly. On the positive side, it calls us to poverty of spirit and generosity of heart.

Part Four – Prayer: The Faith Prayed

The two chapters that make up Part Four nicely explain the call to prayer and suggest guidelines that assist one in praying. Every chapter in the USCCA, moreover, suggests a thought for meditation and the text of a short prayer because sound catechesis may never be disconnected from prayer, the soul of truth.

The important place that a daily hour of prayer had in the life Archbishop Fulton J. Sheen is described in the introduction to Chapter Thirty-Five. In his autobiography he wrote, "Sitting before the Presence is like a body exposing itself to the sun to absorb its rays. In those moments one does not so much pour out written prayers, but listening takes place." The chapter has four sections: Scripture, the sources and manner of prayer, guides for prayer, and expressions of prayer.

The *United States Catholic Catechism for Adults* ends, as does the *Catechism of the Catholic Church*, with a reflection on the seven petitions of the Lord's Prayer. The "Our Father" is the central prayer of Scripture as well as an integral part of sacramental liturgies. It is at the heart of every individual and communal prayer. It teaches not only what to ask God for but also in what sequence we should desire them. Prayer and doctrine go together: Doctrine draws us to prayer and prayer deepens our personal relationship with God in whom we believe.

Chapter Thirty-Five. Noting that "a high number" of Americans report that they pray each day, the USCCA discusses obstacles to prayer and the need for fidelity to times for prayer, constant conversion of heart, and watchfulness.

Chapter Thirty-Six. The spirit of prayer runs through the whole of the USCCA and the fact that certain parts (two and four) treat it more explicitly does not imply some kind of false separation between doctrine and prayer.

The bishops of the United States offer the USCCA as a "Source of Meaning and Hope" in a hectic world. The *Catechism* concludes with a brief summary highlighting the main theme of each of the four parts. It speaks again of the role of the Church over time and calls its members "to transform society not by power but by persuasion and by example." It challenges the view that the nation's founders saw religion as a purely private matter. "Catholics," it says, "must participate in political life and bring to bear upon it... what they have learned about human nature, human destiny, and God's will for human beings from his self-revelation." The purpose of the *Catechism* is to provide Catholics "with a knowledge and understanding of the Gospel that enables them to give an account of their faith... with clarity and persuasiveness."

11. Ecumenism and Inter-Faith Dialogue

The Second Vatican Council's Decree on Ecumenism, *Unitatis Redintegratio*, states that the restoration of unity among Christians is a concern that "involves the whole Church, faithful and clergy alike" (n. 5). The Decree outlined general principles that guide the Catholic approach to ecumenism. Subsequently the Vatican Secretariat for the Promotion of the Unity of Christians published a *Directory Concerning Ecumenical Matters* in two installments (1967, 1970) that the Pontifical Council for Promoting Christian Unity later updated under the title *Directory for the Application of Principles and Norms on Ecumenism* (1993).

In 1998 the Council issued another document, *The Ecumenical Dimension in the Formation of Those Engaged in Pastoral Work* that makes more explicit points made in the 1993 Directory, especially in Chapter Three, regarding the settings and means through which ecumenical formation takes place. The Congregations for the Doctrine of the Faith and Catholic Education were involved in its preparation.

Meanwhile in October 1974 Pope John Paul II established a special Commission for Religious Relations with the Jews, joined to the Secretariat for Promoting Christian Unity, to foster religious relations between Jews and Catholics—and to do so eventually in collaboration with other Christians. The purpose of the Commission is to implement correctly and effectively the intention of the Second Vatican Council. Its first act was to publish *Guidelines and Suggestions for Implementing the Conciliar Declaration "Nostra aetate"* (n. 4). In 1982 the Commission issued another document that further elaborated and explained the *Guidelines and Suggestions* to remedy "a painful ignorance of the history and traditions of Judaism, of which only negative aspects and often caricature seem to form part of the stock of ideas of many Christians" (Conclusion). (See, *The Bible, the Jews, and the Death of Jesus. A Collection of Catholic Documents*. Washington, DC: United States Conference of Catholic Bishops, 2004.)

Directory for the Application of Principles and Norms on Ecumenism

The *Directory for the Application of Principles and Norms on Ecumenism* (APNE) cites the publication of the Codes of Canon Law for the Latin and Eastern Churches (1983, 1990) and the *Catechism of the Catholic Church* (1992) (See, *The Ecumenical Christian Dialogues and the Catechism of the Catholic Church*, edited by Jeffrey Gros, F.S.C. and Daniel S. Mulhall. New York/Mahwah, NJ: Paulist Press, 2006) as the reason for the revision: these documents created "in ecumenical matters a disciplinary situation... which is partly new" (n. 2). The APNE itself provides an outline of its five chapters (n. 7):

1. "The Search for Christian Unity" reaffirms the Catholic commitment to ecumenism based on the doctrinal principles of Vatican II "inspired and guided by a true understanding of the Church as a sacrament or instrumental sign of intimate union with God, and of unity of the whole human race." (n. 9)

2. "Organization in the Catholic Church at the Service of Christian Unity" lists the persons and structures involved in promoting ecumenism at all levels and the norms that direct their activity. (nn. 37-54)

3. "Ecumenical Formation in the Catholic Church" identifies the categories of people to be formed, including those responsible for formation; the aim and methods of formation; its doctrinal and practical aspects. (nn. 55-91)

4. "Communion in Life and Spiritual Activity among the Baptized" explains the communion that exists among Christians on the basis of the sacramental bond of Baptism, and the norms for sharing in prayer and other spiritual activities. (nn. 92-160)

5. "Ecumenical Cooperation, Dialogue and Common Witness" describes principles, different forms, and norms for cooperation between Christians. (nn. 161-218)

At the beginning of Chapter Three, APNE cites the Decree of Vatican II to reiterate that "concern for restoring unity pertains to the whole Church, faithful and clergy alike," and that "all the faithful are called up to make a personal commitment toward promoting increasing communion with other Christians" (n. 55). Ecumenism requires a pedagogy and formation adapted to concrete situations and "respects the need for gradualness in an effort of continual renewal and of change in attitudes" (n. 56). Among the means of formation the *Directory* lists "hearing and studying the Word of God," preaching, catechesis, liturgy, the spiritual life, and collaboration in social and charitable initiatives (nn. 59-64).

The APNE follows Pope John Paul II's Apostolic Exhortation *Catechesi tradendae* in stating that catechesis, in addition to the teaching of doctrine, is "initiation into the Christian life as a whole, with full anticipation in the sacraments of the Church" (n. 61). It can help form "a genuine ecumenical attitude" by observing the following directives:

A. First, it should expound clearly, with charity and with due firmness the whole doctrine of the Catholic Church respecting in a particular way the order of the hierarchy of truths and avoiding expressions and ways of presenting doctrine which would be an obstacle to dialogue.

B. When speaking of other Churches and ecclesial Communities, it is important to present their teaching correctly and honestly. Among those elements by which the Church itself is built up and given life, some—even many and very valuable ones—are to be found outside the visible limits of the Catholic Church. The Spirit of Christ, therefore, does not refuse to use these communities as means of salvation. Doing this also puts in relief the truths of faith held in common by various Christian confessions.

C. Catechesis will have an ecumenical dimension if it arouses and nourishes a true desire for unity and still more if it fosters real effort, including efforts in humility to purify ourselves, so as to remove obstacles on the way, not by facile doctrinal omissions and concessions, but by aiming at that perfect unity which the Lord wills and by using the means that He wills.

D. Catechesis will, moreover, have this ecumenical dimension if it sets out to prepare children and young people as well as adults to live in contact with other Christians, maturing as Catholics while growing in respect for the faith of others.

E. It can do this by discerning the possibilities offered by the distinction between the truths of faith and their modes of expression; by mutual striving to understand and esteem what is good in each other's theological traditions; by making clear that dialogue has created new relationships which, if they are well understood, can lead to collaboration and peace.

F. The Apostolic Exhortation *Catechesi tradendae* should be a point of reference in the elaboration of new catechisms which are prepared in local Churches under the authority of the Bishops.

The parish, gathered around the Eucharist, should be the place of authentic ecumenical witness. Along with preaching, especially the homily, catechesis helps educate its members in the ecumenical spirit (n. 67). The same study programs and norms regarding the ecumenical formation of ordained ministers that the APNE spells out in detail need to be adapted for catechists, teachers and other lay collaborators in pastoral work (n. 83).

Chapter Four describes ways that Christians can live and pray together, and Chapter Five describes other forms of ecumenical cooperation, including catechesis, that promote and give witness to Christian unity. In situations of religious pluralism, cooperation in the field of catechesis can enrich the life of the Catholic Church as well as that of other Churches and ecclesial Communities and, in so far as possible, give a common witness to the truth of the Gospel. The basis of this cooperation, its conditions and its limits are spelled out in paragraph 33 of *Catechesi tradendae* that APNE quotes in full:

Such experiences have a theological foundation in the elements shared by all Christians. But the communion of faith between Catholics and other Christians is not complete and perfect; in certain cases there are even profound divergences. Consequently, this ecumenical collaboration is by its very nature limited; it must never mean a 'reduction' to a common minimum. Furthermore, catechesis does not consist merely in the teaching of doctrine; it also means initiating into the whole of Christian life, bringing full participation in the sacraments of the Church. Therefore, where there is an experience of ecumenical collaboration in the field of catechesis, care must be taken that the education of Catholics in the Catholic Church should be well ensured in matters of doctrine and of Christian living. (n. 188)

APNE notes that in some countries a form of Christian teaching common to Catholics and other Christians is imposed by the state, which selects text-books and dictates the content of the course. In these cases, while appreciating the ecumenical value of such teaching, it still remains indispensable to provide a specifically Catholic catechesis for Catholic children (n. 189).

APNE also envisages the teaching of religion in collaboration with members of religions other than Christian. In such cases "a special effort should be made" to present the Christian message in a way that "highlights the unity of faith between Christians about fundamental matters while at the same time explaining the divisions that do exist and the steps that are being taken to overcome them" (n. 190).

The Ecumenical Dimension in the Formation of Those Engaged in Pastoral Work

The stated intention of the 1998 document *The Ecumenical Dimension in the Formation of Those Engaged in Pastoral Work* (EDFPW) issued by the Pontifical Council for Promoting Christian Unity was to reaffirm the principles of the earlier APNE and provide practical directives because ecumenical formation "cannot be limited to a mere course of information on the ecumenical movement" (Preface). It needs to be read together with the passages in APNE (and other documents) referred to in the footnotes (n. 1).

It is vital that everyone who has a role in animating Christian formation, including catechists and others formally involved in religious education, should themselves have a thorough ecumenical formation (n. 3). Catechesis, along with hearing and studying the Word of God, preaching, liturgy, and the spiritual life, is a principal means (n. 4). Because circumstances vary significantly from one country to another, it is neither feasible nor desirable to attempt a blueprint that would be applicable in every formation program. However, the 1998 EDFPW devotes two chapters to "important guidelines" to ensure that an ecumenical dimension permeates every subject taught, and for a specific course of study in ecumenism.

The first chapter explains in some detail three key elements that should be included in every theological discipline: (1) hermeneutics; (2) the "hierarchy of truths"; and (3) the fruits of ecumenical dialogues. It outlines "a fundamental ecumenical method" that comprises an analytical presentation of (1) elements Christians hold in common; (2) points of disagreement; and (3) the results of ecumenical dialogues to be used in the teaching of each discipline. (Pope John Paul II's encyclical letter *Ut unum sint* can assist with regard to the last.) The document recommends several practical ways of implementing these proposals that include the preparation of local directories or guidelines that apply the general principles and norms to particular situations.

The second chapter outlines in great detail the contents of a "compulsory" course of study in ecumenism. Following APNE, it says the course might be organized in two stages: a general introduction that makes it clear that the aim of ecumenism is the restoration of full visible unity among all Christians (n. 58); and an exploration of topics that may require more specialized study, the biblical and doctrinal foundations of ecumenism. This latter stage will also include a consideration of papal encyclicals and other official documents of the Catholic Church as well as official statements of other Churches and Ecclesial Communities. Towards the end it again makes the point that genuine ecumenical formation must not remain solely academic; it should also include ecumenical experience and that the ongoing or permanent formation of ordained ministers and pastoral workers is vital for "continual evolution in the ecumenical movement" (n. 91).

Guidelines and Suggestions for Implementing the Conciliar Declaration "Nostra aetate"

The *Guidelines and Suggestions* issued by the Commission for Religious Relations with the Jews (1974) refers to number four of Vatican II's "Declaration on the Relations of the Church to Non-Christian Religions." The document, notable for its eminently practical nature, does not propose a Christian theology of Judaism. The Preamble recalls the Council's condemnation of anti-Semitism and the obligation of reciprocal understanding and renewed mutual esteem. It expresses hope that Christians will come to a better knowledge of the religious tradition of Judaism and of the manner in which Jews identify themselves. The text then proposes a series of concrete suggestions:

A. The first section calls for fraternal dialogue and the establishment of deep doctrinal research. Prayer in common is proposed as a means of encounter.

B. Although there are many links between the Christian liturgy and the Jewish liturgy, caution is needed in dealing with commentaries on biblical texts, and with liturgical explanations and translations.

C. The third part concerning teaching and education notes that although a great deal of work is still to be done, the study and research of scholars and the beginning of dialogue has contributed to a better understanding of Judaism and its relationship to Christianity: It is the same God who speaks both in the old and new Covenants. At the time of Christ, Judaism embraced many different trends and spiritual, religious, social, and cultural values. Jesus was born of the Jewish people as were his first disciples, and he used teaching methods similar to those employed by rabbis of his time. When he revealed himself as Messiah and Son of God, he did so as the fulfillment and perfection of the earlier Revelation. His passion and death cannot be blamed upon all the Jews then living, without distinction, nor upon the Jews of today. The history of Judaism, though influenced by the coming of Christ, continues a tradition still rich in religious values. The Church awaits the day, known to God alone, when all peoples will address the Lord in a single voice.

D. The final section deals with possibilities of common social action in the context of a search for social justice and peace.

Notes on the Correct Way to Present the Jews and Judaism in Preaching and Catechesis

The Introduction ("Preliminary Considerations") begins with words of Pope John Paul II. Our aim, he said, should be "that Catholic teaching at its different levels, in catechesis to children and young people, presents Jews and Judaism, not only in an honest and objective manner, free from prejudices and without any offense, but also with full awareness of the heritage common [to Jews and Christians]." The *Notes* then recall Chapter Three of the *Guidelines and Suggestions* that recommends special attention be paid to, among other resources, catechisms and religious textbooks, and that the effective use of these means presupposes the thorough formation of instructors and educators in training schools, seminaries, and universities.

The *Notes* are grouped under six headings that reaffirm and elaborate on the earlier *Guidelines and Suggestions.*

Part One – Religious Teaching and Judaism

Because Christianity and Judaism are "linked together at the very level of their identity," the presence of Jews and Judaism should be organically integrated and not simply occupy an occasional and marginal place in catechesis (n. 2). The theologian and the catechist need to show how promise and fulfillment throw light on each other; there is continuity and newness in the two covenants; the singularity of the people of the Old Testament is open, in the divine vision, to a universal extension; and the uniqueness of the Jewish people is meant to have the force of an example (n. 5). Because of the Church's divine mission as "the all-embracing means of salvation," the Church and Judaism cannot be seen as two parallel ways of salvation. The Church must witness to Christ as the Redeemer for all (n. 7). The importance of precise, objective, and rigorously accurate teaching on Judaism is made urgent by the danger of anti-Semitism that is always ready to reappear under different guises (n. 8).

Part Two – Relations Between the Old and New Testament

In emphasizing the unity of biblical Revelation and the permanent value of the Old Testament an endnote explains, "Old" does not mean "out of date" or "out-worn". "We continue to use the expression Old Testament because it is traditional (cf. 2 Cor. 3:14)." The events of the Old Testament, in the sight of God who reveals his purpose, take on universal and exemplary significance. They concern not only the Jews; they touch us personally (n. 2). From apostolic times the Church, especially in the Liturgy and writings of the Church Fathers, relied on a typological interpretation that read the Old Testament as preparation and, in certain aspects, a foreshadowing of the New (cf. Heb. 5:5-10).

Christ is henceforth the key and point of reference to theScriptures. It should be stressed that the Church reads the Old Testament in light of the event of the dead and risen Christ. Thus Christian identity and Jewish identity should be carefully distinguished in the respective reading of the Bible, but this does nothing to hinder Christians from profiting from the traditions of the Jewish reading (n. 6). In underlining the eschatological dimension of Christianity we reach a greater awareness that the people of God are tending toward a like end in the future, the coming or return of the Messiah, even if they start from two different points of view. Jews and Christians meet in a comparable hope, founded on the same promise made to Abraham (cf. Gen. 12:1-3; Heb. 6:13-18). Attentive to the same hope in him who is the master of history, we must prepare the world for the coming of the Messiah by working together for social justice, rights of persons, and for social and international reconciliation. Transmitted by catechesis, such a vision would teach young Christians, going beyond simple dialogue, to cooperate with Jews (n. 11).

Part Three – Jewish Roots of Christianity

Jesus was and always remained a Jew. He submitted himself to the law, extolled respect for it, and invited obedience to it (nn. 1, 2). His relations with the Pharisees were not always or wholly polemical. He shared with the majority of Palestinian Jews of that time pharisaic doctrines like the resurrection of the body, almsgiving, prayer, fasting, and the liturgical practice of addressing God as Father, the priority of the commandment to love God and neighbor. This is also true of Paul who considered his membership as a title of honor. It is noteworthy, too, that the Pharisees are not mentioned in accounts of the Passion. An exclusively negative picture of the Pharisees is inaccurate and unjust (nn. 5-8). All of this helps us understand better what St. Paul meant about the "root" and "branches" (Rom. 11:16ff). Christianity finds its origin in the Jewish milieu and more deeply still in the "design of God" realized in the Patriarchs, Moses and the Prophets, down to its consummation in Christ Jesus.

Part Four – The Jews in the New Testament

The *Notes* explains that "an objective presentation of the Jewish people in the New Testament should take account of these various facts":

A. The Gospels are the outcome of long and complicated editorial work. Hence it cannot be ruled out that some references hostile or less than favorable to the Jews have their historical context in conflicts between the nascent Church and the Jewish community. Certain controversies reflect Christian-Jewish-relations long after the time of Jesus. To establish this is of capital importance if we wish to bring out the meaning of certain Gospel texts for the Christians of today. All this should be taken into account when preparing catechesis and homilies for the last weeks of Lent and Holy Week.

B. It is clear that there were conflicts between Jesus and certain categories of Jews of his time, among them Pharisees, from the beginning of his ministry (cf. Mk. 2:1-11.24; 3:6 etc.).

C. There is, moreover, the sad fact that the majority of the Jewish people and its authorities did not believe in Jesus—a fact not merely of history but of theological bearing, of which St. Paul tries hard to plumb the meaning (Rom. chap. 9-11).

D. This fact, accentuated as the Christian mission developed, especially among the pagans, led inevitably to a rupture between Judaism and the young Church, now irreducibly separated and divergent in faith, and this stage of affairs is reflected in the texts of the New Testament and particularly in the Gospel. There is no question of playing down or glossing over this rupture; that could only prejudice the identity of either side. Nevertheless it certainly does not cancel the spiritual "bond" of which the Council speaks (*Nostra aetate,* 4) and which we propose to dwell on here.

E. Reflecting on this in the light of Scripture, notably of the chapters cited from the epistle to the Romans, Christians should never forget that the faith is a free gift of God (cf. Rom. 9:12) and that we should never judge the consciences of others.

F. There is no putting the Jews who knew Jesus and did not believe in him, or those who opposed the preaching of the apostles, on the same plane with Jews who came after or those of today. If the responsibility of the former remains a mystery hidden with God (cf. Rom. 11:25), the latter are in an entirely different situation. Vatican II in the declaration on *Religious Liberty* teaches that "all men are to be immune from coercion" in such wise that in matters religious no one is to be forced to act in a manner contrary to his own beliefs." (n. 2). This is one of the bases—proclaimed by the Council—on which Judeo-Christian dialogue rests.

G. The delicate question of responsibility for the death of Christ must be looked at from the standpoint of the conciliar declaration *Nostra aetate,* 4 and of *Guidelines and Suggestions* (III): "What happened in (Christ's) passion cannot be blamed upon all the Jews then living without distinction nor upon the Jews of today." The *Catechism of the Council of Trent* teaches that Christian sinners are more to blame for the death of Christ than those few Jews who brought it about - they indeed "knew not what they did" (cf. Lk. 23:24) (See, *Catechism of the Catholic Church*, nn. 597, 598) and we know it only too well (Pars I, caput V, Quaest, XI). In the same way and for the same reason, "the Jews should not be presented as repudiated or cursed by God, as if such views followed from the holy Scriptures" (*Nostra aetate,* 4), even though it is true that "the Church is the new people of God" (*Nostra aetate,* 4).

Part Five – The Liturgy

Jews and Christians find in the Bible the very substance of their liturgy. The Liturgy of the Word originates in Judaism. The prayer of Hours and other liturgical texts have parallels in Judaism. The Eucharistic prayers also draw inspiration from the Jewish tradition. Jewish practices can greatly help us to understand better certain aspects of the life of the Church as is particularly evident in the great feasts of the liturgical year like the Passover.

Part Six – Judaism and Christianity in History

The history of Israel continued after 70 A.D. in numerous Diaspora that allowed Israel to carry to the whole world an often heroic witness of its fidelity to the one God. Christians are invited to understand their religious attachment to the memory of the land of their forefathers that finds its roots in biblical tradition without making their own any particular religious interpretation of its relationship to the State of Israel. The political options of the State of Israel should be envisaged in reference to the common principles of international law.

The permanence of Israel is a historic fact and a sign to be interpreted within God's design. We rid ourselves of the idea of a people punished, preserved as a living argument for Christian apologetic. We must remind ourselves how the permanence of Israel is accompanied by a continuous spiritual fecundity down through modern times that greatly helps us to understand certain aspects of the life of the Church. Catechesis should help people to understand the meaning for the Jews of the extermination during the years 1939-1945 and its consequences. In light of the spiritual bonds and historical links binding the Church to Judaism and in light of the dignity of the human person education and catechesis should be concerned with the problem of racism, still active in different forms of anti-Semitism.

12. Catechetical Personnel

A*d gentes,* the Decree of Second Vatican Council on the Church's Missionary Activity, recognized the importance of catechists. Wherever there has been missionary activity, catechists have made and continue to make "an outstanding and indispensable contribution to the spread of the faith and the Church" (n. 17). The Decree assigned the task of directing and coordinating missionary work throughout the world to the Sacred Congregation for the Propagation of the Faith, now known as the Congregation for the Evangelization of Peoples (CEP). In 1970, the CEP published some practical directives for catechists that, after "a wide-ranging consultation with bishops and catechetical centers," were revised and updated in a *Guide for Catechists* (1993). It presents a synthesis of official statements beginning with the documents of Vatican II. Although it had taken shape before the *Catechism of the Catholic Church,* the final text of the Guide links it, particularly in the notes, to themes in the catechism. The *General Directory for Catechesis* refers to the *Guide* several times, especially in Part Five. The *Guide* focuses primarily on full-time lay catechists in mission lands, but its description of their roles has universal validity.

Late in 2006 the United States Conference of Catholic Bishops (USCCB) issued a pastoral statement *Co-Workers in the Vineyard of the Lord: A Resource for Guiding the Development of Lay Ecclesial Ministry.* It outlines and applies the theological principles underlying lay ministry and, in a third part, presents a rationale for the authorization and certification of lay ministers. It cites a document developed jointly by the National Association for Lay Ministry, the National Federation for Catholic Youth Ministry, and the National Conference for Catechetical Leadership, *National Certification Standards for Lay Ecclesial Ministers Serving as Parish Catechetical Leaders, Youth Ministry Leaders, Pastoral Associates, and Parish Life Coordinators.* Previous to its publication in 2003, these standards were approved by the USCCB's Commission on Certification and Accreditation. The *National Certification Standards* were then expanded in 2006 in collaboration with the National Association of Pastoral Musicians to include Directors of Music Ministries. The expanded edition was also approved by the USCCB's Commission on Certification and Accreditation. *Co-Workers* says "the standards are a resource that can be helpful in identifying prospective lay ecclesial ministers as well as in setting goals for the formation and certification of those who are completing programs."

Guide for Catechists

The Guide has three main parts in 37 numbered sections.

(See, n. 1) The Introduction explains that the *Guide* is addressed first to lay catechists themselves, and also to bishops, priests, religious, formators, and all members of the ecclesial community. It is based on information that came from a wide-ranging consultation with bishops and catechetical centers in mission territories. The three parts treat the principal aspects of the catechist's vocation; the selection and training, missionary and pastoral tasks of catechists, and their remuneration. The directives are general, leaving it to pastors to make them more specific in keeping with the requirements and possibilities of the individual Churches.

Part One – An Apostle Ever Relevant

(See, n. 2) The catechist's vocation in a missionary Church is twofold: (1) In addition to the specific task of catechizing, the catechist collaborates in a general way in whatever apostolic services are useful for the building up the Church. (2) The Church's Magisterium and legislation clearly recognize that the identity of catechists in mission territories differs from that in the older Churches.

(See, n. 3) The Magisterium makes frequent reference to the role of catechists "in mission lands." The description given by Pope John Paul II in the encyclical *Redemptoris missio*, and the description in the Code of Canon Law (785; see, cc. 773-780) corresponds with that given by the CEP in its 1970 Plenary Assembly: "The catechist is a lay person specially appointed by the Church, in accordance with local needs, to make Christ known, loved, and followed by those who do not yet know Him and by the faithful themselves."

(See, n. 4) In mission territory, catechists fall into categories of full-time and part-time catechists. The tasks assigned to catechists who "collaborate in different forms of apostolate" with ordained ministers are multiple: catechizing catechumens and those already baptized; leading community prayer, especially at the Sunday liturgy in the absence of a priest; helping the sick and presiding at funerals; training other catechists and guiding volunteer catechists in their work; taking charge of pastoral initiatives and organizing parish functions; helping the poor and working for human development and justice. Catechists may be old or young, male or female, married or single, and these factors should be taken into account in assigning tasks in various cultural settings. Finally, there are religious men and women who, carrying out catechesis, are able to bear a unique witness because of their own special consecration.

(See, n. 5) The number of workers is important, but the character of the catechist is of prime importance in the criteria for selecting catechists and the program for training and guiding them. Concrete programs should be drawn up, adequate structures and financial support provided, and qualified formators secured to provide the catechists with a solid formation. In the young Churches, where the services of the lay apostolate are multiplying, specialized catechists should be trained for challenges which already face us today and will become greater in the future: urbanization, increasing numbers going on to third-level education, the world of youngsters, migrant and refugees, political changes, the influence of the mass media, etc.

(See, n. 6) The need for a spirituality proper to catechists springs from their vocation and mission. It is closely bound up with their status as lay Christians, made participants in Christ's prophetic, priestly, and kingly offices.

(See, n. 7) The office of catechist is basically that of communicating God's word, and so the fundamental spiritual attitude should be one of openness to this word, contained in revelation, preached by the Church, celebrated in the liturgy and lived out in the lives of the saints.

(See, n. 8) Before *doing* catechesis one must *be* a catechist whose life confirms the message. Authenticity of life means a life of prayer, experience of God, and fidelity to the action the Holy Spirit. The more intense and real one's spiritual life is, the more convincing will his or her witness and activity be.

(See, n. 9) By reason of their baptism and special vocation, catechists cannot but feel moved by missionary zeal and Christ's words: "Other sheep I have that are not of this fold, and these too I must lead" (Jn. 10:16); and "go out to the whole world and preach the gospel to every creature" (Mt. 16:15). The final stamp of the missionary spirit is the cross. Catechists should be prepared to live in hope the mystery of the Death and Resurrection of Christ in the midst of difficult situations and personal suffering.

(See, n. 10) The spirituality of the catechist, like that of every other Christian, will be enriched by a deep devotion to the Mother of God. Catechists will find in Mary a simple and effective model for themselves and others.

(See, n. 11) Catechists will try to promote communication and communion and try to understand the needs of the community as a whole and particular needs of various groups: young people and adults; students and workers; catechumens preparing for Baptism; etc. They should give special attention to the sick and aged, and show sensitivity in dealing with people in difficult situations: couples in irregular marriages; the children of broken marriages; etc.

(See, n. 12) Like other forms of evangelization, catechesis works to bring the Gospel into the heart of different cultures. The process of inculturation takes time, as it is a deep, gradual, and all-embracing process. Catechists should be specially prepared to understand their own culture and become aware of the guidelines that the Church has laid down. The Gospel is a force for renewal, and can rectify elements in cultures that do not conform to it. Popular piety, understood as an expression of Catholic devotion colored by local values, traditions, and attitudes is a privileged form of inculturation of the Gospel. Catechists should contribute to inculturation by fitting into the overall pastoral plan of the local church and avoiding adventures into particular experiments that might upset the faithful.

(See, n. 13) The preaching of the Gospel and the promotion of human development are both included in the Church's mission. To be incarnated in real life means to take the values of the Gospel into the economic, social, and political fields. Catechists, living as lay people in society, are in a position to interpret and try to bring solutions to personal and social problems in light of the Gospel. When necessary they should have the courage to speak out for the weak and defend their rights. The preferential option for the poor that Pope John Paul II described as "the driving force of mission," means that the poor should have a prior claim on the attention of catechists without neglecting others. They should also pay special attention to other groups in need: the oppressed, persecuted, marginalized, handicapped, prisoners, drug addicts, those suffering from AIDS, etc.

(See, n. 14) Catechists should have a deep desire for Christian unity and promote an ecumenical spirit in the community. They should willingly engage in dialogue with Christians of other denominations and commit themselves generously to ecumenical initiatives. They should avoid stirring up useless rivalries and help the faithful to live in harmony and respect for other Christians. They should join other believers in working for peace.

(See, n. 15) Inter-religious dialogue is another way of making Christ known, and it is essential that the Catholic Church maintain good relations with those of other faiths. Catechists should be taught to realize its value and put it into practice following the Church's guidelines. They should acquire accurate knowledge of the religions practiced in these areas, their history and organization, the values in them which can be a "preparation for the Gospel," as well as their limitations and errors. Dialogue, however, does not dispense them from proclamation that the Church is the ordinary way of salvation and that only she possesses the fullness of revealed truth and salvific means. There should be cooperation with non-Christian religious bodies in bringing about peace, justice, development, etc. Even when it see,ms difficult or misunderstood, one should continue to believe in dialogue.

(See, n. 16) Catechists would see,m to be particularly suitable for counteracting the spread and influence of sects. Catechists should first of all study what the sects teach and particularly the points on which they attack the Church. They should give positive instruction and encourage the Christian community to greater fervor so as to forestall the encroachment of the sects. Constructive dialogue with many sects, intolerant and hostile toward Catholicism, is often not possible, but here too one must have respect and understanding for persons.

Part Two – Choice and Formation of Catechists

(See, n. 17) Because of the varying levels of religious maturity in different ecclesial communities, the scarcity of suitable personnel, financial difficulties and other factors, it is difficult to lay down universal criteria, but these difficulties should not lead to lower standards. Pastors should aim for candidates of high quality and, even though the goal may be achieved only gradually, they should not settle for less. They should explain the role of catechists so as to awaken in the community, especially among the young, an interest in this form of ecclesial service. "A fulfilled, responsible, and dynamic catechist... appreciated and properly remunerated, is the best promoter of other vocations."

(See, n. 18) The criteria for choosing candidates should be precise, realistic, and controllable, adapted to local conditions by the local authorities, who are best able to judge the needs and possibilities of the community. In addition to human and moral qualities, criteria for judging the *person* of the catechist should include motivation, faith manifested in their way of living, love for the Church, apostolic spirit, and missionary zeal. There should be criteria governing the *process* of selection, including the role of the community and official approbation of the bishop or his representative. Each training center will have its own criteria—scholastic achievement, conditions for participation, etc.—for acceptance.

(See, n. 19) The general formation of catechists should be concerned with developing the person's whole character and personality, with specific attention given to the particular tasks they will be charged with (e.g. preaching the word, presiding at liturgical prayers, etc.). In the words of Pope John Paul II, "To set high standards means both to provide a thorough basic training and to keep it constantly updated."

(See, n. 20) Catechists must integrate the values and demands of their *spiritual* life with their *secular* life and the requirements of an *apostolic* life. Temperamental, intellectual, or emotional traits that are obstacles to an ordered lifestyle must be overcome. The unity and harmony in their personalities should be built upon "a deep intimacy with Christ and the Father."

(See, n. 21) It should be clear from the beginning that candidates possess basic human qualities that can be further developed. The aim of catechetical formation is to build on these qualities and add the necessary skills for a fruitful ministry.

(See, n. 22) The need of catechists to have a deep spiritual life is the most important aspect of their personality and the one to be most stressed in formation. Sanctity of life, lived as a lay apostle, is the ideal to be striven for. Key elements in the prayer life of catechists should include regular reception of the Eucharist, lived liturgy, recital of parts of the Divine Office, daily meditation, personal prayer, frequent reception of the Sacrament of Penance, and participation in spiritual retreats. Spiritual direction should be available to help catechists in their spiritual life.

(See, n. 23) Candidates should be able to follow a course of "higher religious education" based on the program for "doctrinal, anthropological, and methodological formation" presented by the *General Directory for Catechesis*. There should be an overall vision of faith that brings unity and harmony to the knowledge acquired, to the catechists' personalities, and to their apostolic service. The *Catechism of the Catholic Church* contains an orderly synthesis of Revelation and Church teaching and a mine of knowledge for the catechetical mission. To provide adequate training requires personnel, structures, and financial support. In view of the importance of catechists, these challenges should be faced courageously, with realistic and intelligent planning.

(See, n. 24) The theoretical part of the pastoral course will deal with the different types of work and the different groups to be addressed (e.g. children, adults, etc.). The practical part will include exercises, especially at the beginning, under the direction of an experienced catechist. Special attention will be paid to the sacraments, not forgetting the Anointing of the Sick, as catechists often have to assist the sick and dying to accept their sufferings in a spirit of faith. The section on "elements of methodology" in the GDC should be consulted.

(See, n. 25) The missionary dimension is an essential part of the work and identity of catechists. They should be taught, therefore, theoretically and practically, how to: proclaim the truth about Jesus Christ whom God sent into the world for the salvation of all; meet followers of other religions in a spirit of openness and dialogue; introduce catechumens to the practice of evangelical norms and the community life of the People of God, and help candidates prepare for the sacraments of Christian initiation.

(See, n. 26) The role of catechists is eminently ecclesial. Their work is always carried out in communion with the local and universal Church. Churches are encouraged to confer a canonical mandate or mission to bring out the link between the catechists' work and that of Christ and his Church. The bishop or his delegate should present catechists with "some suitable sign" such a crucifix or a bible.

(See, n. 27) When we speak about the agents of formation, catechists should be convinced that the most important formator is Christ himself, who forms them through the Holy Spirit. The catechists themselves are formators in that they are responsible for their own interior growth. The community as a whole is called to cooperate in the formation of its catechists, providing them with an atmosphere of acceptance and encouragement. Formators, in the strict sense, i.e. those designated by the Church to train catechists, should be chosen with care, good Christians, with proper intellectual qualifications, and personal experience in the catechetical field. It is good when they work as a team.

(See, n. 28) Although initial formation, the basic training period, differs according to local conditions, it should meet the following criteria: knowledge of the candidates and their background; training should be rooted in the real life situations of the people and be methodical and gradual. The training should be based on experience and aimed at developing the whole person. It should promote dialogue between the candidate and God, the formators and the community. The candidates should be helped to draw up a life program with realistic goals and means to achieve them. Spiritual direction is important, as it touches on depths of a person's soul.

(See, n. 29) Catechists should pursue a process of ongoing formation during the whole course of their service. In the early stage of their apostolate it will be largely the reinforcement of the basic training. Later, it will entail updating so as to keep in touch with developments in theology and changing circumstances. It is can be a source of renewal and revitalization in the face of burn out and discouragement. Every effort should be made to overcome obstacles to ongoing formation (distance, lack of funds, resources, personnel, etc.). There should be organized programs by catechetical centers and other agencies covering every aspect of catechists' work; haphazard, individual initiatives are not enough. Ongoing formation depends to a large extent on the catechists recognizing the need for renewal and updating.

(See, n. 30) Church documents stress the importance of special centers or schools for training catechists. They vary in size and structure, methods and length of program, and make-up of the student body. It is important to promote contacts between centers, especially at a national level. The centers should be places of research and reflection on themes such as inculturation, interreligious dialogue, pastoral methods, etc. In addition, there should be courses and encounters as means of ongoing formation, and each diocese should provide books and other teaching aids necessary for catechetical training. Proposing high objectives in formation is not enough; centers and dioceses must be able to identify and use efficacious means as well.

Part Three – The Responsibilities towards Catechists

(See, n. 31) Proper financial remuneration for catechists is a difficult problem. Their salary, especially when they have families to support, must take into account the full cost of living. Inadequate salaries have negative consequences on the choice of candidates, because the more capable can take better-paid jobs; on commitment, because they might see,k other work to make up the deficit; on formation, because training courses are beyond their means. In many cultures a job is respected only if it is a well-paid one.

(See, n. 32) Remuneration must be considered a matter of justice and not mere benevolence. Both full-time and part-time catechists must be paid according to precise norms. Special consideration has to be given to old, invalid, and sick catechists. The good will of volunteers who are willing to devote part of their free time to catechetical work is certainly to be encouraged. The problem of remuneration has to be solved basically by the local Church. It is important that the faithful be educated to support their work.

(See, n. 33) Catechists should have a place of honor in their communities and be well represented in pastoral councils and other diocesan and parish committees. Their ministry is such that catechists should be strengthened and their numbers increased by an adequate vocational program.

(See, n. 34) Bishops and Episcopal Conferences are urged to continue and to even increase their attention and care for catechists. They should, as far as possible, have a personal relationship with them. They should draw up national or diocesan catechetical directories so as to apply and adapt the guidelines in this *Guide* and other Church documents to local conditions. They provide teaching aids and resources for the formation of catechists, and, where possible, establish and improve catechetical centers.

(See, n. 35) Priests, especially pastors, should have a particular interest in catechists who share with them the task of instructing people in the faith. Parish priests should encourage catechists to be creative and look on them as cooperators and not as subordinates carrying out instructions. Future priests should be taught to value and respect catechists and apostles and fellow-workers in the Lord's vineyard.

(See, n. 36) Formators of catechists should be aware of the responsibility that is theirs. Every diocese will do its best to have a team of formators, made up of priests, brothers, sisters, and lay people, who can be sent to parishes to help in the selection and training of catechists.

(See, n. 37) In conclusion, the *Guide* quotes the words of Pope John Paul II to the catechists of Angola:

> So many times it has fallen to you to strengthen and build up the young Christian communities, and even to found new ones through the first proclamation of the gospel. If missionaries could not be there for this first proclamation or had to leave before it could be followed up, it was you, the catechists, who instructed the catechumens, prepared people for the sacraments, taught the faith, and were leaders of the Christian community. Give thanks to the Lord for the gift of your vocation, through which Christ has called you from among other men and women to be instruments of his salvation. Respond with generosity to your vocation and your names will be written in heaven. (cf. Lk. 10:20)

National Certification Standards for Lay Ecclesial Ministers

Although each of the national associations—NALM, NCCL, NFCYM, and NPM—that developed the *Standards* has its own mission statement, goals, organizational structures, and constituencies, as described in the Introduction, they share a common understanding of lay ministry. Lay ministry is partly a matter of personal awareness and intentionality and partly a matter of recognition by official Church authority. Lay ministers bring their personal competencies and gifts to serve the Church's mission and do so with community authorization and support. National certification standards help shape the field of Church ministry by identifying core and specialized competencies. They have wide-ranging uses, both by lay ecclesial ministers themselves and by those who educate, support, or supervise them (pp. 2-3).

Part One – The Introduction

The Introduction presents a profile that describes expectations and ethics for the Lay Ecclesial Pastoral Associate (PA), Parish Life Coordinator

(PLC), Parish Catechetical Leader (PCL), Youth Ministry Leader (YML), and Director of Music Ministries (DMM). It outlines the specific responsibilities of each and, in some cases, their place on the organization chart of the diocese or parish (pp. 10-16).

The National Association for Lay Ministry developed a Code of Ethics designed as a guide for all lay ministers including Parish Associates and Parish Life Coordinators. Along with vision and mission statements, a code of ethics makes explicit the primary goals and core values of the organization. The code assists the individual's growth in professional identity and fosters a sense of unity and cohesion among members. It provides the framework for acceptable conduct in relationships and in the exercise of their ministry. The code, originally approved in 1994, was updated in 2003 to bring it into full compliance with the USCCB *Charter for the Protection of Children and Young People*. Both NCCL and NFCYM endorse the same code adding particulars peculiar to members of their own organizations.

Part Two – Certification Standards, Core Competencies, and Specialized Competencies

The heart of the document identifies five "certification standards," the "core competencies" connected with each and, where applicable, the "specialized competencies" required by a particular lay ministry. A glossary of terms defines certification standards as "published statements related to a ministry's focus, activities, and responsibilities that identify expectations of a competent minister." Professional organizations identify broad areas of ministerial competence as the norms by which an individual's performance may be assessed. They include specific knowledge, skills, abilities, attitudes, values, and/or traits. Core competencies are foundational and common to all five ministerial roles. Specialized competencies are either unique to a particular ministry or need to be expressed distinctly within the context of that ministry (pp. 41-42). The detailed list of the specialized competencies required of the Parish Catechetical Leader (PCL) for each certification standard is given in full.

Certification Standard One. A lay ecclesial minister demonstrates personal and spiritual maturity in ministry with the people of God. The core competencies focus on a balanced lifestyle, positive self-image, and appropriate relationships. The minister views God, Church, and the world in a holistic manner, engaging in communal worship and social justice.

The Parish Catechetical Leader (PCL) shall have the specialized competency to:

- Identify the various Christian spiritualities informing personal faith development.
- Recognize God's activity in personal life experiences and articulate this understanding with others.
- Give witness to compassion, justice, and charity in personal and pastoral relationships.
- Engage in intentional evangelization efforts consistent with the Church's mission.
- Identify with Jesus Christ by striving to acquire his zeal for forming disciples.

Certification Standard Two. A lay ecclesial minister identifies the call to formal and public ministry as a vocation rooted in baptism. This implies that the minister is competent to balance ministry, community, family, and personal and pastoral relationships. The minister shall identify with the universal Church and its global mission so that all ministerial activity flows from it.

The PCL shall have the specialized competency to:

- Engage in ongoing professional education and formation.
- Exercise flexibility in ministerial situations.
- Respond to the grace of leadership in catechetical ministry as a response to baptism.
- Give witness to the faith through worship and service.

Certification Standard Three. A lay ecclesial minister integrates knowledge of Catholic faith with ministry. Among the minister's core competencies will be the ability to know and integrate into ministerial practice: a theology of revelation as embodied in Scripture, tradition, and creation; a theology of God as one and triune; a theology of Church as it developed through history; a theology of liturgy/worship; a theology of sacraments; a theology of pastoral ministry; a theology of the moral life, including Catholic social teaching; a theology of Catholic spirituality and prayer; a respectful understanding of ecumenism and other faith traditions.

The PCL shall have the specialized competency to:

- Convey a Catholic understanding of conscience formation and the process of moral decision making.
- Identify the major themes relating to peace, justice, and Christian living in the sacred scriptures, the documents of Vatican Council II, encyclicals, and statements of the U.S. bishops.
- Explain in age-appropriate manner the core themes of Scripture and tradition.
- Articulate an understanding of the relations of the person of the Trinity with the mission of Jesus.
- Explain the Church's historical development and its relevance to the modern Church.
- Describe the activity of the Spirit in the Church as sustaining the proclamation of the Gospel in every corner of the world.
- Promote the ecclesiological renewal confirmed by Vatican II.
- Interpret life in the light of theology.
- Explore the meaning of inspiration, historical development, literary criticism, and biblical themes in an age-appropriate manner.
- Demonstrate an understanding and appreciation of the various rituals of the Catholic Church.
- Identify the elements of our Catholic faith that are rooted in Jewish traditions.
- Explore the impact of Mary and the saints on contemporary culture.
- Develop programs that create openness to interaction with persons of other faith traditions.

Certification Standard Four. A lay minister engages in pastoral activity that promotes evangelization, faith formation, community, and pastoral care with sensitivity to diverse situations. The list of core competencies includes the many and varied situations created by the needs of persons with disabilities, signs of physical and sexual abuse, crises of one kind or another, cultural diversity, etc.

The PCL shall have the specialized competency to:

- Guide and assist the catechists in parish catechetical ministry.
- Implement the catechumenal model in age-appropriate ways.
- Contribute to developing the parish as an evangelizing and catechizing community.
- Involve the family as an essential partner in the faith formation process.
- Demonstrate awareness and sensitivity to all ethnic and cultural groups in catechesis.
- Develop all opportunities for faith formation inclusive of and accessible to persons with disabilities.
- Implement approved liturgical principles for the celebration of the sacraments.
- Utilize a variety of prayer experiences in catechetical sessions.
- Serve as a resource regarding the catechetical dimension of initiation into the Church.
- Integrate Catholic social teachings into all faith formation.
- Promote faith formation as a lifelong process for all parishioners.
- Design, implement, and evaluate parish catechetical experiences.
- Promote media literacy and the use of media.

Certification Standard Five. A lay ecclesial minister provides effective leadership, administration, and service, in the spirit of collaboration. This standard requires visioning, planning, communication, decision-making, delegation, conflict management, and the ability to work with parish and diocesan personnel and structures.

The PCL shall have the specialized competency to:

- Direct the parish catechetical ministry.
- Develop parish catechetical policies in accord with diocesan policies and guidelines.
- Collaborate with the parish staff regarding catechetical ministry.
- Develop a comprehensive vision and plan for parish catechesis based on ecclesial catechetical documents.

- Advocate for quality education for students in both public and Catholic schools.
- Demonstrate effective oral and written communication skills for catechetical purposes.
- Provide orientations for and in-servicing of catechetical committee members and formation teams in their areas of responsibilities.
- Implement catechetical programs that are in accord with the Code of Canon Law and diocesan policies.
- Demonstrate an understanding of civil law and legal issues as these apply to the parish catechetical program.
- Develop professional skills for catechetical ministry.
- Exercise effective supervision of catechetical employees and volunteers.
- Recognize and foster leadership ability among volunteers.
- Demonstrate the ability to motivate others.

A table correlates each of the core certification standards with section in the USCCB pastoral statement *Co-Workers in the Vineyard of the Lord* (see, p. 6).

13. Religious Education and Catechesis

E very important document of the Second Vatican Council emphasizes the Church's role as teacher, but it is only the Declaration on Christian Education, *Gravissimum educations*, that deals directly with education. The Declaration promulgated some fundamental principles, especially in regard to schools, but the task of developing them fell to the Congregation of Catholic Education. *The Religious Dimension of Education in a Catholic School* (1988) closely subsumes two earlier documents published by the Congregation: *The Catholic School* (1977), and *Lay Catholics in Schools: Witnesses to the Faith* (1982). The first statement outlined specific characteristics of the Catholic school and its mission. The second described the valuable contributions of lay people who assist Religious Congregations of men and women in the educational ministry. *The Religious Dimension of Education in a Catholic School* concentrates on "educational institutions, of whatever type, devoted to the formation of young people at all pre-university levels," that are dependent on ecclesiastical authority (Introduction, n. 4). It intentionally leaves many questions untouched, but one issue it does clarify is the distinction between "catechesis" and "religious instruction." While the terms are complementary, the goal of catechesis is "maturity: spiritual, liturgical, sacramental and apostolic" that takes place in the local church community over a whole lifetime. The aim of religious instruction in Catholic schools is systematic "knowledge" of the nature of Christianity and Christian living (nn. 68-69).

The Religious Dimension of Education in a Catholic School

The Congregation for Catholic Education describes the document as "guidelines for reflection and renewal," an instrument that "should lead to concrete decisions about what can and should be done to make Catholic schools more effective in meeting the expectations of the Church, expectations shared by many families and students." Focusing as it does on Catholic schools, the document leaves many related questions to future consideration.

The guidelines are general; their adaptation to local situations is left to those in charge of the schools. In acknowledging that not all students in Catholic schools are Catholics and that some are not Christian, the Congregation, citing Vatican II, insists that the religious freedom and personal conscience of individual students must be respected. However, a Catholic school cannot relinquish its own freedom and duty to proclaim the Gospel and to offer a formation based on Christian values (Introduction, nn. 1-6). The document has 115 numbered paragraphs distributed in five parts.

Part One – The Religious Dimension in the Lives of Today's Youth

Part One calls on educators to analyze the present situation of young people at the local level. It acknowledges that "young people today are, in some respects, different from those that the Council had in mind." Changes in outlook and life-style, generated by socio-economic factors and the media expose them to a wide variety of opinions on every possible topic, but they are not yet capable of ordering or prioritizing what they learn. Often they do not have the critical ability to distinguish the true and good from their opposites. They have not yet acquired the necessary religious and moral criteria to remain objective and independent in the face of whatever is popular at the moment. Even a culture resistant to change is being influenced by the all-pervasive mass-media (nn. 7-10).

Although local situations differ greatly, educators need to be aware of characteristics that are common to today's young people. Many live in a universe whose only value is economic and technological progress. Others live in an environment devoid of truly human relationships, suffering from loneliness and lack of affection. Large numbers worry about an uncertain future, brought about by the threat of nuclear annihilation, wide-spread unemployment, divorce, etc. Their worry and insecurity fosters violent behavior. Unable to find meaning in life and seeking ways to escape from loneliness, many turn to alcohol and drugs (nn. 11-13).

In places where there is high economic development and rapid social and cultural change, many young people abandon religious practices. Often they develop a hostility toward Church structures and a crisis of conscience regarding the truths of faith and their accompanying moral values. Certain patterns of behavior are attempts to fill the religious void with some sort of a substitute: the cult of the body, massive "youth events" that generate fanaticism and alienation from reality (nn. 14-16).

Educators must search for the causes of these behavior patterns. Although there are positive signs in Catholic schools that offer grounds for encouragement, Christian formation in the home and parish is not always proof against the influence of environment. "For some of today's youth, the years spent in a Catholic school seem to have scarcely any effect." They have a negative attitude toward and even reject the ways in which Christian life is expressed: prayer, participation in the Mass, frequenting the sacraments. "If a school is excellent as an academic institution, but does not witness to authentic values... it is obvious that renewal is called for—not only in the content and methodology of religious instruction, but in the overall school planning which governs the whole process of formation of the students." To respond to the questions that come from the restless and critical minds of the young the Catholic school must be guided by an educational philosophy illumined by the Gospel message and conditioned by each student's unique situation (nn. 17-23).

Part Two - The Religious Dimension of the School Climate

Part Two embraces all the components which interact with one another in such a way as to create favorable conditions for a formation process: personnel, space, time, relationships, teaching, study, and other activities. On entering a Catholic school a student should have the impression of entering a new environment, one permeated with the Gospel spirit of love and freedom. Teachers, as individuals and as a community, have prime responsibility for creating the religious climate. Through their daily witness the students will come to appreciate the uniqueness of the environment (nn. 24-26).

An adequate physical facility helps create a pleasant environment. Students can be made to feel "at home" even when the surroundings are modest, if the climate is humanly and spiritually rich. Simplicity and evangelical poverty are not inconsistent with having the materials needed to educate properly. The physical proximity of the school to a church can contribute to achieving its educational aims. Liturgy planning should bring the school community and local Church together (nn. 27-30).

Vatican II's *Declaration on Christian Education* notes that thinking of the Catholic school as a community rather than an institution represents an important advance. In the Council texts the community dimension is primarily a theological concept rather than a sociological category. Everyone directly involved in the school—teachers and administrative staff, parents and students—is a part of the school community. The Church offers encouragement to members of Religious Congregations who have dedicated their lives to education on behalf of young people who are the hope of the Church. The Congregation for Christian Education has devoted a specific document to lay teachers, meant to remind them of their apostolic responsibility in the field of education and to summon them to participate in the Church's common mission. When lay people establish schools, they should be concerned to create a community climate permeated by the Gospel spirit of freedom and love. Considering the age group primary schools are working with, they should try to create a community climate that reproduces, as far as possible, the warm and intimate atmosphere of family life (nn. 31-41).

Close cooperation of the school with families is especially important when treating sensitive issues such as religious, moral, or sexual education, or the choice of a vocation in life. The Catholic school is aware that the first and primary educators of children are their parents, but the same is not always true of the families themselves. The school has the responsibility to give them this awareness (nn. 42-43).

Just as the Church is present in the school, so the school is present in the Church. The Catholic school receives its spirit from the Church through which the Redemption of Christ is revealed and made operative. The educational goals of the school include a concern for the life and problems of the Church, both local and universal. Direct contacts between the school and Church authorities establish mutual esteem and collaboration (n. 44).

Catholic schools help form good citizens and promote respect for the State, observance of just laws, civil values, and the need to pursue social progress. Christian education sees all humanity as one family, divided perhaps by historical and political events, but always one in God who is Father of all. The Catholic school should help promulgate appeals for peace, justice, and assistance for countries in need that come from the Church and recognized international organizations such as UNESCO and the United Nations (nn. 45-46).

Part Three – The Religious Dimension of School Life and Work

Part Three recognizes that classes and lessons are only a small part of school life. There are exercises, para-curricular activities, class meetings, group meetings, school assemblies, student-teacher and student-student relationships, etc. While this complex variety of events are part of the life of all schools, the Catholic school is different in that it draws its strength from the Gospel. The educational process is a genuine Christian journey towards perfection. Students, sensitive to the religious dimension of life, realize that the will of God is found in school-work and the human relationships of each day. Intellectual work is involved in loving God and doing his will. It stimulates a desire to know the universe as God's creation and enkindles a love for truth. It impels the mind to learn with careful order and precise methods and to work with a sense of responsibility (nn. 47-50).

As students grow, it is imperative that a Catholic school help them become aware of the relationship between faith and human culture. Culture and religion are not like two parallel lines that never meet. A believer is both human and a person of faith who searches for and will be able to find points of contact between religion and culture. It is the task of all teachers, not only religion teachers, to help students in this search and see beyond the limited horizon of human reality. A Catholic secondary school will help students meet the challenges that culture poses for faith and attain that synthesis that is necessary for faith to mature. Academic studies cannot completely solve all the problems of religion and faith, but a Catholic school is a privileged place for finding ways to deal with them. While faith is not to be identified with any one culture and is independent of all cultures, faith that is detached from culture is not received fully, not assimilated entirely, not lived faithfully (nn. 51-53).

Science and the technology allied to it is part of the universe created by God. The wonder recorded by the biblical authors is still valid for students today who have a knowledge of creation that is much more vast and profound. Students who discover the harmony between faith and science will be better able to put science and technology to the service of men and women and to the service of God (n. 55).

A Catholic school must be committed to overcoming the problems of a fragmented and incomplete curriculum. Teachers dealing with the social sciences and philosophy have the opportunity to present a complete picture of the human person, including the religious dimension. They should help students see the human person as a creature having both a physical and a spirit nature. Older students can gradually come to a mature understanding of all that is implied in the concept of "person," the capacity to be an active and creative agent, called to a specific mission in the world. The religious dimension makes possible a true understanding of the dignity of human beings as having both a divine origin and an eternal destiny that transcends the physical universe (nn. 55-56).

The Gospel message embraces and integrates the wisdom of all cultures. A careful and reflective study of philosophy brings human wisdom into an encounter with the divine. Students should be encouraged to develop a taste for historical truth and to discover a religious dimension in human history. The drama of human history is a monumental struggle between human grandeur and human misery subject to moral judgments. To this end teachers should help students see history as a whole and reflect on the fact that this struggle takes place within the divine history of universal salvation (nn. 57-60).

The artistic and literary heritage of each society represents the sum total of its cultural wealth. The vast artistic and literary patrimony of Christianity gives testimony to a faith that has been handed down through the centuries. The Christian perspective offers penetrating criteria for understanding the human struggle and the mysteries of the human spirit. Students in the upper grades can appreciate artistic works as a reflection of divine beauty in tangible form. St. Augustine finds God's eternal order reflected in art, and St. Thomas finds the Divine Word in art (nn. 60-61).

Teachers of pedagogical science can help those preparing to become teachers by helping them reflect, judge, and choose elements that are true and useful in formulating a carefully thought out synthesis. The Christian model for future teachers begins with the human and enriches it with supernatural gifts, virtues, and values. Proper pedagogical formation leads to a self-formation that is both human and Christian, because this is the best possible preparation for one who is preparing to educate others (nn. 62-63).

Religious themes should be included in interdisciplinary studies. They arise naturally when dealing with such topics as the human person, the family, society, or history. Religion teachers can assist in clarifying religious questions just as colleagues in other fields might provide expert help in the religion class when dealing with specific questions. A cooperative spirit among teachers impresses students (nn. 64-65).

Part Four – Religious Instruction in the Classroom and the Religious Dimension of Formation

Part Four treats the underlying reason for the existence of the Catholic school and the reason that Catholic parents should prefer it. The task of bringing the two aspects together—the school as a "civic institution" and as a "Christian community"—requires constant attention so that the effort to transmit culture and at the same time witness to the Gospel does not turn into a conflict harmful to both (nn. 66-67).

Although there is a close connection between religious instruction and catechesis, there is, at the same time, a clear distinction. Unlike religious instruction, whose aim is transmitting knowledge, catechesis presupposes that the hearer is receiving the Christian message as a salvific reality in the context of a faith community. Religious instruction can strengthen the faith of a believing student just as catechesis can increase one's knowledge of the Christian message. The distinction notwithstanding, religious instruction and catechesis are complementary. Religious instruction should have a place alongside other classes so that there is a coordination between human learning and religious awareness (nn. 68-70).

Teachers must be aware that young people bring into the classroom what they see and hear in the world around them, along with impressions gained from the mass media. Teachers will accept students as they are and let them talk. Various questions will come up naturally, questions that make a calm study of the Christian faith very difficult. The teachers own experiences and the carefully worked out responses given by Vatican II can be used to help the students (nn. 71-72).

It is not easy to develop a course syllabus that will present the Christian faith systematically and in a way suited to young people today. While waiting for the new catechism proposed by Second Extraordinary Synod of Bishops in 1985, the document presented an outline that is the fruit of experience, faithful to the Gospel message, and developed according to a methodology based on the words and deeds of the Lord (n. 73).

Christology should present some ideas about Sacred Scripture, especially the Gospels, Divine Revelation, and Tradition as a basis for learning about the Lord Jesus, his person, message, deeds, and the historical fact of his resurrection. For more mature students, this study can include Jesus as Savior, Priest, Teacher, Lord of the universe, and Mary his Mother who cooperates in his mission (n. 74).

Through the Lord Jesus we come to the mystery of God the Father, who created the universe, and to the Holy Spirit, sent into the world to bring the mission of the Son to fulfillment. It is this mystery of the Holy Trinity that the Church venerates and proclaims when it recites the Creed (n. 75).

Christian anthropology is where students discover the value of the human person, with a mission on earth and a destiny that is immortal. As students see that all types of people, as if representing all of humanity, surrounded Jesus, they will begin asking themselves why Jesus loves everyone, why he gives his life for all. They will conclude that each person must be a privileged creature of God. At this point they will begin to discover that human history unfolds within a divine history of salvation. As a result they learn the virtues of self-respect and love for others (n. 76).

Ecclesiology shows how the history of salvation continues in the Church. Students will discover the Church as the People of God, composed of women and men like themselves, guided by the Spirit who sustains it, and by the Holy Father with bishops, assisted by priests and other collaborators in ministry. The Creed celebrates and proclaims the mystery of the One, Holy, Catholic, and Apostolic Church (n. 77).

The essential point is that Jesus Christ is truly present in the sacraments that he instituted, and his presence makes them efficacious means of grace. The moment of closest encounter with the Lord Jesus occurs in the Eucharist, which is both sacrifice that renews the mystery of salvation for us and sacrament wherein our Lord is truly present to us (nn. 78-79).

The Lord proposes an effective approach to the teaching the last things. In the parable of the rich man he teaches that a personal judgment awaits each one. In Matthew 25 he points to an eternal destiny. The good or evil done to each human being is as if it were done to him. From the pattern of the Creed, students learn that the Kingdom of Heaven consists of "saints," who believed and spent their lives in the Lord's service. They are not separated from us and together with us they form the one Church, the People of God, the "communion of saints" (nn. 80-81).

A systematic presentation of Christian ethics is also needed; a sample outline is presented. By way of introduction to the relationship between faith and life, it is helpful to reflect on the first Christian communities where the Gospel message was accompanied by prayer and the celebration of the sacraments. Liturgical prayer is the official prayer of the Church, which makes the mystery of Christ present in our lives especially through the Eucharist and the Sacrament of Reconciliation. Thus the virtues of faith and religion are cultivated during childhood, youth, and in all the years that follow (nn. 82-83).

Students may object that we are a long way from the ideal, but it is better to present a positive picture of personal Christian ethics than to get lost in an analysis of human misery. We must cultivate intelligence and other spiritual gifts. We must learn to care for our body and its health. We must be careful of our sexual integrity because it is also a gift of God contributing the perfection of the person and having a providential function for the life of society and the Church (n. 84).

Christian love is a new reality born of faith. The Lord Jesus lived among us in order to show us the Father's love and to model the love that we should have for one another. It stands in opposition to all that is evil and every form of egoism. Beginning in the family and school affection, respect, obedience and goodness must be cultivated, and all manifestations of egoism, rebellion, hatred, or revenge must be rooted out. The Church, laboring to relieve human suffering, must witness to a love that excludes no one so that all may know the Lord. Inspired by love in the Church, young people may respond to a call to the priesthood or to Religious Life. As they prepare for marriage, young people should discover the newness and depth of Christian love between man and woman, including the mutuality and reserve with which it is expressed and the tenderness by which it is preserved. They should experience love in this way from their first friendships until finally they consecrate their love in the Sacrament of Matrimony (nn. 85-87).

Christian social ethics, founded on faith, sheds light on disciplines that study the human situation such as law, economics, and political science. God has put the world at the service of the human family. The basic elements of a Christian social ethic is the human person, the central focus of the social order;

justice, honesty, and freedom. World peace must be founded on justice; national and international well being depend on an equitable distribution of the goods of the earth. Misery and hunger weigh on the conscience of humanity and cry out to God for justice (nn. 88-89).

Students enriched by the Church's social doctrine will find their service of society more effective. They must have a clear awareness of the evil that is at work in the world and in the human person. By examining their own consciences they will acquire a sense of sin: the great sin of humanity as a whole and the personal sin within ourselves. But it is not a hopeless situation. In the light of faith this reality has another side to it. To be a Christian involves a call to help liberate the human family from its slavery to sin and from the effects of sin in the cultural, economic, social and political orders (nn. 90-94).

Perfection is a theme that must be part of this systematic presentation of the Christian message. The Christian perfection to which we are called is a gift of Jesus through the mediation of the Spirit, but it requires our cooperation. Once students get beyond the feeling that too much is being asked of them, they will realize that perfection is within their grasp if they live their lives in study and work as best they can: put into practice the virtues, especially love, in the classroom, at home, and among friends; accept difficulties with courage; help those in need; find inspiration in the words and example of Jesus. The ideal is for each student to have an opportunity for spiritual guidance that helps integrate the religious instruction given in the classroom into their personal experiences (n. 95).

The religion teacher is the key to achieving the educational goals of the Catholic school. The effectiveness of religious instruction is closely tied to personal witness given by the teacher. Religion teachers must be endowed with many gifts, both natural and supernatural, and have a thorough cultural, professional, and pedagogical training. Everything possible must be done to insure that religion teachers in Catholic schools be adequately trained. An unprepared teacher can do a great deal of harm. Ecclesiastical universities and faculties should develop appropriate programs for the teachers of tomorrow (n. 97).

Part Five – A General Summary: The Religious Dimension of the Formation Process as a Whole

Part Five might be described as an organic set of elements with the single purpose of developing the capability of every student within a context that recognizes the help of grace. Although Christian education is a movement or a growth process, directed toward an ideal goal beyond the limitations of anything human, it takes place within human formation (nn. 98-99).

A Catholic school needs to have educational goals that are "distinctive" in the sense they define the school's identity, course content, organization, and management in relationship to Gospel values. Care must be given to the development of general criteria that will enable each aspect of school activity to direct the attainment of its educational objective so that the cultural, pedagogical, social, civil, and political aspects of the school are integrated. Educational goals, quite distinct from internal school regulations or teaching methods, are not just descriptions of vague intentions. They should be revised each year on the basis of experience and need and, at the end of each school year or some other appropriate time, the degree of success in achieving them should be evaluated. The evaluation is the common responsibility of teachers, students, and families (nn. 100-102).

Conditions that create and strengthen a positive climate require that everyone—teachers, students, and administrators—cooperate in achieving the educational goals. The climate must welcome the participation of families, the local Church, and civil society. It is an added advantage when all share a common faith. Everything possible must be done to eliminate conditions that threaten a healthy climate and the religious dimension of the school. When an authentic Christian witness is absent from the school, religious instruction falls on deaf ears (nn. 103-104).

The Christian process of formation is the result of a constant interaction involving teachers, students, and the help of grace. It is impossible for education to be genuine without the active involvement of the one being educated. The more students realize that a school and all its activities have the sole purpose of helping them to grow to maturity, the more they will become actively involved (nn. 105-107).

In situations where the student body in a Catholic school includes young people of different faiths and ideological backgrounds, evangelization is not easy and may not even be possible. It is essential, therefore, to clarify the relationship between religious development and cultural growth. The transmission of culture ought to strengthen those aspects that make a person more human, and paying special attention to its religious dimension and the ethical requirements found in it. There can be unity in the midst of pluralism. We need to discern between what is essential and what is accidental. A genuine pre-evangelization that leads to integral human development may at some future time bear fruit (n. 108).

The formation process in the Catholic school is a constant interplay of action and reaction. The interplay has both a horizontal and vertical dimension that makes the Catholic school distinctive. The horizontal dimension manifests itself in the mutual respect, trust, and love teachers and students have for one another. There is also a continuous vertical interaction through prayer. Teachers pray for the students. Students pray for the teachers. A relationship is built up in the Catholic school that is both human and divine. The flow of love and also of grace makes the Catholic school truly authentic. As years pass, students will realize, when they look back, that the educational objectives have become a reality. And as they look forward, they will feel free and secure in facing new, and now proximate, life commitments (nn. 109-112).

Conclusion

The Congregation for Catholic Education asks local ordinaries and superiors of Religious Congregations to bring these reflections to all teachers and directors of Catholic schools. The Congregation thanks everyone engaged in the educational mission of the Church, often in the face of political, economic, and practical difficulties. The Congregation suggests further study, research, and experimentation in all areas that affect the religious dimension of education in Catholic schools (nn. 113-115).

Appendix

Most of the documents discussed in this book can be found online at the Vatican website, www.vatican.va, or can be purchased through the United States Conference of Catholic Bishops; go to www.usccb.org. A few documents are out of print and can be found at a theological library.

A Vision of Youth Ministry
Out of print.

Adult Catechesis in the Christian Community: Some Principles and Guidelines
http://www.vatican.va/roman_curia/congregations/cclergy/documents /rc_con_cclergy_doc_14041990_acat_en.html

Basic Teachings for Catholic Religious Education
Out of print.

Catechesi tradendae (On Catechesis in Our Time) (CT)
http://www.vatican.va/holy_father/john_paul_ii/apost_exhortations/ documents/hf_jp-ii_exh_16101979_catechesi-tradendae_en.html

Catechism of the Catholic Church (CCC)
http://www.vatican.va/archive/ENG0015/_INDEX.HTM

Code of Canon Law (CIC)
http://www.vatican.va/archive/ENG1104/_INDEX.HTM

Compendium of the Catechism of the Catholic Church (C-CCC)
http://www.vatican.va/archive/compendium_ccc/documents/archive_ 2005_compendium-ccc_en.html

Compendium of the Social Doctrine of the Church (C-SD)
http://www.vatican.va/archive/compendium_ccc/documents/archive_
2005_compendium-ccc_en.html

Directory for Masses with Children (MWC)
http://www.fdlc.org/liturgy_resources/Directory_Masses_Children.htm

Directory for the Application of Principles and Norms on Ecumenism
(APNE)
http://www.vatican.va/roman_curia/pontifical_councils/chrstuni/doc
uments/rc_pc_chrstuni_doc_25031993_principles-and-norms-on-
ecumenism_en.html

Evangelii nuntiandi (*On Evangelization in the Modern World*) (EN)
http://www.vatican.va/holy_father/paul_vi/apost_exhortations/docume
nts/hf_p-vi_exh_19751208_evangelii-nuntiandi_en.html

Familiaris consortio (*On the Family*) (FC)
http://www.vatican.va/holy_father/john_paul_ii/apost_exhortations/
documents/hf_jp-ii_exh_19811122_familiaris-consortio_en.html

General Catechetical Directory (GCD)
http://www.vatican.va/roman_curia/congregations/cclergy/documents
/rc_con_cclergy_doc_11041971_gcat_en.html

General Directory for Catechesis (GDC)
http://www.vatican.va/roman_curia/congregations/cclergy/documents
/rc_con_ccatheduc_doc_17041998_directory-for-catechesis_en.html

Guide for Catechists (GCM)
http://www.vatican.va/roman_curia/congregations/cevang/documents
/rc_con_cevang_doc_19971203_cath_en.html

Guidelines and Suggestions for Implementing the Conciliar Declaration "Nostra aetate"
http://www.vatican.va/roman_curia/pontifical_councils/chrstuni/
relations-jews docs/rc_pc_chrstuni_doc_19741201_nostraaetate
_en.html

Guidelines for Doctrinally Sound Catechetical Materials (GDSCM)
For purchase from the USCCB: http://www.usccbpublishing.org/
productdetails.cfm?PC=47

National Certification Standards for Lay Ecclesial Ministers
For purchase from any of these organizations: www.nalm.org;
www.nccl.org; www.nfcym.org; www.npm.org

National Directory for Catechesis (NDC)
For purchase from the USCCB: http://www.usccbpublishing.org/

Notes on the Correct Way to Present the Jews and Judaism in Preaching and Catechesis
http://www.vatican.va/roman_curia/pontifical_councils/chrstuni/relat
ions-jews-docs/rc_pc_chrstuni_doc_19820306_jews-judaism_en.html

Our Hearts Were Burning Within Us: A Pastoral Plan for Adult Faith Formation in the United States (OHWB)
http://www.usccb.org/education/ourhearts.htm

Reconciliatio et paenitentia (*Reconciliation and Penance*) (RP)
http://www.vatican.va/holy_father/john_paul_ii/apost_exhortations/
documents/hf_jp-ii_exh_02121984_reconciliatio-etpaenitentia_en.html

Renewing the Vision: A Framework for Catholic Youth Ministry (RV)
http://www.usccb.org/laity/youth/rtvcontents.shtml

Rite of Christian Initiation of Adults (RCIA)
For purchase from the USCCB:
http://www.usccbpublishing.org/showproducts.cfm?FullCat=120

Sharing the Light of Faith: National Catechetical Directory for Catholics of the United States (SLF / NCD)
Out of print.

The Challenge of Adolescent Catechesis: Maturing in Faith
For purchase from NFCYM:
https://store.nfcymoffice.net/shop/pc/viewCategories.asp?idCategory=6

The Ecumenical Dimension in the Formation of Those Engaged in Pastoral Work (EDFPW)
http://www.vatican.va/roman_curia/pontifical_councils/chrstuni/documents/rc_pc_chrstuni_doc_16031998_ecumenical-dimension_en.html

The Religious Dimension of Education in a Catholic School
http://www.vatican.va/roman_curia/congregations/ccatheduc/documents/rc_con_ccatheduc_doc_19880407_catholic-school_en.html

To Teach as Jesus Did: A Pastoral Message on Catholic Education (TTJD)
For purchase from the USCCB:
http://www.usccbpublishing.org/searchproducts.cfm

United States Catholic Catechism for Adults (USCCA)
http://www.usccbpublishing.org/client/client_pdfs/Organization.pdf

Rev. Berard L. Marthaler, O.F.M. Conv., S.T.D., Ph.D.

Rev. Dr. Berard L. Marthaler is a friar of the Louisville Province of the Conventual Franciscans. He is an Emeritus Professor in the Department of Religion and Religious Education at The Catholic University of America, having taught full time from 1963 to 1997, and periodically since. He has contributed nationally and internationally in historical theology, catechetics and the development of catechetical directories and commentaries. He edited the national catechetical journal, *The Living Light,* for forty years.

Fr. Marthaler holds the S.T.D. from the Seraphicum University in Rome and a Ph.D. in ancient history from the University of Minnesota. He became head of the Department of Religious Education in 1967 and formed generations of catechetical leaders over the years. He has published widely in journals and contributed to many collections.

He is the author of *Catechetics in context: Notes and commentary on the General Catechetical Directory* issued by the Sacred Congregation for the Clergy. Huntington, IN: Our Sunday Visitor, 1973; *Sharing the Light of Faith: An official commentary.* Washington, DC: United States Catholic Conference, 1981; *The Creed: The apostolic faith in contemporary theology.* (Rev. ed.). Mystic, CT: Twenty-Third Publications, 1992; *The catechism yesterday and today: The evolution of a genre.* Collegeville: Liturgical Press, 1995; *Sowing seeds: Notes and comments on the General Directory for Catechesis.* Washington, DC: United States Catholic Conference, 2000. He was the editor of the 2nd edition of the revised 15 volume, 12,000 article *New Catholic Encyclopedia* (2002).

In 2006 Fr. Marthaler was named recipient of the National Association of Parish Catechetical Directors (NPCD) Emmaus Award through NCEA.

Index

A

A Family Perspective in Church and Society (USCC, 1988) 85

A Message to Youth: Pathway to Hope (USCC, 1995) 85

A Vision of Evangelization 170

A Vision of Youth Ministry (1976) 81–83, 84, 85

Acerbo nimis, Encyclical of Pius X, 1905 5, 6, 7

Ad gentes (AG), Decree on the Church's Missionary Activity 13, 15, 23, 37, 92, 126, 241

Adult Catechesis in the Christian Community. Some Principles and Guidelines (1990) 81, 86-89

Apostolicam actuositatem (AA), Decree on the Apostolate of Lay People 13

Authoritative Statements 2

B

Basic Teachings for Catholic Religious Education 41, 47-49, 50, 52, 56, 57, 58, 75, 76, 77

Beatitudes 49, 50, 65, 112, 139, 177, 188, 190, 221

Benedict XIV, pope 2, 4, 5

Benedict XVI, pope xi, xiii, 106, 115

Biblico-theological formation 48, 166

C

Catechesi tradendae (CT), Apostolic Exhortation, John Paul II, 1979 33, 77, 84, 86, 100-103, 106, 107, 109, 110, 123, 127, 230

Catechesis for a Worshiping Community 16, 39, 59, 70, 73, 83, 86, 179, 186, 193, 199, 200, 218, 222, 252

Catechesis for Liturgy 58–61

Catechesis for People with Special Needs 58, 61, 64, 67, 68, 71, 194, 203, 205

Catechesis for Social Ministry 50, 51, 62-64, 87

Catechesis for the Aged 66

Catechesis in a Worshiping Community 57, 58-61

Catechesis of Adolescents and Youths 28, 29, 35, 45-47, 81-86

Catechesis of Adults xii, 8, 23, 30, 35, 44-45, 51, 65, 86-90

Catechesis of Infants and Children
28, 35, 65

Catechesis Toward Maturity in Faith
64-68, 81

Catechesis, Definition 23, 55

Catechetical Leaders xv, 11, 14, 70,
74, 76, 197, 198, 201, 202, 203,
204, 207, 208, 209, 241

Catechetical Personnel 31, 51, 68,
69–71, 205, 241-255

Catechetical Resources 51, 73–75

Catechism as the norm and source for
catechetical instruction 4

Catechism of St. Robert Bellarmine 3

Catechism of the Catholic Church
xii, 11, 12, 24, 76, 86, 105,
106–115, 116, 123, 135, 139,
140, 142, 143, 150, 158, 166,
167, 170, 175, 190, 191, 198,
200, 201, 206, 207, 208, 213,
214, 215, 216, 218, 221, 225,
228, 237, 241, 247

Catechism of the Council of Trent 6,
7, 107, 108, 237

Catechisms, general 3–5, 38

Catechist Formation 31, 36, 67, 126,
160, 161, 163–167, 199-201,
245-246, 249

Catechists xiii, 8, 15, 16, 17, 22, 23,
26, 28, 29, 30, 31, 32, 34, 36, 37,
55, 56, 61, 63–65, 67, 68-69,

72–75, 84, 86, 88, 91–95, 102,
107, 114, 126, 144, 148, 149,
151, 152, 154, 155, 158,
160–167, 176, 179, 180, 183,
191, 194–201, 206, 207, 209,
210, 230, 231, 241–250, 254

Catechumens/Catechumenate 17, 22,
23, 27, 29, 30, 32, 37, 93–95,
100, 115, 128, 129, 132, 134,
138, 141, 150, 151, 153, 159,
161–162, 181, 182, 197, 204,
207, 244, 247, 250

Catholic Education 34, 38, 41, 42,
44, 47, 70, 120, 257, 268

*Catholic Higher Education and the
Pastoral Mission of the Church*
170

Catholic School Principals and Teachers
68, 70, 84, 209

Catholic Schools 17, 38, 43, 46–47,
48, 68, 70, 83, 199, 200, 203,
257, 258, 260, 266, 268

Catholic Social Teaching 62, 77, 101,
106, 118, 120, 124, 126, 130,
143, 170, 224, 252

Christian Anthropology 26, 88, 207,
264

Christian Doctrine 2, 3, 5, 6, 7, 8,
15, 16, 17, 21, 24, 30, 31, 34, 35,
36, 38, 43, 44, 48, 54, 55, 57, 69,
76, 77, 78, 105, 106, 107, 113,
115, 116, 140, 141, 157, 158,
170, 175, 187, 195, 207, 209,
212, 214, 225, 227, 229–231

Christian Family 16, 28, 34, 35, 40, 43, 102, 110, 113, 116, 118–119, 131, 132, 152–155, 159, 163, 171, 179, 181, 183, 186, 190, 194, 196, 203, 219–223, 252, 254, 260, 262, 265, 266

Christian Morality 49, 53, 54, 57, 113, 116, 120, 137, 151, 176, 190, 196, 215, 221

Christifideles laici, Apostolic Exhortation, John Paul II, (1987) 77, 88, 103, 120

Christus Dominus (CD), Decree on the Pastoral Office of Bishops in the Church 13, 14, 16, 17, 19, 23, 35, 92, 99

Church as the People of God 26, 33, 92, 100, 102, 111,158, 183, 185, 191, 264, 265

Code of Canon Law 7, 12, 19, 33–40, 72, 242

Communities of Salt and Light (USCC, 1993) 85

Compendium of the Catechism of the Catholic Church 106, 115–116, 117, 120

Compendium of the Social Doctrine of the Church 116–121

Confraternity of Christian Doctrine 2, 6, 7, 16, 48

Constitution on the Sacred Liturgy 13, 40, 58, 59

Council of Trent 2, 3, 5, 6, 7, 107, 108, 139, 237

Co-Workers in the Vineyard of the Lord—A Resource for Guiding the Development of Lay Ecclesial Ministry (2006) 241, 242, 255

Creeds 27, 108

D

De parvo catechismo, Constitution of the First Vatican Council 4

Deacons xiii, 68, 70, 91, 93, 160, 185, 198

Decalogue (See also, Ten Commandments) 49, 113, 139, 140, 190, 206

Declaration on Certain Questions Concerning Sexual Ethics, Congregation for the Doctrine of the Faith (1975) 57

Deductive Method 27, 44, 45, 65, 146, 178

Dei Verbum (DV) Dogmatic Constitution on Divine Revelation 13, 14, 22, 54

Devotional Life 61, 65

Dignitatis humanae (DH), Declaration on Religious Liberty 13

Diocesan Bishops 4, 35, 36, 38, 71, 76, 84, 268

Directory Concerning Ecumenical Matters (1967, 1970) 227

Directory for Masses with Children (MWC), (1973) 61, 95, 96, 97, 181, 183, 184

Directory for the Application of Principles and Norms on Ecumenism (1993) 195, 227, 228-231

Divine and Human Methodology 177–180

Divine Law 2, 26, 62, 189

E

Eastern Churches 13, 51, 56, 59, 60, 62, 169, 183, 185, 213, 228

Economic Justice for All: Pastoral Letter on Catholic Social Teaching and the U.S. Economy 77

Ecumenism 13, 15, 19, 55, 72, 195, 227-230, 232, 234, 236, 238, 252

Education in Sexuality 45, 66-67, 193, 224

Educational Mission of the Church 43, 46, 47, 268

Empowered by the Spirit 170, 205

Etsi minime, encyclical of Benedict XIV, 1792 2

Eucharistic Banquet 25

Evangelii nuntiandi Apostolic Exhortation, Paul VI, 1975 33, 88, 99-100, 123, 127

Evangelization xiii, 8, 15, 22, 27, 34, 37, 38, 40, 53, 84, 85, 86, 88,

99-103, 110, 120, 123-125, 127-130, 133, 137, 139, 143, 148, 153, 156, 157, 159, 160, 161, 164, 166, 170, 171, 172, 174, 175, 182, 187, 193, 199, 200, 203, 207, 208, 210, 218, 241, 244, 252, 253, 268, 272

Ex debito pastoralis officio, papal brief of Pius V, 1571 2

F

Faith and Culture 20, 21, 24, 30, 46, 76, 77, 78, 82, 107, 111-124, 125, 131, 137-138, 140, 141, 142, 143, 145, 149, 150, 157, 158, 164, 171, 173, 174, 175, 176, 178, 180, 187, 188, 193, 195, 205, 206, 207, 213-225, 244, 253, 258, 261, 262, 262, 268

Faith and Technology 21, 42, 44, 52, 74, 76, 171, 177, 180, 207, 261

Familiaris consortio, Apostolic Exhortation John Paul II (1981) 102–103

Fidei depositum, Apostolic Constitution, John Paul II (1992) 105

fides qua 135, 145

fides quae 23, 135, 145

First Vatican Council 4

Follow the Way of Love (USCC, 1994) 85

Formation of Conscience 66, 155, 189, 192

Formation Process 148, 254, 259, 267, 268

G

Gaudium et spes (GS), Pastoral Constitution on the Church in the Modern World 13, 14, 62

General Catechetical Directory (1971) xi, xii, 19-33, 41, 44, 45, 48, 49, 51, 52, 53, 56, 57, 60, 61, 64, 65, 66, 72, 81, 91, 92, 96, 99, 123, 140, 169

General Congregation of the Council/ Congregation of the Clergy 19, 20, 33, 50

General Directory for Catechesis (1997) 86, 89, 93, 116, 120, 121, 123-167, 169, 170, 175, 198, 208, 213, 241, 247

Go and Make Disciples: A National Plan and Strategy for Catholic Evangelization in the United States 172

Goals and Norms for Catechesis 11, 17, 23, 24, 25, 28, 30, 31, 39, 41, 47, 53, 54, 67, 70, 71, 82, 85, 86, 89, 99, 100, 135, 139, 141, 160, 172, 181, 191, 192, 194, 197, 198, 201, 202, 204, 242, 248, 250, 251, 260, 266, 267

Gospels 127, 134, 135, 144, 182, 206, 236, 264

Gravissimum educationis (GE), Declaration on Christian Education 13, 16-17, 46, 66, 69, 257, 259

Guide for Catechists (1993) *241, 242-250*

Guidelines and Suggestions for Implementing the Conciliar Declaration "Nostra aetate" (1974) 232-238

Guidelines for Doctrinally Sound Catechetical Materials 41, 75-78

H

Higher Education 31, 38, 45, 71, 73, 170

Home Schooling 204

Human Experience xii, 13, 27, 29, 35, 37, 44, 45, 59, 69, 71, 74, 75, 76, 82, 83, 90, 95, 96, 118, 134, 143, 144, 145, 147, 148, 149, 150, 166, 178, 189, 191, 194, 204, 218, 220, 232, 248, 263, 267

Humanae vitae, Encyclical of Pope Paul VI 25

I

In Dominico agro, encyclical of Clement XIII (1761), See also *Roman Catechism* 3, 4

Inculturation of the Gospel message 120, 124, 134, 137-138, 142-143, 157-159, 174, 176, 244, 248

Inductive Method 27, 64, 65, 146, 178

Initiation 22, 23, 27, 30, 37, 60, 93, 94, 111, 126, 128, 129, 132, 134, 142, 145, 152, 153, 161, 182, 183, 229, 252

Inter mirifica (IM), Decree on the
Mass Media 13, 14

International Council for Catechists
(COINCAT) 86-89

J

John Paul II, pope xiii, 12, 33, 63, 79,
85, 102, 103, 105, 106, 116, 123,
174, 213, 222, 224, 227, 233,
242, 244, 246

John XXIII, pope 1, 8, 11, 12, 33, 63,
215

Judaism 196, 227, 233-238

Justice in the World 62

L

Last Things 26, 57

Life in Christ (See also Christian
Morality) 112, 126, 188, 190,
191

Liturgical Catechesis 58-61, 87, 217,
264

Local Catechisms 105, 135, 138, 140,
141, 142, 143, 158, 175, 206, 213

Lumen gentium (LG), Dogmatic
Constitution on the Church 13,
14, 15, 25, 26, 62, 91

M

Mary, Mother of God 26, 57, 77, 78,
79, 219, 244, 253

Media 11, 13, 14, 21, 32, 38, 39, 42,
51, 52, 64, 74-75, 85, 110, 125,
146, 148-149, 155, 158, 175, 176,

180, 192, 205, 207-208, 223, 243,
254, 258, 262

Memorization 11, 65, 107, 114, 147

Method of Evangelization 27

Methodology 20, 24, 25, 26, 31, 50,
51, 64, 120, 124, 145, 146, 177,
178, 180, 198, 209, 247, 259, 263

Mission of the Church 8, 20, 43, 57,
103, 170, 174, 198, 210, 216,
218, 268

Missionary Action of the Church 8,
37, 57

Mystery of Salvation 16, 24, 34, 37,
115, 264

N

National Association for Lay Ministry
(NALM) 241, 250

National Catholic Educational
Association (NCEA) xv, 275

*National Certification Standards for
Lay Ecclesial Ministers Serving as
Parish Catechetical Leaders, Youth
Ministry Leaders, Patoral Associates,
and Parish Life Coordinators* (2003)
241, 250-255

National Conference for Catechetical
Leadership (NCCL) 241, 250

National Conference of Diocesan
Directors of Religious Education
(NCDD) 83

National Directory for Catechesis
(2005) xii, 121, 168-210

National Federation for Catholic
Youth Ministry (NFCYM) 83, 85,
241, 250, 251

Neophytes 27, 37, 95, 115

New Testament xi, 62, 65, 139, 234,
235, 236

Non-Christian Religions 23, 25, 26,
56, 123, 196, 232

Norms for "The First Reception of
the Sacraments of Penance and
the Eucharist" 20

Nostra aetate (NA), Declaration on
the Relation of the Church to
Non-Christian Religions 13, 15,
16, 226, 232, 233, 236-237

*Notes on the Correct Way to Present
the Jews and Judaism in Preaching
and Catechesis* 233-238

O

Old Testament 65, 111, 114, 137,
138, 176, 196, 234, 235

Optatam totius (OT), Decree on the
Training of Priests 13, 16, 142

Orbem catholicum, Motu proprio of
Pius XI establishing catechetical
office (June 23, 1923) 7

Organization of Catechesis 204

Orientalium ecclesiarum (OE), Decree
on the Catholic Eastern Churches
13

*Our Hearts Were Burning Within Us,
A Pastoral Plan for Adult Faith
Formation in the United States*
(1999) 81, 89-90

P

Parish Catechetical Leader 70, 198,
200, 251, 252

Parish Priests 5-6, 13, 70, 84, 197,
249

Pastores do vobis, Apostolic Exhortation, John Paul II (1990) 103

Pastores gregis, Apostolic Exhortation,
John Paul II (2002) 103

Pastors 2, 3, 5, 6, 8, 16, 35-36, 38,
39, 70, 114, 152, 159, 169, 197,
204, 209, 242, 245, 249

Paul VI, pope 12, 23, 33, 63, 78, 99,
100, 101, 223

Pedagogy of God 24, 144-146

Perfectae caritatis (PC), Decree on
the Up-to-Date Renewal of
Religious Life 13

Pius V, pope 2

Pius IX, pope 4

Pius X, pope 5, 6, 7, 8

Pius XI, pope 7, 8

Planning 42, 43, 47, 67, 70-73, 75, 83, 89, 120, 125, 155, 161, 193, 198, 202, 247, 254, 257, 259

Pluralism 20, 155, 159, 194, 230, 268

Popular Piety 15, 21, 65, 112, 114, 156, 180, 187, 244

Prayer 6, 26, 31, 39, 48, 58, 59, 61, 65, 68, 71, 76, 84, 86, 90, 92, 95, 107, 110, 114-115, 132-134, 139, 140, 142, 145, 147, 148, 152, 154, 166, 172, 179-182, 186, 187, 193, 194, 196, 200, 203, 207, 213, 214, 218, 220, 224-225, 228, 232, 235, 237, 242, 243, 246, 252, 254, 259, 265

Preachers 2, 5, 16, 34

Preaching 5, 16, 17, 22, 33, 34, 35, 37, 53, 70, 103, 124, 128, 136, 156, 171, 196, 229, 230, 231, 233, 236, 244, 246

Presbyterorum ordinis (PO), Decree on the Ministry and Life of Priests 13

Principal Elements of the Christian Message 51, 56, 58

Profession of the Christian Faith 34, 108-109, 129, 132, 173, 176, 200

Provido sane consilio, Instruction "On Better Care for Catechetical Teaching" (1935 published) 7

Provincial Council of Baltimore 4

Putting Children and Families First (USCC, 1991) 85

R

Reconciliatio et paenitentia, Apostolic Exhortation, John Paul II (1984) 103

Renewal xi, xv, 8, 11, 12, 21, 22, 120, 123, 124, 132, 155, 172, 218, 229, 244, 248, 253, 257, 259

Renewing the Vision: A Framework for Catholic Youth Ministry (1997) 81, 85, 86, 170

Revelation 13, 20, 22, 24, 27, 32, 50, 54-55, 64, 81, 108, 116-118, 124, 127-129, 137, 138, 142, 143, 145, 146, 147, 156, 171, 176, 178, 210, 215, 216, 225, 233, 234, 243, 247, 252, 264

Rite of Christian Initiation of Adults xii, 30, 60, 61, 91, 94, 95, 151, 123, 172, 191, 192, 213

Role of Family in Catechesis 16, 28, 40, 42, 66

Roman Catechism 3, 4

S

Sacrament of Confirmation 2, 5, 7, 30, 36, 57, 60, 84, 92, 95, 152, 162, 182, 218, 219, 220

Sacrament of Penance 3, 5, 7, 20, 36, 39, 60, 61, 91, 95, 103, 162, 184, 219, 220, 246

Sacrament of Reconciliation 20, 58, 59, 61, 103, 120, 204, 235, 265

Sacraments of Commitment 59

Sacraments of Healing 59, 112, 184

Sacraments of Initiation 59, 60, 95, 129, 134, 141, 164, 182-184, 218

Sacraments, general xiii, 2, 6, 25, 31, 35, 39, 40, 57, 58, 61, 65, 77, 79, 86, 100, 107, 111-112, 127, 129, 132, 134, 138, 140, 142, 148, 150, 151, 172, 173, 177, 180, 181, 182, 184, 185, 187, 200, 204, 207, 213, 218, 219, 222, 229, 231, 247, 252, 254, 259, 262, 265

Sacred Congregation of the Council 7, 19

Sacrosanctum concilium (SC), Constitution on the Sacred Liturgy 13, 40, 58, 59

Sanctifying Mission of the Church 34, 39, 40

Scripture 17, 22, 31, 34, 39, 53, 55, 69, 84, 105, 109, 118, 125, 126, 132, 135, 141, 142, 144, 152, 156, 166, 171, 172, 175, 179, 190, 191, 195, 198, 201, 206, 207, 208, 225, 236, 252, 253, 264

Second Vatican Council xi, xii, xiii, xv, 1, 2, 8, 9, 11-17, 19, 21, 22, 23, 33, 41, 46, 49, 52, 53, 54, 59, 75, 76, 77, 81, 83, 91, 93, 94, 99, 105, 106, 123, 124, 125, 140, 141, 142, 166, 223, 227, 228, 237, 241, 253, 257, 258, 263

Sharing Catholic Social Teaching 170

Sharing the Light of Faith, National Catechetical Directory for the United States 41, 43, 47, 49-75, 77, 81, 169

Small Christian Communities 204

Social Justice 62-64, 72, 90, 172, 203, 221, 223, 233, 235, 252

Social Sin 63, 189, 190

Statement in Support of Catechetical Ministry 170

Statement in Support of Catholic Elementary and Secondary Schools 170

Synodal Documents 62, 99, 103

Synods 19, 33, 62, 77, 99-103, 105, 123

Systematic and Intentional Catechesis 45, 87, 183

T

Task of Catechesis 11, 16-17, 28, 131-134, 160, 162, 171-174, 191, 242, 246

Ten Commandments (See also, Decalogue) 6, 49, 113, 190, 196, 221

Textbooks 32, 38-39, 55, 75, 78, 206-210

The Catholic School (1977), and Lay Catholics in Schools: Witnesses to the Faith (1982) 257

The Challenge of Adolescent Catechesis: Maturing in Faith (1986) 81, 83-85

The Challenge of Catholic Youth Evangelization: Called to Be Witnesses and Storytellers (NFCYM, 1993) 85

The Commentary on the Revised Liturgical Year 61

The Ecumenical Dimension in the Formation of Those Engaged in Pastoral Work (1998) 231-232

The General Norms for the Liturgical Year and Calendar 61

The Ministry of the Word 21, 31

The Religious Dimension of Education in a Catholic School (1988) 257-268

The Rite of Initiation for Children of Catechetical Age 94-95

The Teaching Ministry of the Diocesan Bishop 170

The U.S. Catholic Catechism for Adults xii, 213-225

To Live in Christ Jesus, Pastoral Letter on the Life of Grace and the Church's Moral Teaching (USCC 1976) 57

To Teach as Jesus Did: A Pastoral Message on Catholic Education and *Basic Teachings of Catholic Religious Education* (USCC, January, 1973) 41-49, 69

Transubstantiation 25

Trinitarian Christocentricity 24, 25, 60

U

Uniformitas, Letter of Pius X to the Cardinal Vicar of Rome (June 14, 1905) 6

Unitatis redintegratio (UR), Decree on Ecumenism 13, 15

United States Conference of Catholic Bishops (USCCB; also NCCB/ USCC) 2, 41, 42, 50, 51, 73, 75, 81, 83, 89

USCCB's Commission on Certification and Accreditation 241, 242

Ut unum sint 232

V

Vita consecrata, Apostolic Exhortation, John Paul II (1994) 103

Y

Youth Ministry xii, 81-85, 198-199, 203, 241

Youth Ministers 47, 81, 83-84, 198-199